Contents

Pitlane Lessons

ALSO BY MARC PRIESTLEY

The Mechanic: The Secret World of the F1 Pitlane

Pitlane Lessons

What F1 Can Teach You About Life and Work

MARC PRIESTLEY

THE BODLEY HEAD

LONDON

1 3 5 7 9 10 8 6 4 2

The Bodley Head, an imprint of Vintage, is part of
the Penguin Random House group of companies

Vintage, Penguin Random House UK, One Embassy Gardens,
8 Viaduct Gardens, London SW11 7BW

penguin.co.uk/vintage
global.penguinrandomhouse.com

First published by The Bodley Head in 2025

Typeset in 12.8/16pt Dante MT Pro by Six Red Marbles UK, Thetford, Norfolk
Printed and bound in Great Britain by Clays Ltd, Elcograf S.p.A.

The authorised representative in the EEA is Penguin Random House Ireland,
Morrison Chambers, 32 Nassau Street, Dublin D02 YH68

A CIP catalogue record for this book is available from the British Library

ISBN 9781847928955

Penguin Random House is committed to a sustainable future
for our business, our readers and our planet. This book is made from Forest
Stewardship Council® certified paper.

To my wife Clare, and our four children, Lexi, Leo, Rex and Ginger, with thanks for their patience, support and love whilst I live my dreams. Love you all.

Foreword

It's Jake Humphrey here.

I first met Marc many years ago in the Formula One paddock when I was presenting the BBC's coverage of this amazing sport. Whilst we were on separate paths within F1, it's fair to say it's left a lasting impression on us both.

I was fascinated by the intensity of the on-track battles and the entertainment the racing offers, but I also grew obsessed with learning more about the inspirational people I found myself surrounded by.

What I quickly realised is this sport isn't just about winning a race; it offers us an incredible insight into the behaviours, thought processes and cultures that drive success. What you see on track is just the tip of a very big and complex iceberg.

Thousands of people, meticulously filtered from all walks of life, come together to produce excellence in almost every area they set their minds to. It's a sport that embraces failure. They thrive under pressure and are comfortable pushing the boundaries. It generates the kind of innovative thinking most of us would love to foster in our own lives.

My journey through F1 and beyond sparked a curiosity in me to learn more, which led to me creating *High Performance*, where I'm lucky enough to interview some of the world's most extraordinary people.

Many of our biggest episodes feature guests from the elite environment of Grand Prix racing, just like Marc, as we all wake up to the incredible lessons that the sport can teach us.

Marc's packed this excellent book full of great stories, expertise and insight, but also the kind of useful tips that businesses, parents and every single one of us can put into practice to get a little bit closer to our own version of living a high-performance life.

Jake Humphrey, 2025

Introduction

I come from a world in which almost everyone is willing to do almost anything if it means getting an edge over their competitors, because F1 is a sport where even fractions of seconds can have an explosive impact.

For a long time that meant its teams pursued the most innovative, daring technological methods available in the relentless chase for speed. They were uncompromising in their desire to explore the outer limits of what was possible with their cars. Later, that furious ambition and obsessive attention to detail was unleashed on every single aspect of a team's performance. Earlier than most, they understood that when it comes to winning races, human beings are as important as engines.

I had a ring-side seat for much of this, spending the most amazing decade in various roles at the illustrious McLaren Formula One Team. I started as a mechanic, working on the racing cars and playing my part in the pressure-cooker environment of pitstops, before taking a wider role in programmes within the organisation dedicated to understanding and improving the team's human performance and collective mindset.

What I didn't appreciate back then was that the elite-level people I was lucky enough to work with, and the groundbreaking things we were able to discover, would go on to change the rest of my life for the better. In passing some of what I learnt on to you in the pages of this book, I'm hoping we might just be able to help change yours too.

Helping to transform an organisation from one that focused almost all its resources and attention on designing and engineering a faster car, towards one that realised it couldn't have the *fastest* car without focusing resources and attention on the people that created it, was an area that fascinated me. I convinced our CEO, Ron Dennis, to let me have a go at improving our outcomes by learning how to get the best out of the brilliant people in the team. My new mission in life began.

Together we helped bring significant change and, in doing so, helped Lewis Hamilton to the first F1 World Title of his career. I'm very proud of that. But mostly I'm proud to say we laid the foundations for a new way of thinking at one of the sport's oldest and most successful teams.

And that's what this book's about: new ways of thinking. My own journey of self-discovery and personal development changed direction through understanding the brilliance of what the extraordinary people in F1 could offer when truly enabled. We can all do the same.

Each chapter takes a different topic that F1 teams exploit extremely well and that I believe can help us all. It breaks down the 'hows' and 'whys' of each and combines this with real-life stories and examples from my Formula One experience. Embedded in each chapter is a 'Marginal Gain', something I think is worth pursuing in order to reach the very highest standards possible in whatever mission you're on. Then each chapter closes with a set of 'Pitlane Lessons', or bitesize tips, to summarise what you've learnt and help you to implement them in the framework of your own life.

I worked with, and learnt from, elite performance coaches and leaders from other sports and industries, all the while trying to understand more about humans and how we perform best. I got the opportunity to share insights with and from Olympic athletes and titans of business, as well as the world-class drivers and people within our own team. Upon finally leaving McLaren, I only became hungrier for more learning and so went on to study and read subjects like team psychology, high-performing team cultures and lots more.

Alongside a growing broadcasting career, I began giving talks at big public and private events about the things I'd learnt in Formula One that I knew could help others. I set up my own companies, helping businesses to achieve great things through consultancy and executive mentoring programmes, and today I travel the globe providing these services to some of the biggest organisations in the world.

A few years ago I had the realisation that whilst the privileged existence I've been lucky enough to have in the high-performance world of F1 is enormously valuable to the business world, the same things I teach my corporate clients can be just as valuable to you and me. So I started a podcast, *Pitlane Life Lessons*.

The ethos behind it, and this very book, is to help you to think more about the challenges you face in life, in the way a successful F1 team might approach them. I want to help you to get a little bit closer to living your own version of a high-performance existence by developing a Formula One mindset.

I hope you enjoy reading.

Marc

@marc_priestley / @f1elvis

1.

GOALS ARE MORE THAN PLANS – THEY'RE FUEL
How to Set World-Champion-Worthy Goals

It is almost impossible to overestimate the sheer scale of the challenge facing Formula One teams. What's required just to get their two cars onto the Fi grid is so demanding, relentless, expensive and punishing that many good teams have tried and failed even to do that. The competition for those who've managed to establish themselves is so intense, and at such a high level, that whilst designing and building a car to take part is one thing, creating and operating one that can compete at the front is another altogether.

The biggest teams employ over a thousand of some of the best people in the business to spend around twelve months coming up with a car they think can beat the other teams, whose own thousand of the best people in the business are trying to do the same. All are working within the same strict, but regularly changing, regulations set by the sport's governing body, the FIA.

If the initial design process starts in February, the car needs to hit the racetrack for pre-season testing the following February. In the meantime, there's the small matter of competing in the ferociously competitive World Championship with the car that began its own design journey twelve months earlier than that. And that car doesn't just get designed once and then raced for a season, it gets redesigned almost every week as regular

upgrades and new components get rushed through a staggeringly rapid production system. All of that takes the highest
possible levels of coordination and a relentless drive from every
single person involved. And, of course, it never stops. When
the season finally comes to a close in December, production
of the following year's brand-new car, and the myriad intricate
parts it consists of, is ramping up to full capacity ahead of the
new campaign. The everlasting cycle continues . . . the winter
'off season' is often the busiest time of all inside each team's
factory.

> Just doing a good job, or even a *very* good job, isn't enough
> to survive, let alone win in Formula One. You need brilliant
> individuals operating at their highest levels.

Which is why keeping motivated and energised teams of
that many people, with such a demanding and ongoing workload that never seems to let up, is one of the biggest challenges
these elite organisations face. It's a challenge they take seriously and I was privileged to spend almost a decade benefitting
directly from McLaren's groundbreaking efforts in this area.
We employed leading doctors, therapists and psychologists. We
collaborated with other extremely high-performing organisations in and outside of professional sport. We conducted our
own research and ran experiments, collected and forensically
analysed data and went deep into trying to understand anything that might help us win.

The continual and relentless pursuit of ultimate performance
means that teams are as invested in financing and innovating
in the human performance sphere as they are aerodynamics
and technology. Having a system of meticulously curated and
measurable goals is one of the ways they manage this.

Although each has their own specific approaches, the

process is similar up and down the pitlane. Engineering and team debriefs happen daily and their conclusions help to form job lists and a strategic run plan for the next time the car hits the track. These ever-flexible plans are documented, distributed and used as guides for the team to make the most efficient use of the available time they have.

In the bigger picture, teams identify performance-based as well as halo-like idealistic targets that stretch them, but with excellence across the board, they're able to work towards or hit them over an extended period. This happens in the sporting context, but also in the business sense, with phenomenal amounts of data continuously gauging progress across both.

But the way they do this has evolved over time. When I was starting out, each season McLaren began with the single over-arching target of aiming to score more points than every other team and be crowned as champions by its end. On any given race weekend, the way we were most likely to achieve that was to go out and win the Grand Prix. The trouble is that everyone else at the top end of the sport set out with what *they* hoped was the fastest car the rules would allow, to achieve exactly the same thing. Even if we'd done an exceptional job by the time the car first hit the track in testing, we still had Everest-scale mountains to climb whilst others around us did anything they could to climb them faster and better. Our biggest annual aim, the reason we existed, was the same one that everyone else aspired to: to become champions. And yet the nature of F1 is such that, clearly, we couldn't all win it.

On thirty separate occasions during my years there we hit the goal of winning an F1 race and, I can tell you, it felt amazing every single time. That's a lot of celebrations under the podium, a lot of champagne sprayed, parties enjoyed and bonuses earned.

But . . . during that same period with the team we entered 180 Grand Prix.

To put it another way, we failed to achieve our goal 83.33 per cent of the times we tried.

Of the ten seasons I was directly involved in at the team, we managed to accomplish the one humongous goal we were led to believe defined us, winning an F1 World Championship . . . just once. And yet we carried on.

In life it can be the same. Things go wrong. There isn't always a neat link between effort and reward. Everyone's journeys are full of their own versions of an untimely engine failure or an unfortunate mid-race puncture. In response, we can always take the easy option and give up. We can feel sorry for ourselves and rue the unfairness of 'bad luck', retreat to lick our wounds and think about perhaps having another go on a 'better' day. But there is another way. So how can one sustain the constant drive to accomplish your goals for inordinate amounts of time, often without much to celebrate along the way?

The best teams have come to realise that the targets they used to set themselves – winning the world championship, or a certain number of races – are no longer enough by themselves (though they remain incredibly useful, as we'll see) to ensure that they have the edge over their competitors. Instead, they set themselves infinite goals. These are inspirational aspirations that don't have a defined end-point but are pursued continually. These are what can drive you on when the going gets tough; they lend meaning to your life, and push you to reach levels that you might never have thought possible.

They were a game-changer for us, and transformed the way we conducted every aspect of our operations. In this chapter, I'm going to show you how you can do the same to your life. In the process, I hope I'll be able to help you think more like an F1 team and positively reframe both what you're aiming for and why you might be chasing after it.

How to set the right goals

I believe that we should all have goals in our lives. They help us to know where we're heading, like the North Star, and give us reason to push through tough or difficult times. I can tell you that on a day when the world seems against you in the pitlane, because your car's engine blew up in the final practice session just a couple of frantic hours before qualifying, fixating on that North Star can often be the only thing that keeps you relentlessly ploughing on against the odds. When that exact scenario played out with us at McLaren, I remember the sense of pride I felt as our entire crew threw themselves into the task of rebuilding the car in the impossibly short timeframe. No one questioned it. No one needed instructions. Everyone just knew that's what we had to do, even though the chance of actually being ready for our immovable qualifying time slot might be slim.

We made it, just.

You can also think of goals as future rewards. They're the delayed payback or gratification for the effort you're putting in today and that *can* be a powerful motivator. When I look back at some of the heart-wrenching sacrifices and soul-crushing moments I went through along the way, when we finally did hit that enormous goal of winning the F1 World Championship at the end of 2008, the reward more than justified it all.

If you don't set the correct goals in the correct way, they can easily end up holding you back. For me the process is important. They should have meaning and a good reason behind them. They should be important enough that they're of the highest priority, otherwise they simply become a 'nice to have', rather than a 'must achieve' and only one of those normally gets done. And they should motivate, not demotivate. That sounds obvious, but striving for a singular goal for a decade like I did, where the success rate is just 10 per cent if you're lucky, can easily morph from one to the other as more unfulfilled time passes.

That's why, these days, teams invest an enormous amount of effort into setting the right goals for everyone to chase. That process has developed through an intense search for the highest possible levels of performance. It embraces psychology and the understanding of how we, as humans, operate. In exactly the same way that we need to try and learn everything about our car in order to hopefully get the best out of it, it's also true of the people in our team. This is because the human performance element of an F1 operation is seen today as *the* most important element, without which none of the technical or sporting achievements are possible. The teams always look for innovative solutions to help them get the best possible results from the resources available. It's what matters most and so looking at how best to enable a team's brilliant collection of people is now a major focus.

After years of trying different solutions and studying different organisational cultures, my own preferred option for goal setting is, perhaps unsurprisingly, broadly the way most F1 teams work in the modern era.

Today I set my own goals on three main time horizons.

- Short-term goals. These are anything less than a month, but can be as short as hourly or even less. I have many of these on the go at any one time. For an F1 team on race weekends these could range from getting the car ready within the event schedule timings, to winning the

Grand Prix. I try and write three simple ones in my diary before bed for the next day and the first one's always '1: Make my bed'. It's simple to achieve, I manage it within seconds of waking up and it immediately gives me a winning feeling by ticking the first goal off so early that it helps push me on to the next.

- Long-term goals. I typically have one or two of these in my life to focus on at a time and they can be anything up to a year or more away. The obvious F1 team example is the major goal of winning the World Championship. They're incredibly difficult, but certainly not impossible to achieve, but the reward for hitting them is appropriately significant.

- The infinite goal. I have only one. This is something that's always there in the background of everything I do and I spent a long time working out what it was. It's a goal I can never actually achieve, hence its 'infinity', but it's the most important of them all. I'll tell you what mine is a bit later on, but this is also something we introduced at McLaren.

Each set of goals should contribute towards the next set and all should be aligned with the infinite goal. Although on very different timescales, your goal levels should all be linked to each other. Your short-term goals should all contribute to achieving your longer-term goals, and everything you do should remain true to the infinite goal. If at any point you check in and suspect this not to be the case, then spend time (add it to a list) questioning which one or more of them have become misaligned and then rectify it.

The truth is that most people have both short- and long-term goals – they just don't realise it. Which means that they're less likely to achieve them. And the reason many people aren't consciously aware of their own goals is that they rarely document, or often even acknowledge them. But, as I'm about to show you, they *really* should.

Writing your targets down makes you more likely to reach them

During my time at McLaren and in the years since, I've been lucky to have the opportunity to work with several psychologists across different fields. I was once in a race team meeting towards the end of the 2000s, where McLaren had linked us up with an external Olympic team sports psych to share experiences and ideas on how to reach a greater level of achievement. The highly professional, suit-clad man in front of us that day shared advice he swore by when it came to training his accomplished Olympic athletes for their big event. Goal setting! He told us he couldn't recommend highly enough the value of specifically writing down a list of targets we wanted to hit every single day. He suggested writing in a diary, or on a phone app. What was important, he said, was that we actually dedicated the time to document our goals as part of our regular daily schedule. All of his athletes did it.

I remember one of my more sceptical colleagues openly scoffing at the idea and suggesting that preparing for an event that only happened once every four years sounded like it gave these athletes a lot more time than any of us seemed to have spare each day! People chuckled under their breath. But then the man went on to share a statistic from a recently published study that I've never forgotten and still use in much of my consultancy work today. That study came from Dr Gail Matthews, a psychology professor at the Dominican University of California, and it concluded that people who specifically write down their goals are up to 42 per cent more likely to achieve them than those who simply conceptualise those goals in their minds. Forty-two per cent! Stacking the odds in favour of accomplishing the things you want, by that much, instantly seemed like a no-brainer.

In Formula One today, sports psychologists form part of a group that helps us to operate at higher levels by trying to maximise every detail of what goes into our performance. I've worked with businesses and high-performing individuals who use similar methods to help them accomplish great things. After all, we're very happy to use a physical trainer or coach to get our bodies in shape to be able to achieve something big, so why not give the same attention to detail when it comes to our brains? Goal setting's a technique that each psychologist I've encountered has recommended, and writing down the goals we set ourselves is proven to be surprisingly beneficial.

Nearly twenty years on, I still write down my personal and professional goals almost every single day.

Ironically, given my colleagues' early scepticism on that day, we were already practising a version of this in our professional lives at McLaren. I normally encouraged my teams to actively write down what it was we were trying to achieve. Sometimes that was almost done for us in the form of our race weekend schedule. A minute-by-minute document detailed what state the car needed to be in by a certain time, or when we needed, within the regulations, to be completely off the grid ahead of the race start on Sunday, for example. It might be that the event scrutineers were coming to inspect the car's build specification at 4:35pm on the Thursday, in which case we knew the whole thing had to be together and in an inspectable condition by 4:30pm. That same car might be scheduled to be used for pitstop practice out in the pitlane at 2pm on the same day. So that was another milestone requiring the car in a different state, with pitstop practice brakes and brake ducts, pitstop wheels, the dummy crash structure (which would inevitably get smashed to bits by the rear jack) and protective covers on the floor and other sensitive components. The timeline was set and immovable, therefore it dictated the workload. That formed a series of short-term goals that we all knew we needed to hit hour by hour, that were documented and available for everyone in the team to see.

Aside from timetables and event schedules giving us timelines to work to inside the garage, we also wrote down our own work goals so that everyone knew what we were trying to achieve. These often took the form of simple job lists. Writing down or printing out a checklist of what physically needed to be done to the car was essentially a catalogue of our short-term goals. It gave us a guide to help navigate the day, it helped me to distribute tasks amongst my crews and, most importantly, it gave us all something we could satisfyingly tick off when we'd accomplished anything on it.

In addition to this, at regular intervals – the end of every day, after each track session and race weekend, once the season was over – we'd get together to assess our own performance. The term we use is 'debrief'. The mechanics got together to review how well their goals, or tasks on job lists, had been met. Other departments did the same. The engineering teams sat down with the drivers and analysed what we'd learnt. The point of each debrief was to check in with the goals we'd set ourselves and share what we'd discovered since. Had we achieved them? If so, how well? If not, why? The aim of every single debrief was to come up with a new set of goals. They might be completely new, or adaptations of previous ones, but the goals we set ourselves should always be evolving and moving forward as we learn more and develop.

This all highlighted an undoubted truth. People are far more likely to physically document their targets in their professional lives than they are in their personal lives. We present annual or quarterly budget targets to the shareholders. We 'pitch' goals to potential clients. We agree on the milestones we want to hit over the next twelve months in our end-of-year reviews with the boss. And so on. But we rarely do anything like this at home.

Using these powerful techniques away from work, when no one's watching and there's no accountability at stake, is somehow a lot harder to do. It's a bit like a professional footballer that 'piles on the pounds' as soon as they retire . . . they suddenly understand it was a lot easier to get up and train every single day when it was literally their job and they were being paid to do it.

What McLaren realised was that our success wasn't solely built on the way our team went about its business during the working hours of a season. The way each person lived their personal lives, how they behaved away from work, was intrinsically linked to how they showed up at the office or in the pitlane. The desire to continuously improve could be a holistic mindset applying to everything, but often only if there was deliberate intention for it to be that way. So could the team teach its people techniques that we could show them would improve their chances of success in Formula One, but also away from it in everything else they did? We had to do some learning.

Finding myself in that room with an Olympic sports psychologist was part of that learning process, and it kickstarted a fascination in my own life and work to discover more, as I know it did for lots of people in the end. Here's what I now know about setting goals, which I certainly didn't appreciate to the same extent back then.

That staggering revelation that we can increase our chances of accomplishing goals by more than 40 per cent just by writing them down seems absurd, but here's the reasoning behind it.

Committing goals to a page is also a commitment to oneself. When we write things down we usually take the time to articulate them in a clearly defined way. Even that short mental process means we're forced to think more about them than we otherwise might, and that creates a deeper internal connection.

Even the physical action of writing with a pen, or typing onto a screen, means we also have something visual in front of us to mirror back the thoughts we just had. It adds a level of subconscious reaffirmation, helping to confirm their credibility or importance in our minds.

Of course, having a document in front of us detailing the things we want to achieve also gives us a reference point to keep coming back to. That can help remotivate us in times of waning enthusiasm. When we do come back to it, hopefully we're able to tick off an item on the list and that creates a sense of achievement, which is powerful. The brain's reward centre fires up and makes us feel good through a release of dopamine, and that's addictive.

That list of goals also acts as a road map that can help you recover your direction and purpose if ever you stray during your journey.

MARGINAL GAIN
Write down short-term goals every single day, using a diary, a notepad, or even the notes or calendar app on your phone.

I find three to five easy-to-achieve things make a great starting point and I write them before bed the night before or first thing in the morning. Make one so easy you can tick it off with hardly any effort in the first thirty minutes of your day; it provides an early 'win' and helps you launch onto the next one. Keep the list with you. Add to it if you need to and celebrate the significant achievement of ticking something off along the way. This short-term goals list can be a guide for your day or week, eliminating aimless wandering and assisting in the pursuit of time and energy efficiency. By its very nature it literally helps you to get done what you need to do, so do it.

Gail Matthews' revelatory study noted three other factors that contribute to enhancing the likelihood of achieving the things we desire. If you want to level up your goal setting and increase the odds of success further, try this. As well as writing down goals, think a bit more about how you're going to hit them. Noting down the steps you'll take on the way to getting there amplifies all of the points above. Reason the problem out. Make assessments of what actions you can take, in turn giving yourself an even smaller set of very achievable goals to hit frequently along the way. This is exactly what an F1 team's debrief does. We don't just come out of the post-qualifying meeting saying we want to go out and win the race on Sunday; we also generate the necessary stepping stones to make it happen. That's where most of our time is actually spent.

If we've qualified near the back of the field, then maybe winning the Grand Prix might now be unrealistic. So we set an achievable goal that pushes us, perhaps finding a way to move forward from our lowly grid slot and get into the points-scoring places. We then need to look at our general car performance relative to our competitors' . . . did we qualify badly because that was our genuine pace, or have we actually got a much faster car, but made a mistake or had some bad luck? We conduct the same analysis for those cars around us on the grid and try to understand what they might be able to achieve on Sunday too. Can we set up the car to increase its ability to overtake on this track? Perhaps by lessening the wing angles, reducing downforce which might compromise cornering stability, making it harder to drive, but importantly reducing aerodynamic drag for higher top speeds along the straights where most overtaking's done? That might be a step we can actively take to move us closer to our goal. It goes on the list and, when the mechanics have completed the set-up change, it gets ticked off and we're one small step closer, or hopefully a little bit further along our road map, to success.

Another key understanding to come from Dr Matthews' study is that sharing those goals with other people can also be a significant factor in actually accomplishing them. It falls under the heading of accountability. It's much easier to turn up for training or deliver the project on time if you're directly accountable to someone else for it. When we leave work or retire, who's going to know, or care, if we actually hit the goals we set ourselves? We can tell ourselves we want to go to the gym, but when the alarm goes off early in the morning, there's no one to stop us hitting the snooze button. So, finding someone or a group of people we can share our targets with can really help to drag us out of bed so we don't 'disappoint them' or 'feel ashamed' of quitting. An F1 team will share its goals internally. The entire team's able to see what we're trying to do and how we're trying to do it. I know from my own personal perspective there was no way I was ever going to allow myself to feel like

I'd let my teammates down by not delivering what I set out to do. Perhaps you can set up a WhatsApp group amongst other gym-going friends to help push each other along the health journey you're on?

The last discovery from Matthews' study was the importance of putting in place a means to regularly revisit your goals. That might be structuring a defined schedule through which you come back at the end of every day or every week to check in with progress. It could be setting up a regular meeting that everyone involved needs to attend . . . like an F1 team debrief . . . or it could be making revisiting the list before you go to bed part of your daily routine. Coming back to look at the goals you set yourself has a number of benefits. It reminds you of the mission you're on, which is important. The way you felt when you constructed your goals, motivated and driven, may not necessarily be the same way you feel days or weeks later, or after the enormous disappointment of that catastrophic engine failure. Nudging yourself regularly back on track can really help you to recall why you're putting the effort in.

It also gives you a chance to amend the goals. Being determined, yet flexible, in your approach is by far the best way to achieve most things in life. The world has a way of throwing curveballs at us that change the game, like a disastrous qualifying. In Friday night's post-practice debrief, we may've been all set on winning the race and coming away with maximum points, the best possible stepping stone to achieving our longer-term goal of winning the title. Perhaps everything was looking good until it all went wrong for whatever reason on Saturday afternoon. If, in Saturday night's debrief, we just blindly ploughed on with the same lofty targets, we'd almost certainly feel demotivated because they were out of reach, and be disappointed on Sunday. But if we're flexible and revisit what we believe to now be possible, we can adapt the goals, or the path to achieving them, to something that feels difficult enough to push us, but realistic enough to be attainable, and then we have something sensible to aim for. Motivation returns.

So, to help you achieve your long-term goals, you could use your diary or journalling app and, as well as documenting your goals, use it as a debrief tool to check in every day or week with your progress towards them. If you didn't make progress, write that down too – don't pretend or leave out the days you struggled; they're a critical step towards the day you succeed. Tell someone else what your goals are. It could be a friend or family member, a personal confidant, or you could find it more helpful to tell the world. Social media can be a powerful way to increase accountability and help with motivation. I deliberately announced on Instagram that I was writing this book when I first began and I'm super grateful to all those who checked in every now and then to see how I was getting on. There was no way I could've ever gone back to Instagram to announce that I'd given up and quit – and as a result, you're reading it now.

Infinite goals

All of this is well and good when it comes to keeping the show on the road. But one thing that working in F1 taught me is that there always needs to be something more.

What I've come to appreciate since leaving McLaren is that many of the behaviours and thought processes I saw as 'normal' aren't as ubiquitous outside of the sport as I'd imagined. I'd become conditioned to operate at such a consistently high level, to demand so much of myself and others, that it subconsciously became my 'baseline'. In all honesty I've struggled on many occasions to adapt back into the 'real world' since leaving the team because I've become impatient with what I see as inefficiencies, laziness or corner-cutting. I've frustratedly 'sacked' at least one set of builders and 'trades' on every one of the five major home improvement or renovation projects my wife and I have undertaken – often more than one!

That's not to say I'm perfect, because I'm far from it – just ask my wife! I don't do everything to F1 standards all of the time; in fact I'm sure she'll tell you there's an awful lot that I definitely don't! But when it comes to something that I deem important, or that might create an advantage for me, I'll immediately go into my F1 mentality of doing whatever it takes. You'll never find a hotel bed that I've slept in unmade when I leave, because I believe in respect. I regularly unpack the loaded dishwasher, only to reorganise and reload it when in almost everyone else's eyes it would be just fine, because I believe in efficiency. I become almost instantly frustrated, to a level I know is ridiculous and even sometimes unfair to those around me, with what I deem to be poor timekeeping, even by the smallest amounts, because I believe in punctuality. In my mind I just try to always do the things that I think matter to the best standard possible and I sometimes find it very hard to understand why everyone else in the world doesn't do the same. When chatting recently to my friend and former teammate David Coulthard on my *Pitlane Life Lessons* podcast, he explained that the mentality he came out of the team with was that 'everything matters' and it resonated extremely well with me.

That striving for more, that uncompromising desire to be better today than I was the day before, was what helped me become successful in F1. It's something that most people in the top teams shared. But its effect was supercharged once we embraced the concept of infinite goals.

Many big companies I work with today have 'mission

statements', many of which could sometimes be described as infinite goals. But I think it's also true to say that some of those companies seem to have them because they look good emblazoned across the wall above main reception, or as a hashtag on Instagram, rather than for what they actually stand for. The concept of an infinite goal is to some extent similar to the carrot suspended in front of the nose of a donkey. It can never actually be reached, but is always there as something motivating to chase. Part of its beauty is that it avoids the very real possibility of motivation falling away once a major target's reached. If the donkey actually got the carrot one day, why keep moving forward?

The well-documented phenomenon of 'Gold Medal Syndrome' is a great example of this. An athlete has a monumental goal in their life: winning an Olympic gold medal, the biggest prize in the sport. As a youngster it seems so big it can feel infinite, like they can never really achieve it, but it's the dangling carrot that gets them up early every day of their lives to train hard. They progress up the ladder and the goal becomes more real; they're openly chasing it as the ultimate target. Perhaps they might even make it to an Olympic squad, a huge accomplishment which becomes part of who they are in life. They're now an Olympian. Then one day many, many years, even sometimes decades, after they dedicated their life's work to it, they win the elusive Olympic gold medal. They finally get the carrot they've been chasing. The feeling's incredible, the celebration huge . . . but then, the very next day, the carrot's gone. The thing they've been hunting and struggling for, sometimes their entire identity, has been ticked off the list and vanished. Now what?

The sad truth is that many end up in a downward spiral of

mental and emotional struggle. I've seen people in F1 teams have similar experiences after winning the F1 World Championship, our equivalent of the Olympic gold medal. It's probably no coincidence that after almost a decade of trying, not to mention the many years struggling to break into F1 in the first place, once I finally became part of a title-winning team, I began to think about my own exit strategy.

On one hand you could say asking an Olympic athlete to switch their life's focus from winning medals to some kind of higher-level infinite goal might be hard, impossible even, given how deeply ingrained in their make-up it's been since they were young. But the point about setting the correct infinite goal is that if you are able to make that the overall focus, the thing that all other goals point towards, it should inevitably lead to the Olympic gold medal or F1 World Title along the way. Except, crucially, it doesn't have to represent an abrupt end to the journey. An Olympic athlete might choose something like 'To strive for continuous improvement in mental and physical performance without limits,' or 'To always do whatever it takes to show up as the best I can be.' If an athlete truly focuses on goals like these, there's a high chance it will lead to medals, but importantly there's a high chance it will lead to many medals over an extended period of time.

The idea is to move what someone values as true 'success' from a moment in time, or a tangible reward, to an ongoing set of positive habits. A lifestyle, or the *process* of striving for those prizes, rather than the prizes themselves. It's the way of living and operating that creates happiness or effectiveness, not something you attain along the way. Winning one F1 title won't, by itself, set you up to win more of them, but an ongoing highly effective set of habits and determined mindset just might.

At McLaren, during my time trying to help forge new horizons for the team and pushing us towards new ways of thinking in this regard, our first informal version of an 'infinite challenge', as we called it back then, was simply 'To be the best Formula One team we could be.' I still think it stands as a solid infinite goal. It's open-ended, clear, performance-driven and aspirational. It might be basic, but that's exactly what we thought would work best and I for one pushed for simplicity during the initial discussions I was involved in. Something that's broad enough to apply in all scenarios and give everyone in the team a distinct vision they'd be proud to be a part of. We figured that an 'infinite challenge' should continuously push us in the right direction and that no matter what the present state of play at any time, even if we were up to our eyes in the broken bits of a smouldering crashed racing car, a mini and momentary debrief in anyone's mind could help us appreciate that what we were doing was just part of the overall process to be the best Formula One team we could be. Even a crash could be reframed as the driver learning where the limits of grip were, which could make him faster next time. In the garage we could be understanding how best to prepare the spares and sub-assembly departments for even more time-sensitive occurrences of incidents like this one in the future . . . and so on.

On any given day we could ask ourselves if what we were doing was getting us closer to it, which of course it always should. It was constantly referred to in meetings and internal communications as we began to get used to the idea of chasing this new North Star. In all honesty it took a lot of people a long time to really embrace the idea of striving for something so seemingly immeasurable in a sport where everything else was so data-driven.

To truly believe in shifting the overall focus of a well-established group from a distinct end-point, or globally celebrated goal, to being focused on the everyday habits we cultivated wasn't easy or fast. Sport, in particular, is so binary in the way it measures success. You often either win or you lose and that result's not even always in your control, yet the prize is what's celebrated, not the performance. Inside the team we needed a cultural change where everyone's individual and collective behaviours became the measure of us, not just the awards that someone else gave us if the result went our way. We still aimed to win, but we did it by aiming to maximise the process of trying to win. It took time, years, and was difficult to quantify in any scientific way, but I personally have no doubt that focusing on what we did, as opposed to what we wanted to achieve, led to us winning the title in 2008.

Our 'infinite challenge' was simply a philosophy we were all working towards, something many people had inadvertently always done, just without openly acknowledging it. With it established as a guiding principle, something we continuously checked in with, we began to appreciate that everything we did should align with it and that if we continually pursued that goal, the on-track wins would eventually take care of themselves.

Of course in a team environment it may not prevent people like me from seeing the hitting of a major milestone, like when we did win that World Championship with Lewis Hamilton, as a rational 'jumping off' point, but it does give the team a continued and endless pursuit of greatness.

In my own life it was only years later that I finally worked out what I thought my own infinite goal should be. My career's taken a number of twists and turns through writing and TV broadcasting to the many other things I cover today like public speaking, consultancy, F1 commentary and podcasting, to name a few. Each one of those things, though, is inextricably linked to my journey through F1. I've developed a real appreciation for the privileged existence I've had, living and working as part of an elite F1 organisation. Almost all the work I do today is in some way designed to share that with those not lucky enough to have been exposed to the same experiences.

The infinite goal I've set myself is 'Do the right things, do the things right, and help as many people as possible through sharing.'

I find it broad enough to not be too restrictive, yet specific enough to keep me focused on what I'm trying to do. The first part of it is something regular listeners and viewers of my *Pitlane Life Lessons* podcast will be familiar with. I say it at the end of every episode as a suggestion to those listening for something to strive for until the next show, but in my own life I try to remember it always. For me, 'Do the right things' means trying to make the best decisions I can, making the right choices as I go through my days. Then 'do the things right' means to try and do the things that matter to me to the best of my ability, to do things properly. The second part I added in later and of course I hope it helps others to benefit from what I know and am lucky enough to have access to. It can never be 'completed', but allows room to be innovative and creative about how I pursue it, and it also gives me enough scope to point almost all the many aspects of my personal and professional life in that direction. I share what I've learnt, my experiences, my time, my love and more, and reminding myself constantly that this is my infinite goal keeps me deploying those things for what I believe in most, helping people. I hope this very book is a great example of trying to help you to achieve more by sharing what

I know, which you may not get the opportunity to experience first-hand yourself.

This is your chance to start thinking about what your infinite goal might look like. It might take you a while and you may well change your mind over and over before settling on something you think encapsulates your mission. Try to be as self-aware as you can about who you are and who you want to be. For the infinite goal to have a positive effect on your life, you need to truly believe that it aligns with the person you're striving to become. If you fast forward to a point in your mind, years, even decades, from now, what sort of life would you be proud to have lived? Don't just think about the achievements you want to collect along the way: think about the way you want to collect them. If you won nothing, but stayed true to this infinite goal, could you be happy and content that you did your best? Would you be proud of the way you did it?

Once you've landed on your infinite goal, write it down somewhere prominent, make it your screensaver, get it tattooed on yourself, whatever works for you, but make sure it can't get forgotten. It should describe, in a nutshell, the journey you're on, your purpose, and perhaps even why it matters.

Because it's infinite, it'll always be there to refer back to and that's important. Everything you do should be aligned with this top-level goal. I find it a really useful way to help me make the big decisions I face. If you're presented with two options at a 'fork-in-the-road' moment, it's highly possible that upon reflection one will lead towards your infinite goal whereas one may not. If you truly believe in the goal you've set for yourself, you've probably got your answer right there. Don't be afraid to change it; in fact, it's worth constantly re-evaluating it. We evolve as people. I think quite differently today in my forties than I did in my twenties, so my mission's also changed along with that. Don't hold on to a goal just because it sounds good; make it something that serves you in this phase of your life.

PITLANE LESSONS

- Create a range of short-term goals that you can tick off each day to give yourself 'wins' that can create valuable momentum.
- Make your longer-term goals deliberately difficult, but possible. Make them mean something to you personally. Aiming for someone else's goals rarely works.
- Writing your goals down increases your chances of achieving them exponentially.
- Make yourself accountable by sharing your goals with other people.
- Create an infinite goal for yourself that will help lead to a permanent shift in your habits and behaviour.

2.

INNOVATION ISN'T WHAT YOU DO – IT'S HOW YOU THINK
How You Can Innovate Your Way to Success

There was always one department at McLaren that intrigued me more than any other. R & D. The Research & Development group, based in a far corner of the futuristic McLaren Technology Centre, were the ones charged with experimenting with new ideas. If someone had a technical brainwave anywhere in the business that might somehow improve performance, no matter how far-fetched it seemed, R & D had the freedom to find ways of figuring out if it could actually work. They'd build scale models, devise tests and conduct investigations on some of the most top-secret ideas in F1. So potentially valuable were some of the innovations coming through R & D, that it was a highly restricted area even to most McLaren staff. It was only when I progressed into a more senior position in the company over time that I was given the required clearance to be able to freely enter. The potential value of these technical innovations was of course that they were indeed innovative, meaning no one else in this highly competitive sport had thought of them, or made them work yet. The ideas needed to be protected from escaping the team's four walls until they were ready for deployment in the field.

I used to think of it as McLaren's version of Q Branch in the James Bond films and, once I got my security clearance, I was in there as much as I could be.

I'd go there at lunchtimes and just hang out with the guys. I'd make ridiculous detours on my way to see someone else in the building, just so I could pop in and see what was going on. I'd even come in early some days just to spend an hour in there before officially starting work. I was eager to know what we had coming through the system and hopefully be able to offer my own ideas and feedback from my perspective on whatever was being researched and developed. I felt an air of excitement and anticipation each time I swiped my security pass and walked in.

Over the years I saw some amazing inventions at different stages of gestation. I remember one day walking in and asking what was new and the guys in there all laughed as they explained this mad idea they'd been asked to test.

They had a spare F1 car chassis and inside they'd mocked up some ducting running along the chassis wall from the inside of the nosecone at the very front, through the cockpit next to where the driver would sit and all the way out towards the rear of the car. There was a deliberate and intriguing hole in the ducting about halfway between the pedals and where the steering wheel sits.

They went on to detail how an aerodynamicist had had the idea of channelling high-speed air from an inlet at the front of the car, through the ducting, with it exiting at a very specific point near the rear wing at the back of the car. At first it made little sense as the rear wing was already in the path of high-velocity airflow; it was obviously designed that way to generate maximum downforce and increase grip so the car could corner at high speed. Blowing some of the rear wing's airflow through the ducting wasn't necessary and wouldn't seem to add anything.

But innovation's about solving problems and one of the perennial challenges facing F1 car designers and aero teams is the fact that whilst we want to maximise downforce and therefore grip through the corners of a racetrack, that downforce also comes with the associated and inevitable penalty of aerodynamic drag forces that slow us down along the straights where we just need all-out speed. So ideally you'd have wings for the turns and no wings at all on the straights, but with any form of moveable wings banned in the regulations at the time, that wasn't physically possible.

The innovative thinking behind the unusual ducting was all about the positioning of that mysterious hole in the cockpit. In normal running conditions, the airflow being channelled through the ducting would pass from the front of the car and the hole was designed in such a way that it became the path of least resistance, and the air would naturally exit through the hole and inconsequentially escape to atmosphere through the cockpit. It would never reach the end of the ducting at the back and the car's aerodynamics would behave as normal. However, that clever little hole was placed very specifically so that as the car came out of a corner on track and onto a straight, where downforce was no longer required and drag became a hindrance, the driver could move his now redundant left knee as he came off the brakes, against the ducting and block the hole. This meant that the air flowing through the duct could no longer escape and therefore travelled along its length to the back of the car. Its exit point was directed very specifically at the rear wing in a way that disrupted, or rerouted, the optimal flow over its surface and the wing effectively 'stalled', or stopped generating downforce and drag. In turn that meant the car could reach higher maximum speeds until the driver then moved his knee again at the end of the straight to hit the brake pedal, re-opening the hole and reengaging the optimal airflow over the rear wing to maximise downforce for the approaching corner. It was genius.

At the time it seemed like a crazy idea that surely couldn't actually work. But as it got developed by the R & D team and tried in the wind tunnel, it became clear it was something of a masterstroke. It didn't contravene the regulations preventing moveable aerodynamic surfaces and it was largely hidden from view. The ducting was eventually integrated into the chassis design and was fed by a small intake on the top of the mono-coque near the front of the car. The intake's exact positioning happened to align perfectly with the letter 'F' in our main sponsor, Vodafone's, branding and so, some time later, once eventually discovered by the media and rival teams, it became famously known as the 'F Duct'.

On another day, I swiped and walked into R & D to find they had one of our pitstop refuelling rigs set up. It was a familiar piece of equipment to me as I'd previously been trained as the back-up refueller in the crew. The rules stated that every team had to use the same standard rig from the approved supplier and in no way was anyone allowed to modify it.

The limiting factor when it came to pitstops back in the early 2000s was almost always delivering the required amount of fuel into the car. The aerospace-designed rigs pumped it in at twelve litres per second and that was the same for every team in the pitlane. This was the process.

The desired fuel quantity was inputted into the system's software program and, as the car stopped in the pitstop box in a race, the aircraft-style rig was jammed onto a heavily sprung valve on the side of the car. Once fully connected and latched, the system would automatically begin pumping petrol in. The tyres were changed and then we'd wait for the fuel. When the preset fuel quantity was delivered a motorised mechani-cal valve inside the refuelling nozzle would wind closed before we'd finally get a green light on the rig's display to let us know.

Only at that point could we react and begin the slightly clunky two-stage process of detaching from the car. Firstly releasing a safety latch and then three people lifting the heavy nozzle and pipework away from the car for it to be dispatched back into the race.

It was frustratingly slow, but with such tight rules around using the standard rigs and not modifying them in any way, there seemed little anyone could do to speed it up. Until we innovated in the most brilliant way.

Someone had realised that one of the most infuriatingly slow parts of the process were the multiple steps to remove the rig once the fuel was in the car. Of course it had to be safe, which is why the steps were there, but we'd had a brilliantly simple idea on how to speed it up without compromising safety.

Once all the pre-programmed fuel had been delivered, the rig shut off its pumps. Then this motorised valve sealed the pipe before illuminating the green lights to tell us to begin detaching the nozzle from the car. With no more fuel flowing, we figured that we could actually safely remove the nozzle immediately, but had no indication of when that was until the lights went green after the valve had fully closed.

After a routine visit for a medical checkup, one of the team had walked into work one day inspired with a brainwave.

The genius idea was to run a doctor's stethoscope down the sleeve of the pitstop refueller, with one end in his ear and the other, the bit the doctor places on your chest when listening to your breathing, in the palm of his glove. Whilst the fuel was being delivered, he'd surreptitiously place it on the side of the fuel nozzle and once all the petrol was in and the pumps had stopped, he could hear the internal whirring of the valve closing over the noise of the car's engine through the stethoscope. As the valve began to close, instead of waiting for that to slowly complete and then illuminate the lights, we started to decouple the safety latch from the car and by the time the lights had gone green we were almost stepping away from the car. We hadn't modified the rig in any way and we were able to keep it secret from the prying eyes of other teams: it was brilliant innovation at its best. It saved us perhaps a second in each pitstop, which doesn't sound like much, but in F1 terms that was huge.

There were many days like these, where I was blown away by the creative thinking of some of the best minds in F1. I felt proud. I feel proud now, sharing these innovative solutions with you. It inspired me to believe that there was always a way around a problem, even within the tight confines of F1, or whichever framework or rules we operate in. I still believe it today. Some of the experiments I watched unfolding went on to become well-known, successful car developments that perhaps helped us win races and occasionally even revolutionised the industry. Others didn't ever make it out of that room in our factory, but that's the nature of being innovative.

Innovation refers to something new, which solves a problem, that's never been done before and, as such, we tend to think of it as unusual, unfamiliar, even rare. In F1 circles, though, not only is it not rare: it's simply the norm. The sport and all of its participants are in a constant state of innovation in the endless race towards ultimate performance. Even small, seemingly insignificant innovations, like the 'F Duct' or the redeployment of the doctor's stethoscope, can have an outsized impact. Every second matters.

Not only is everyone in continuous competition with each other at the very highest level, but the framework in which they operate, F1's technical, sporting and now financial regulations, are forever being reviewed, tweaked and even overhauled. It often means the amazing technical idea on your car that's giving you a significant advantage right now will become out-lawed or obsolete before the next season starts, sometimes even before. It can be frustrating and infuriating, but it's also part of the reason this industry's developed a culture where innovation's seen as much as a necessary requirement to get ahead as it is an absolute minimum standard for not being left behind.

Of course the wider environment, the world that F1 and all of us exist within, is also forever evolving. It presents new challenges for some and opportunities for others across an infinite spectrum of scale and complexity, for which many of the solutions rely on an innovative approach.

> Being innovative isn't just the process of inventing something like a clever technical trick on an F1 car, or a revolutionary new product; it describes the traits of certain people or groups. Innovation's a way of thinking.

Having spent most of my working life in and around this sport as a competitor, broadcaster and businessman, the idea of thinking this way is just a part of who I am today. Throughout this chapter I hope to be able to explain the techniques, tips and mindset required to innovate like an F1 team in the everyday context of life.

Innovation needs time and space

For the best F1 teams, innovation starts with the creation of the right environment.

The R & D department at McLaren were never once told how to overcome a problem we'd identified; they were just presented with the challenge and left to try and find a solution in whatever creative ways they could dream up. In some ways, that might seem contradictory to Ron Dennis's desire to control every detail of the company, but although it appeared as if he might've liked to prescribe a company hairstyle at times, he also knew that what mattered most was winning. To do that we needed to have better ideas than the competition.

A company culture that enables and encourages innovation is one where members of the team feel like they have an element of space and freedom.

The 'space' is to allow for people to think outside the traditional box. If they feel restricted, either physically, mentally or metaphorically, it's much harder to have any spare capacity for creative or inventive thinking. More 'space' is required because the innovative development process isn't linear; it can be all over the place at times. It's often branching off on a tangent idea simultaneously or in replacement of the original train of thought, halfway through. It's messy. Think of it as working in narrow channels leading to narrow trains of thought. Innovators need vast spaces in which to throw around vast ideas before eventually trying to narrow them back down in the end.

The 'freedom' part is about instilling a company or team culture that allows, even encourages, failures. Ron Dennis once told me that if we delve into our failures as a team in the same forensic way we analyse the milliseconds of lap time gained or lost by our car through a corner, we'll find our biggest successes. He hated losing, maybe more than anyone else I know, but he didn't necessarily hate the idea of failure, not when it led to winning in the end. He gave us freedom, in many aspects of what we did, to try new things and embrace the failures that came from them. That freedom allowed us to be open-minded about taking risks and opening new doors without the fear that, if it didn't work out, it would be the end of the world. It might take longer to get there, but if you get to a place no one's ever been before and reap the untapped rewards for doing so, it's worth it. Especially in a competitive environment like Formula One. Feeling 'free' to get things wrong helped to generate many of the crazy ideas that came through the R & D department over the years and many of those helped us to win World Championships.

In the 'real world', these concepts just need to be a perception felt by those involved. That can come from the boss openly celebrating the ambition of a failed attempt at finding a new solution to a problem and encouraging the team to have another go. If it was easy, someone would've done it already, and if the team sees the boss taking that viewpoint, it begins to set the culture. The most innovative companies and F1 teams don't need a handbook or set of rules to outline how you should feel or think. They don't prescribe a set number of failed attempts at an idea before the idea has to be shelved in favour of a known solution. They place trust in those that have the crazy ideas, to try and make them work as long as they believe they can. They create 'space' and 'freedom' and then have faith in the people they've hired.

Ask what it's worth to you, not what it costs

For that to work, the company has to truly want to be the best at something and be willing to take hits along the way in order to get there. They need a big-picture mindset with 'getting there' as the biggest priority over and above the intricate details of exactly *how* they get there. They sometimes need to have their judgement so naively clouded by their own self-belief that it *'might just work'* that they're able to somehow fight off the naysayers and make it happen despite the resistance.

It probably doesn't need to be said that not all the innovations I saw being developed saw the light of day on an F1 car in the heat of battle. The exact 'hit rate' would've ebbed and flowed at different times, but it's probably safe to say there were more ideas that never ended up going racing than those that did. That's innovation.

It's generally not a very efficient process, which is partly why not everyone can or wants to do it. It's a process of trial and error, of experimentation and testing. Because, by its very nature, no one's done it before; there is no blueprint or instruction manual for what you're trying to achieve and that means that, on the way to finding the right answer, there's a high chance you'll hit plenty of wrong answers first. Innovators need to be comfortable with that.

When I worked with Adrian Newey, the most successful and decorated car designer in F1 history, he was convinced he could find an innovative way to utilise the highly energised hot gases exiting the exhaust pipe to improve aerodynamic downforce by rerouting them through the car's floor. He was given total freedom to explore the idea and we tried multiple solutions on our cars, all of which failed for various reasons. Running the extremely hot exhaust through the tightly packaged confines of the carbon fibre floor meant the car regularly came back from a run on fire or with the surrounding carbon melted. The theory was good, but neither the materials science of the time, nor our ability to execute the idea in reality, was advanced enough. It appeared it just wasn't going to work. That didn't stop Adrian though. He never gave up on the idea, having total belief in the advantages it could offer, and after literally years of trying, going back and forth to his drawing board, and even moving on later in his career to Red Bull Racing, the concept of F1's Exhaust Blown Diffuser was ultimately so successful it later defined an era of the sport.

When an innovative team or person has identified a problem

they want to solve, they go all in: the only thing that matters is getting to the right solution in the end. If finding that solution is important enough, it won't matter how many steps it takes to get there, or often even how much it costs to achieve it. Solving the problem is the driving force, not the efficiency of the process.

You could of course argue that Formula One's an industry with enormous budgets where they can easily afford to think this way. There is some truth to this. But I have a different perspective. Formula One's an industry that's evolved and shaped itself to look the way it does due to the necessity to innovate in competition. Rather than innovation being a product of a large budget, the large budget is, at least in part, a product of the need to innovate. At the highest level of sport or business, in a landscape that's constantly evolving, finding new ways to solve problems that might otherwise hold you back is an essential component. The size of the budget itself is not the most important thing, more the relative portion of it you see fit to dedicate to thinking outside the box.

And that's where the same philosophy can be applied to people living lives outside F1. When we're faced with a particular problem that needs to be solved, the first question we should ask ourselves is 'How high up our priority list does this sit?'

At McLaren we'd weigh up the value that would come with solving that problem against the expenditure in resources (not least time) it would involve.

So, when we were inventing the 'F Duct' at McLaren, the problem was the 'benefit of aerodynamic downforce versus the penalty of aerodynamic drag' conundrum that everyone in Formula One faces when designing cars. The potential upside was an increase in performance that no one else could easily match at the time because of the integral way it had to be designed into the car's DNA and our ability to keep much of it hidden from view of other teams. So the advantage in our world of competition was substantial. The cost when we started was that we had no idea if it would or could work and the lengthy experimentation process to find out took resources away from other exploratory performance avenues we were pursuing at the same time. If we hadn't managed to 'blunt force engineer' it into existence, by trying things, having them fail and then trying again, we could find ourselves behind the curve of others who developed along a much safer but less optimistic path.

It's not always a simple answer. At different times, different problems in our lives become more or less important, dependent on all sorts of factors. So it's fine for our drive and ability to innovate to vary along with that. If we can make an argument to ourselves that it's OK to 'get around', or to 'live with', a certain issue, then we're highly unlikely to be motivated to go and find a way to fix it, especially if doing so is a time-, energy- and finance-consuming operation.

But when you've identified the area you want to innovate in, you should prepare to push yourself as far as you're able to go to find the solution. In F1's intense competition, the theory's generally that if we're not aiming to be the best, those around us will be and therefore we'll get left behind. Pushing the boundaries is part of operating at the very highest level and so the question often comes down to 'Are we *really* willing to do whatever it takes to get to where we want to be?'

So it's here where you need to be honest with yourself. Most people aren't willing to push the limits of what's possible. Maybe because they either don't deem the problem to be severe enough, or they assume the cost of doing so is too great. But that internal assessment, quite often in my experience, doesn't always align with the external projection of a lot of people's ambitions or goals.

Someone might declare that their number-one priority for the new year is to get fit. They might tell the world on social media. They join a gym and start going on 1 January and then regularly for a couple of weeks, posting pics from the cross-trainer. But by now enthusiasm's beginning to wane, they're tired and the commute to get to the gym in the morning's becoming a pain, it takes too much time, so they don't go as much. Then they realise the cost of the gym is a lot and they're not really using it as much as they used to, so it doesn't really seem worth the money. The Instagram pics fade away and they cancel the membership. The problem they were trying to solve, getting fit, is not *really* the most important thing to them, otherwise even if time and money were factors, they'd still find a way to achieve the goal. They'd innovate.

They could work out at home, for free, using objects around the house as weights for resistance. They could join, or even create, a community, either online or local to them, to help with accountability and support. Maybe they could run or cycle to work to save time and money, whilst still helping to solve the problem. Simple ideas, but the point is that only if the motivation's high enough to succeed will the drive to innovate win through.

A good example of people willing to do whatever it takes to innovate their way to success are a lot of the founders of companies I speak to. If someone starts a business and it scales to become successful in the corporate landscape, a few things have likely happened.

- They will either have had an idea, or at least been brave enough to take an idea and push it through so much resistance, even when it didn't seem to make sense. Quite often both.

- They'll have overcome enormous hurdles, perhaps ones they only discovered when it was too late to turn back.
- They'll have had to get very creative in the way they think, just to survive.
- I'm sure there'll have been plenty of people along the journey that were all too ready to point out that it was highly likely to fail.
- But somehow they got through these and every other challenge that came their way to make it a success in the end . . .

These founders are innovators by nature. They understand that on the other side of closed doors, doors that can seem so hard to open for most people, are amazing opportunities for those willing to force them ajar. They've done it, and especially in the case of someone who's scaled to a substantial level, they've had that belief affirmed in the most impactful way. Because it's part of their character, they carry that mindset into the new business as it grows and it infects others as the team builds out.

How to do it

I'm often asked to come into an organisation to help foster this kind of innovation culture and one of the first things I try and do is sit down with the CEO and leadership team. Despite whatever official brief I've been given, I can often tell within the first ten minutes of conversation whether or not the company actually lives by the mission statement it claims it's beholden to. A lot of companies want to be innovative, they want the potential that can come from it, but they aren't really ready for what that entails.

In recent F1 history there are good examples, which I often use with clients, to demonstrate how creating a culture of innovation can lead to massive and sustained success, but also how doing the opposite can lead to a very different outcome.

When Austrian businessman Toto Wolff came in as Team Principal, Executive Director and a major shareholder of the Mercedes F1 team in 2013, he came in with a long-term vision for the company which was a bit different to the way it had been run previously.

The overall goal was still to try and win F1 races and eventually world titles, but the team's order of priorities changed. Toto walked into a team full of great people, with great resources, desperately trying to design and build a great racing car for their two great drivers. But for all the great things he saw, he was immediately drawn to some of the things he noticed as being not-so-great. He took over an organisation focusing almost everything on its core product, the F1 car.

Toto had a different, bigger vision. He saw a future where the great F1 car they needed would be an almost inevitable byproduct of creating the right environment in which it could be dreamt up and manufactured. He didn't just want to turn up and compete in the sport; he wanted to revolutionise and dominate it.

He spent time building and developing that environment and between 2014 and 2021 the team won a record-breaking eight consecutive Constructors' World Titles.

The results obviously speak largely for themselves, but it's the way the team operated in the background that I find really interesting. Following the thesis of giving every member of the organisation 'space' and 'freedom', placing total trust in the

people behind the scenes, the group naturally began to innovate. Toto cultivated a no-blame culture, where the cliché of
winning and losing as a team became the reality and the brilliant men and women at Mercedes felt empowered to find
solutions to problems that might otherwise hold them back.
He repeatedly told them failure was just part of the process of
winning and was very quick to admit publicly when he didn't
get things right himself.

Attention to detail was spread into everything, not just the
car. The team presented itself more professionally, the factory
was developed to be more operationally user-friendly and they
deliberately chose to try and do things the 'right way'. They
formed an image of a team with morals and values that those
working in it could be proud of. The culture in the team began
to focus on the people in the team, not just on what those people
were producing and it made them feel valued, supported and,
ultimately, happy. They embarked on innovative marketing campaigns that had deep social and cultural messaging in a bid to
help change the sport for the better alongside Lewis Hamilton,
who was now driving for them. All things that, on the face of it,
didn't make the car go faster, but the truth is that they really did.

Changing who they were and what they stood for as a team
in F1 went against the traditional grain of just winning at all
costs and shifted how they were perceived by those watching
on. They became loved from the outside by more than just
their own fans, which I can tell you from my own experience at
McLaren has a really positive impact on everyone on the inside.
The legacy they began to generate created respect and a sense
of pride from within and when people are proud to work for a
team, when they feel valued by that team, they behave differently as a result. They walk differently, they talk differently and
most importantly they think differently.

In early 2020 as F1's annual pre-season testing got underway in Barcelona, I was watching the on-track coverage from home. In one of the first laps for the Mercedes team I noticed something very strange as Lewis Hamilton exited a corner and put the power down onto the straight . . . he was seemingly pulling back on the steering wheel, like an aircraft pilot taking off on a runway, and the wheel and steering column, components that are always firmly fixed in their fore and aft position in an F1 car, were sliding backwards! It caught me by huge surprise, as it did with everyone watching on, and the speculation as to what on earth they were trying to do exploded online as we all tried to figure it out.

Mercedes had found an ingenious way, within the regulations, to adjust the steering geometry of the car's front wheels at different parts of the racetrack. They could change the toe angle, the angle the wheels sit at relative to the car's centre line when viewed from above, to give different benefits at different times. The innovative idea could be used to allow the wheels to run dead straight, or true, when looking for max speed and therefore minimum rolling resistance or 'drag' along the fast straights, but then have a small amount of optimal 'toe out' to give better turn-in on the way into a corner. By sliding the steering column rearwards through some clever engineering, they could introduce a small amount of tyre scrub to generate tyre temperature in preparation for a qualifying lap or after a safety car period in a race when everything had cooled off after running slowly for a few laps. It gave an extra element of control, or another tool, to be able to optimise the car for various situations and it was brilliant. They solved a performance-limiting problem by thinking about it in a different way to anyone else.

It was so clever and relatively simple as a concept, like the best innovations often are. Notably it wasn't something that a new change in rules had just allowed to happen, but something that had always been available as an option to every team in the pitlane, yet no one had thought of. Now, though, Mercedes had created an environment where members of the team felt so safe and comfortable sharing even the wildest ideas if they believed they had potential. The pride on the face of James Allison, the team's technical boss, was overwhelming as he fronted up to the F1 media at lunchtime on that first day of testing to clarify what every other team and fan had got themselves into a frenzy over. Even the fact that he came out and explained it to the world was unusual, as opposed to trying to keep it as secret as possible for as long as possible. It was a sign of how comfortable the team felt about their own position; they were proud of what they'd done and wanted to recognise, publicly, the people in the team that had made it happen.

That's how you generate innovation and new ideas. You can't just instruct someone to be innovative; you need to take the right person or people and put them in the right space, with the right amount of freedom and support . . . and then you wait. As I said before, it's not always an efficient process. It takes a strong belief and a lot of patience and trust, which are not always things that everybody finds easy to come by.

I have no idea how many versions of what Mercedes termed 'DAS', or their 'Dual Axis Steering' system, it took before they found the optimum way to make it work, or even how many other ideas they may've had to try to achieve something similar, but they got there in the end and with it they won another two championships.

The sustained years of winning in this highly competitive, elite sport are impressive enough, but to see how the team reacted to being overtaken as the dominant force on track by

Red Bull in recent times gives another hint as to what sort of company they are.

When the tides turned in 2022 and Mercedes got a bit lost with their car development for the next couple of years, they didn't panic, or sack people; they worked through their problems together and trusted that the same philosophy and team that brought them so much success would also be able to innovate their way out of trouble. They continued to believe in each other's ability to come up with great ideas and were comfortable enough to be sufficiently self-critical to accept it when they got things wrong. There was no blame. Instead of playing safe and looking for short-term, limiting fixes, they continued to push the limits in the same way they'd been doing for years and eventually it paid off. They began winning races again.

Throughout the same period there was a very different story unfolding at another team in the pitlane: Ferrari.

How not to do it

Ferrari are the most successful team in F1 history with more world titles than anybody else. They've known how to win over and over again and yet, as I write this chapter in 2025, they haven't won a championship in Formula One since 2007. At times during the period in question Ferrari still came up with a great car. It's testament to the fact that they had some brilliant and experienced people working there, but even with some world-class drivers, there always seemed to be something missing that meant they never got across the line first. As I've said already and it's true with most things in life, symptoms are just that, symptomatic of something further downstream that's causing the problems to arise.

It's true that Ferrari face different pressures than most teams in the sport, holding almost national team, or even religious, status in Italy. If they win, the country celebrates, and if they don't, the nation wants to know why.

But comparing the two teams over the period in which Toto was building the record-breaking outfit at Mercedes, there are a few stark differences on the outside that might hint towards the very different approaches each team took on the inside.

One of the most obvious is the sheer amount of staff turn-over being much higher at one than at the other, notably in the most senior, Team Principal position. Whilst no one got fired for trying but failing at Mercedes, that's exactly what seemed to happen at Ferrari over and over again. Where Toto presided over a stable ship with a long-term vision, Ferrari went through FOUR different Team Principals between 2014 and 2020.

One of the big problems with firing people you judge to have underperformed in the short term, especially the very public-facing, senior people like the person in charge of the team, is the message it sends to everyone else. If your boss is vulnerable when results don't come quickly enough, then surely everyone else is too. And if the staff fear for their jobs, they're far less likely to think boldly and creatively. There's no space to think outside the box and there's certainly no freedom to be able to get things wrong.

When I analysed Mercedes' years of success versus Ferrari's drought in the same period, one thing I picked up on was the way the two teams communicated. In talking to the media, Toto and his team seemed surprisingly open in a world which is traditionally so secretive. The team were noticeably transparent about how they won races when talking afterwards, but also refreshingly honest about why they failed to win when someone else did a better job. They were comfortable admitting when they could've done better.

Of course it's easier to be humble in defeat when you're winning most of the time, but a large part of that comfort and humility comes from feeling that you're safe. Knowing there aren't major repercussions for your job and livelihood coming off the back of a poor result means you conduct yourself very differently. There's an argument to say that even the openness displayed by Toto Wolff's team when speaking to the media was innovative in itself. On the other side of the coin, it felt like the bosses at Ferrari were always trying to find a way to avoid the question of what went wrong. Both the words that came out in interviews and the body language behind them sounded and looked like someone in fear. Explaining another disappointing result came across like an admission of guilt to the world, but perhaps more poignantly, to the Ferrari board who they knew would be watching.

The other aspect of team communication where I found some interesting differences was the way the people in the team spoke to each other in pressurised situations. Looking back at races from this period and listening to the team radio transmissions is a real window into the mentality of those involved.

At Ferrari there seemed to be a lack of trust in the team. Key radio messages and instructions from the pitwall to the drivers in the cars during Grand Prix were frequently questioned by the guys behind the wheel. Quite often a race strategy call from the team, who have a wealth of advanced information and tools to base decisions on, would be transmitted to the driver only for them to come back on the radio and reply with things like 'Are you sure?', or even just a flat out 'NO!' in refusing to comply.

It's easy to understand where that kind of trust breakdown comes from when there's been such a drought of good results for so long. On many notable occasions, Ferrari had got their race strategy wrong, so if recent evidence suggests the team aren't making the right decisions, why should a driver necessarily trust the next one?

The next sign of deeper problems for me was the way in which the race engineers responded to having their decisions questioned by their own drivers. Instead of being totally confident in what they and all of their data and simulation software had concluded was the right thing to do, they instantly sounded unsure themselves of what they'd just instructed their driver to do. Messages like 'Err, let me check . . .' or 'OK, I'll come back to you,' became almost standard responses to being questioned. They were being led into questioning their own decisions, just moments after making them.

Of course, nobody should be above being questioned, and the idea of questioning yourself is not bad per se, but in the midst of the intensity of a Grand Prix, that process should've all happened before the critical communication was made to the guy in the car. In those moments there needs to be trust all the way down the chain so that, when the pressure's on, decisions can be made and then executed efficiently.

That lack of trust at Ferrari looked to me like a symptom of the environment within the organisation. Everyone appeared afraid of getting something wrong, so was reluctant to make the call. I can only imagine the kind of fear-led conversations that must've happened internally to get to the point of deciding what to initially tell the driver, let alone the ones that went on after that decision had been pushed back against on the team radio.

Even the media began to pick up on some of these details, with the drivers being asked about it in post-race interviews. They found it hard to show any sign of confidence in their own team if things had gone badly. I heard Ferrari drivers saying things like, 'They called me in for new tyres at the wrong time,' as opposed to what I'd imagine the equivalent Mercedes driver response would likely be: 'We need to look at whether we got all the pitstop calls right today.' One response outright blames the team and makes a clear distinction between the driver and everyone else; the other uses the term 'we', which signifies that they're in this together and will analyse and learn from it together too.

Whilst I have the greatest respect for Ferrari, it felt to me as if they were driven by fear, not by the collective desire to push the boundaries and think innovatively in the pursuit of greatness.

At Mercedes, almost the opposite seemed to be the case. They still occasionally got frantic messages on their radio from emotionally charged drivers questioning a team decision in a race, but there was almost always an instant response from the engineer confidently confirming they thought it was the right call. At that point the driver has the required belief that an entire team of people have come to that conclusion and they trust them. Like any pressurised decision with risk attached, they didn't all work out perfectly, but there was rarely ever any blame.

Whilst one team had perhaps more than just an eye on the consequences of getting things wrong, the other operated with a freedom that allowed each person to know they were secure, trusted and backed up by every other teammate.

How to be an innovative human being

Being innovative as a character trait isn't just a benefit in the highest echelons of elite sport or business. If we can create the right atmosphere around ourselves and the people closest to us, the benefits of thinking and acting innovatively can be far-reaching.

It's something I'm constantly trying to remind myself in the difficult and ongoing challenge of being a parent. When all four of my children were young they needed absolutely everything doing for them, and then as they got a bit older they needed very clear instructions and help to be able to accomplish most tasks.

One temptation, and definitely something I've been guilty of myself in the past, is continuing to do everything for them as they get older still. Particularly as they became early teenagers it often seemed easier that way than the frustratingly protracted process of issuing an instruction, only for it either to be ignored, or responded to with moans and complaints. So a few years ago, before the hormones and attitude kicked in, I tried something to help give them space and freedom.

During the Covid-19 lockdowns in the UK, like many people, we found ourselves homeschooling our youngest children. In an attempt to bring us together as a family I suggested we play a board game one day, but the idea was rejected because 'We've played them all!' So I came up with a solution I thought might encourage them to get a little bit innovative and solve their own 'problem'.

I gave them a giant sheet of cardboard and some pens and asked them to come up with the best board game they could think of . . . that was it, no further instructions.

We sat together for ages as they came up with all sorts of ideas. I never said no to anything; I just suggested they try. They divided the board up into squares and added a combination of elements of some of their favourite existing games and made up new features of their own to go with them. Some were crazy, like 'if you land on this square, you have to go and get every other player a treat from the fridge', others simply didn't work, like 'if you land here Dad has to give you £10', so after trying them, we stuck a clean square over the top and tried something else instead. By the end of the day we'd created The Priestley Game. I'll admit it wasn't the most innovative title, but the game was great and we still play it occasionally today, with it continually evolving over time by adding new squares or rules and tweaking others.

I created a space to be creative and gave them total freedom to experiment and test ideas through which they came to their own eventual solution. I hope I gave them a small sense of what it's like to innovate.

One of the hardest things to achieve in company culture is to align the motivations and goals of the individuals in the team with those of the bigger organisation. If the business is motivated by profit margins, the workforce are unlikely to feel the same way unless you find a method of linking them in to the same outcome-related rewards. You could offer profit-tracked bonuses if they're motivated by money, or even a share of equity in the firm to give them a powerfully personal reason to feel the same way about success. In F1 teams, there are financial bonuses for winning, but the bigger motivation tends to come from the mutual competitive spirit shared by everyone involved. We all desperately want to win and are made to feel part of that process when it happens.

In parenting my teenage twins, I'm trying to tap into something similar. I appreciate now that their goals at this age are going to be different from mine. I might need a job doing around the house or garden and so my motivation's to get the task completed, because I haven't got time or just need help with it. At fourteen years old, though, they're developing a growing desire to no longer be seen as children and to become adults as quickly as possible as, in their mind, it represents freedom to them. I'm trying more and more to align our goals.

Instead of prescribing exactly how I want something to be done, I'm trying to develop the patience required to simply communicate the problem I need solving, with some guidance which I know they don't always listen to, and leave the exact solution up to them. It's sometimes difficult because I have an innate need to protect them and to keep them safe, and a deep desire to help them along the way. I don't want to see them struggle, yet I know that struggle and failure are exactly what they need to teach them to be resilient, innovative and ready to figure out their own path in life.

It's a journey my wife and I are on right now and it's certainly not a linear path; I'm happy to admit I still get it wrong at times. I can get annoyed when I had a crystal-clear vision of how I thought something should turn out, but it didn't end up going that way at all. I've wanted to step in and course-correct, or even insist that they were doing it 'wrong', but I've had to resist.

I'm trying to see myself as the founder of the operation, which, together with my wife, of course we actually are! I know I need to step back and have that big-picture mentality, take a longer-term view, in that what's really important to me is that they grow up to be happy, healthy and fulfilled. How they achieve that I can't, and shouldn't, want to control. Giving them the space to think differently to me, and everyone else if they want to, is a pretty adult concept and one I know appeals in their quest to be treated like grown-ups. Giving them the freedom to make mistakes, as long as they're well intentioned, without the fear of punishment but with the support to continue trying to succeed, is a challenge for any parent. But creating an environment like this, together with all the other nourishing, protecting and educational foundations that most parents are desperately attempting to find a way to give their children, has the potential to create similar benefits to the ones that some of the world's best Formula One teams enjoy.

MARGINAL GAIN

Being an innovative human being comes with all the benefits of being an innovative business or sports team. You just have to decide on your priorities for any given challenge and conclude how far you're willing to go to accomplish them. It might be that for most things in your life, you're not prepared to go to extraordinary lengths to find solutions that millions of other people haven't yet found themselves. Perhaps being acceptably less than perfect is OK in these areas? But when you do have a problem you'd really like to solve and the reward for doing so is significant enough to you, think like an F1 team. You might need to re-evaluate your budget, both financially as well as in terms of time. Flexibly apportion resources to allow for multiple failed attempts. If you've decided the eventual solution is the top priority, be prepared for a messy and costly journey to get there, but if you believe in it, keep going. Be open to inspiration from the most unlikely sources and don't be restricted by the way things have always been done. Afford yourself the luxury of the space to think big and the freedom to get things wrong.

It can create an abundance of opportunity and potential wealth, depending on where you choose to focus it, by creating advantages over the competition through thinking and behaving differently to them. It can create the kind of resilience that means no matter what gets thrown at you, from global pandemics to job redundancy, social dilemmas or health scares, you have the mindset to just somehow dig deep and try to find a new way through. It can create the kind of people the world needs to continue evolving, the kind of people who solve problems, rather than just create them, and I believe it can help you in almost everything you do in life. If my F1 team can use a doctor's stethoscope to help make pitstops faster, there should be no limit to how you think about solving your own problems.

PITLANE LESSONS

- Innovation comes from removing limitations to the way you think about problems.
- Try to understand the challenge you face in detail, but strip away existing or traditional solutions and look again with a fresh perspective.
- Take inspiration from all around you like McLaren and their stethoscope trick or Mercedes and their aeroplane-inspired controls.
- If the reason for innovating's important enough to you, create the right environment and allow the process to happen. Focus more on the advantage it'll give you in the end and less about exactly how you're going to get there.
- Create space and freedom to encourage an innovative way of thinking. Embrace failure as part of the process.

3.

YOU ALREADY HAVE ALL THE TOOLS
YOU NEED TO CONQUER STRESS
How to Hack Your Body and Mind to Help
You Deal with Pressure and Stress

Formula One's one of the highest-pressure, highest-stress environments you can imagine. Think of the situation the drivers find themselves in every time they jump in a car on a Grand Prix weekend. Nowadays fans of the sport get a real glimpse into what they experience through things like broadcast team radio communications where we hear the drivers' raw emotions and heavy, rapid breathing in response to the pressures they face behind the wheel. We see driver's eye camera views from inside the crash helmet showing the claustrophobic environment and uncomfortable ride as G-forces push their bodies to fighter-pilot-like extremes. They face the brutal reality of not just trying to tame the angry 1,000-horsepower, high-tech machines they're driving at well over 200mph, but doing it centimetres away from the best in the world in their own cars doing the same things. Those speeds distort vision and perception, yet they need to make hundreds of decisions and judgements in thousandths of seconds all the way around a lap for perhaps sixty circulations of the track whilst monitoring what others are doing around them in their attempts to get past or keep them behind.

Whilst all that's happening, the team are talking to them in their earpieces, giving them instructions and information about their own strategy as well as what others are up to. They're getting tones in their ears as indicators on when to change gear or to open the DRS rear wing flap. The steering wheel not only controls the car mechanically, but is a multifunction computer displaying critical data and technical measurements indicating how the car needs to be driven to keep them all in the optimum performance ranges. It's littered with switches and buttons, none of which are just there for show. Around twenty-five buttons or dials can control hundreds of settings and functions throughout a race, requiring the dexterity and cognitive capacity of a surgeon whilst everything else happens at speeds most of us can't comprehend and nineteen other drivers try and make it as hard as they can for them to do it all.

Throw in the precision required to get pitstops right for the team to service the car in less than two seconds and the fact that not only is the world watching, but the prize you've dreamt of since you were a small child's at stake, and you can start to see why it's fair to call it a high-pressure job.

The pressure of the sport can turn the relatively straightforward operations into something that pushes the body and mind into places most people will never experience or, quite frankly, be able to cope with. That extreme pressure isn't just reserved for the role of racing driver in this sport either, as literally everybody faces it: team members in factories around the world, suppliers and sub-contractors, even the F1 media.

I've experienced some of this myself. I don't think I'll ever forget how I felt on the day of my first-ever live Grand Prix pitstop. I was almost crushed by the fear that I was about to mess things up, not just for me, but for my teammates, Kimi Räikkönen my driver, and the millions of McLaren fans around the world watching on with hope and expectation. As the car approached me in the pitlane I convinced myself that it was all about to go wrong and that it was definitely going to be all my fault.

Inside my mind, I began forecasting the impending disaster, my thoughts rapidly darting from one catastrophic scenario to another and back again. I envisaged my friends and family back home watching proudly on the television, only for them to see me become the reason that Kimi and McLaren's day took a horrible turn for the worse. I thought of the TV commentators calling me out as the reason for our failure. I imagined the camera operators zooming in on me as it all unfolded. The back pages of tomorrow's newspapers would surely feature a picture of me with a humiliating headline above. I wondered how I'd explain it all afterwards. My mind was in utter chaos. I tried so hard to focus, but it felt impossible. I was terrified.

All of that was happening in my thought process in the space of a few seconds, yet the wait for the car to trundle along the pitlane towards us and arrive in the pitstop box seemed like it went on forever.

Physically I was shaking uncontrollably. My pulse rate was so high I could actually feel my heart pounding violently in my chest, yet another distraction for my mind to focus on. I became hot. Very hot. I was in Australia, wearing multiple layers of fireproof underwear, race suit, gloves and balaclava, all of which was pretty warm anyway, but my temperature rose to such a level I became acutely aware of it in that moment. Sweat was running into my eyes. They were stinging and blurring my vision. I felt the intense pulsating of the blood vessels inside my head. I couldn't stand still and bounced and adjusted my position at the front of the box incessantly as I waited for the car to arrive. I wanted to run away.

These reactions, apparently uncontrollable as they seemed

at the time, were the inbuilt responses of my body and mind to the very real threats they deemed were heading my way. There was of course the genuine threat of physical danger. A huge, heavy, pointy Formula One car was driving directly at me at 70mph. The brakes on an F1 car are so good that at around 15 metres away from me, it was still going at 70mph and I was expected to trust it would stop right in front of me! I couldn't *fight* this enormous lump of carbon fibre and metal, so it's no real surprise then that I felt like *flying* away.

Very different, but equally powerful, was the threat of impending failure. My brain was convinced I wasn't up to the challenge in front of me and flashed all manner of reasons I should escape into my thoughts. Embarrassment, shame, regret, humiliation, anxiety, discomfort, guilt, fear and many more.

Somehow, my role in that very first pitstop of mine went without a hitch: I changed the nosecone and front wing on Kimi Räikkönen's car in a personal best time. But in all honesty, it was largely down to luck on the day. Because, back then, the team, and even the sport itself, hadn't yet fully appreciated the opportunities that lay within the realms of understanding human performance at all levels, including the techniques to harness those innate human responses and use them to our advantage. That early pitstop experience, once I settled into the team and reflected more deeply upon it, became a catalyst for my own personal development, but also led me down a path of discovery and development within the team that helped change the course of my life many years later. In the following pages, I'll pass those lessons on to you, so that when pressure and stress strike (which they will), they won't hold you back.

The eye of the storm

At McLaren, taking steps to avoid our team-members becoming derailed by stress was something we really began to take seriously in the mid-2000s. We'd been looking at the human performance element of the drivers for a few years, triggered by the great Michael Schumacher leading the way in how he took training, conditioning, nutrition and many other aspects to new levels.

We first employed trainers and therapists dedicated to helping the drivers to be in better physical shape, which inevitably led on to the same philosophy being applied to their mental preparation too. Around 2004–5, under the advice of the inspirational Dr Aki Hintsa who'd been working with our drivers, Mika Häkkinen and then Kimi Räikkönen, we began to put more focus on understanding the physical and mental pressures facing the pitstop crew too. The McLaren Lab programme was born.

We'd moved into our state-of-the-art new factory, the McLaren Technology Centre, or MTC, which had an advanced subterranean health and fitness centre beneath where we designed and manufactured the cars. The McLaren Lab was Aki's vision for understanding and improving human performance and well-being, something that most big organisations around the globe are now starting to take more seriously, twenty-something years later.

As well as dedicating fitness and therapy staff to the pitstop crew and beyond, we also realised the value in searching for expertise outside of the walls of our own team. Although we operated at very high levels ourselves, there are always other industries, sports or individuals that have different views and can offer a new perspective or methods that could help, and if we were truly striving to be the best, we could never be arrogant enough to think we knew it all. So Aki, a highly accomplished Finnish doctor, who'd worked with a number of elite athletes in other sports, opened the doors of the McLaren Lab to collaborate with other global sporting leaders.

The annual visits we began making to the Olympic Training Centre in Kuortane in Finland were some of the most valuable. Working with athletes and coaches across a variety of disciplines at the highest level, we were able to share some of the things we did in our world, but also understand how they approached their own, often quite similar, challenges. We took the revelatory things they told us, especially around mental preparation for competition, then retooled them to make them applicable to our own experiences in F1 and I'm sure they did the same in the opposite direction.

One of the central insights that came from all of this was that when most people are asked to think of the high-pressure and high-stress moments they've faced in life, they firstly tend to think about those two categories as the same thing, and they normally perceive them both as negative. Exams; job interviews; awkward conversations; public speaking, etc.

But stress and pressure are two different sensations and learning to differentiate between the two is important when it comes to managing them. Stress is a physiological and psychological response to external or internal demands that exceed our perceived ability to cope. It often arises from situations that we see as threatening, overwhelming, or beyond our control. Pressure, on the other hand, is the expectation or demand for performance within a specific timeframe or under specific circumstances. It might stem from external sources, such as work deadlines and social expectations, or internally from personal goals; again, like my first-ever pitstop!

And though the circumstances that give rise to these

sensations can seem daunting or unpleasant, and both can certainly be unhelpful, they shouldn't necessarily be seen as only negative.

Stress can place us in a temporarily heightened state of awareness, giving us rapid reactions when we need them most. Pressure can drive us to excel and do great things. And we can use the energy both generate to help us.

Understanding this led to my first epiphany.

Freeze, fight, flight, *thrive*

As I sat there at the Olympic Training Centre I learnt that the physical sensations I'd experienced at that first live pitstop were ancient evolutionary mechanisms designed to protect me both physically and mentally in that moment.

My senses were more alert; pupils dilated to improve vision; hearing and smell in a heightened state to detect danger; my elevated heart rate and blood pressure moved nutrients and oxygen to muscles to prepare for an immediate physical response; limbs were tense and trembling like a sprinter in the starting blocks, ready to go.

This biological stress response has been a crucial factor in our survival as a species. Often referred to as 'freeze, fight or flight', it's the way in which we almost instantly prepare ourselves to deal with a threat by either hiding, fighting for our lives or running away to safety. Although most of us fortunately don't live in constant fear of being eaten by lions or hunted by rival tribes these days, the internal wiring and systems we developed back then to cope still function today.

Even though you're unlikely to experience the exact situation I described at the beginning of this chapter, I am sure that you'll recognise some of the physical and emotional responses to the threats I encountered. If you've walked into a big job interview, turned up nervous on a first date, had to make a huge business decision, even the often monumental decision to start a new business, together with many other significant moments in your life, they can all be interpreted as major threats by your brain. You can feel pressurised to make that decision and to get it right and, as such, the body and mind go into self-defence mode.

I'd always thought that there was little you could do to protect yourself in these scenarios . . . and then I spoke with a Finnish Olympic swimming coach we collaborated with at the team. What she told me has never left me.

'You know the feelings and sensations you get when you're facing a big moment in life, just like my athletes at the start of an Olympic final? Elevated heart rate. Sweaty palms. Nervous shakes. Chaotic thoughts. Struggling to focus. Raised temperature . . . It's really common for people to see those as negative associations. But which feelings and sensations do you experience when you're in your most exciting, thrilling moments in life?'

The body and mind respond in very similar ways to overwhelming fear as they do to overwhelming excitement. Her advice to me was that anyone facing a big moment, like me about to embark on a high-pressure pitstop, needs to learn to reframe the experience as exciting rather than terrifying. This might seem easier said than done, but it is actually just a skill that, like any other skill, can be practised and improved upon.

The revelation, for me, that we can train ourselves relatively easily to harness and optimise the body's response to the threats or challenges we face, has literally changed my life.

How to train your brain

Throughout ten years of working at McLaren, I came to love pitstops. They're one of the things I miss most about working for the team. They were the biggest rush I've ever experienced in my life. I never took them for granted. As I became more experienced my brain and body were still flooded with adrenaline, but instead of paralysing fear I felt only excitement. I'd done so many by the end of my time on the team that my brain had no reason to believe that I was anything other than perfectly capable and that the outcome would be successful. I'd reframed the experience as something I loved and felt privileged to do, rather than one that I feared, something backed up by the years of evidence I'd built up. After all, regular practice over the years honed the skills I needed to know that I was capable of doing the role. My mind knew what was likely to happen and how it would go. My body got so used to the physical movements and actions required, it became almost automatic.

But there's a short-cut. What I've learnt over time is that we can create that game-changing sense of belief right from the very start.

The problem with our brains is that they generally default to a worst-case scenario ahead of trying something difficult, new and unknown, because that's often the evidence it has to go off and a far safer approach to uncharted territory.

Our own life history tells us that the first time we tried to walk it was a disaster, and the first time we got onto a bike we fell off and hurt ourselves. Left to its own devices the brain's highly likely to move into its natural stress response mode and do what it can to help you avoid the incoming threat of anxiety or fear. It'll probably start encouraging you, through those naughty little voices in your head predicting a disastrous outcome, to run away. It'll flash images of everything that could wrong into your mind, like it did for me in that Melbourne pitlane all those years ago. All my mind really knew was that it was highly likely I was going to fail, because I'd never done that task in those circumstances before.

Running away's rarely a good solution to most modern problems – I can only imagine what might have happened had I done that during that first Grand Prix. But in those 'threatening' moments, our brain is thinking very short term and trying to protect us. For those few seconds, the brain doesn't care about our longer-term relationships, or our careers, or helping us to grow as people.

> The good news is that it is possible to overcome the hindrance of our slow neurological evolution. This is because of a simple fact: your mind believes what it hears.

A joint study in 2020 between the Psychology departments of San Francisco and Georgia State Universities confirmed this by concluding that the human brain perceives repeated information as truthful information, whatever its *actual* degree of truthfulness. The phenomenon's known as the Illusory Truth Effect and it helps explain why advertisements and propaganda work and why people end up believing 'fake news' circulated on social media. This means that, accurate or otherwise, your brain listens to the messages it receives over and over again, many of which come from you, and it responds accordingly.

A basic technique I was taught through our team visits to the Olympic Training Centre in Finland that became an annual feature of my later years at McLaren was to think of the brain as a machine or computer. A computer will operate solely based on the commands it's given by the programmer or operator; it won't veer from those commands and will only make a mistake if there was a problem with the information or instruction it received. Our brains are very similar in many regards. They've been taking in and processing information for the entirety of our lives and their outputs today are based on all of that historic, archived data, together with any new inputs we give them. So if we actively choose to give our brains a set of prompts that are more likely to benefit us, we can affect the output in our favour.

In practical terms this means giving yourself new messages.

The coaches in Finland taught me to set aside a period of time each day – they recommended the morning – to literally tell myself that the day ahead was going to be a positive one. They told me to try staring into the bathroom mirror first thing after waking up, looking myself in the eyes and saying out loud the way I wanted the day to go. If I was preparing for an event, the morning of a race for example, I'd say things like 'Today's going to be a great day. I have a really good feeling about the race and the pitstops I'm going to do. I've got this!'

In the beginning, this all felt a bit crazy, but the people that had encouraged me to try it were so accomplished, with so much notable success in their fields, I trusted their advice. I reasoned that if it had helped elite-level Olympic athletes to achieve more, why on earth couldn't it help me? And besides, what did I have to lose?

I know a few of my colleagues at the time thought it was nonsense – they didn't need anyone's help to be better at pit-stops. But it's telling that those who did persist with the practice are evangelical about its results. Lewis Hamilton, one of whose first-ever experiences with us as a new Formula One driver back in 2007 was to come on one of these trips to Finland, embraced the practice of positive affirmations to help him cope with the pressures he was now facing. To my knowledge he still does and it's examples like this, just like it was with the Olympic athletes I first met years ago, that inspire me to keep going in the same way.

The other reason I didn't give up, even though I didn't see dramatic positive changes happening overnight, was that in many of the private conversations I had with Olympic trainers and doctors over the years that we worked together, the biggest message I always took away was that consistency was key to making any meaningful change in your life.

If you join a gym in January, head down there for an intense workout, then come home and look in the mirror expecting a six-pack to have emerged under your t-shirt, you're going to be disappointed. It's why so many people give up on their new year's fitness resolutions and cancel their gym memberships by February every year. The process takes time and we only get the outcomes we're after if we keep going, putting in the work required on a consistent basis. If we trust the methods, if we believe we're doing the right things and do them consistently, one day, maybe months in, we'll catch ourselves in the mirror whilst getting dressed one morning and realise that the six-pack's coming.

Exactly the same theory applies when it comes to giving ourselves positive messages to feed the brain. Telling yourself once how you're going to approach the day or a task at work does very little – even doing so every day for a week won't permanently reprogramme your brain. But doing it every day, consistently for a month, then six months, has the power to really change your behaviour and therefore the outcomes from it.

So I spoke to myself either in the bathroom mirror or in the car on the way to work every day for the next year or so and it changed my life. I changed the messages I gave myself based on what challenges I had in front of me and in the end it developed into an almost conversational-like exchange with my subconscious mind. You might be thinking, 'This guy's lost the plot!', but I bet you've had little conversations with the 'voices in your head' at times? For most of us it happens many times a day without thinking about it, so why not try thinking about those conversations and manipulating them to serve you better? Rather than just your mind talking to you, why not take control of the conversation and steer it the way you want it to go?

Over time, as it became clear the practice was helping me become more confident in new situations, I began to develop the process further to draw out the characteristics I needed for certain challenges or to ensure the right version of me showed up to a particular occasion. I've stood in front of many mirrors, in many hotel rooms around the world, convincing myself that, despite the inevitable difficulties of the day ahead that we faced at the track, I was ready and would help lead my team through it in the most positive way I could.

To this day, I have regular intentional conversations with myself to affirm what I need to do or want to achieve, though many of them now happen silently in my head. It means I can do them anywhere and at any time. I might be standing backstage, waiting to be called out to give a keynote address to a thousand industry leaders and I'll be running through a series of messages, programming my mind for the moments ahead. It's not the content of my speech that I'm reminding myself about, I know my subject inside out now, but it's the way I want to deliver it, the energy I want to give off to the audience, the confidence I need in order to come across as authentic. I remind myself who the crowd's made up of: are they technical people, are they creatives, are they finance execs and therefore what kind of language are they most likely to best respond to? I'm repeating the inputs my computer needs in order to deliver the right outputs.

The gift of the written word

The biggest tweak to the process I've made over the years comes from my appreciation that I tend to retain information more effectively when I write it down. Today, I complement my regular internal conversations with the practice of keeping a journal.

Part of this is about getting to know oneself over time. We're all on a journey of self-discovery and every experience contributes to that. My time on the front line at McLaren pushed me into so many uncomfortable situations, forcing me to find out what I was made of up against some of the best in the world, and as a result I now have a much clearer picture of who I am and what I need to do to succeed. Creating visual representations, either through writing down words, or sketching pictures and diagrams, works so much better for me in terms of learning new things and understanding new concepts.

Each morning I get up early and set some time aside to reflect on the previous day, making notes about what I did and how I felt, but then also to look ahead to the day in front of me and what I require of myself to get through it successfully.

My journal's incredibly positive. Even on days when I've struggled, I try to find a way to put a positive spin on things. It's one of the reasons I choose to write it in the morning after I've slept and not in the evening when emotions might still be a bit raw after something went wrong. It's not that I'm not honest with myself about the tough moments; I am, but I also know that the last thing I write before heading into the day could have a significant impact on my mood and how I'm mentally prepared for the pressures to come.

Writing positively, just like speaking positively, sets the tone for my day and even though it's a conscious act, the subconscious effect on my brain can be long-lasting and have a significant impact on my behaviour. I don't think you'll find many people who would ever describe me as a negative person.

MARGINAL GAIN

Another piece of advice I was once given by a coach during my days in the Formula One garages, to help orchestrate the mood or vibe that might best prepare you for a potentially high-pressure challenge, was to soundtrack periods of your day with well-intentioned music.

There's a huge amount of research showing the effects of music on different times in our lives and I'm sure we can all relate to some degree. Whether it's the sombre break-up music we tend to listen to after a relationship ending that reinforces our temporary low ebb, or the high-energy dance tracks that remind us of the good times on the amazing nights we've shared with others at a club, festival or concert. Music's powerful and, a bit like the visual process of writing and drawing, can add another layer to a memory or idea, making it easier to recall or more impactful when we do. Almost every F1 driver I've worked with has set aside time in the hours before the Grand Prix starts to listen to music whilst preparing themselves for battle. It can help focus and remove distractions from the outside world. As F1 driver Daniel Ricciardo once put it to me in an airport queue as we were chatting, 'Everything just feels better with music.' The actual music choice is of course a personal one, but different tempos and styles can also have different effects on how they make you feel. I know Lewis listens to a variety of genres from Drake to Adele and lots in between depending on how he's feeling and how he wants to feel as a result. When Daniel shared what he was listening to on that particular day waiting for a flight, it was a pretty heavy rock band I'd never heard of, but it helped him to bounce his head back and forth with an enormous smile on his face, so it looked like it was working for him.

Today my own life is full of music. My morning routine has a backdrop of happy tunes to set the mood and I've found it to work tremendously well, even breaking into impromptu dance or singing on my own in a deserted kitchen whilst everyone else sleeps. It's almost impossible not to be in a good mood after an effect like that.

The result of all of this is of course that if I feel more positive about the things coming my way, like a pitstop, or a big presentation, it's far more likely that my brain won't see them as an incoming threat and therefore that it won't initiate the kind of stress response I experienced on that traumatic day in Australia all those years ago.

If I feel more positive, I'm setting myself up for success, rather than preparing myself for failure.

It's all in the breath

Another crucial tool we have in our armoury to either prepare for battle or defend ourselves is our breathing. When the breath is unsteady, all is unsteady. When the breath is still, all is still.

We can all breathe; it's the thing we have most experience of in our lives, having been doing it pretty successfully and instinctively since the first moments we emerged into the world. As a result of it being so effortless, though, most of us naturally take it for granted.

In my description of what happened to me during the intense moments building up to my first F1 pitstop, one of the overwhelming reactions my body had was to increase the rate of my breathing. Short, sharp and incredibly rapid breaths were an involuntary response to the stress I felt at the time. My shoulders would have been rising and falling dramatically as my breathing shifted from my abdomen and diaphragm to my upper chest. I would've struggled to take a deep breath in those moments and that would only have increased the anxiety I felt.

Most modern-day pressurised situations which tend to cause us to feel stressed don't often need the same 'fight or flight' response from our bodies to get the best out of the moment or challenge in front of us. In most cases the rapid delivery of extra oxygen to muscle groups isn't actually required and can in fact have a negative effect on us.

The primary function of breathing is to absorb oxygen and expel carbon dioxide through movement of the lungs, but when our breathing becomes rapid and shallow in stressful times, the exchange of gas becomes far less effective and unbalanced as the body prioritises delivering blood flow to the muscles. As a result we build up excess CO_2 in the bloodstream, which can increase feelings of anxiety and have the effect of making us feel even more stressed. So, if you're heading into a big investor pitch meeting, or a job interview, for which you already feel a little anxious and nervous, this kind of physiological response from your body is particularly unhelpful.

F1 drivers and team members face exactly the same challenges when it comes to the high-pressure stakes of an intense Grand Prix situation. But what the Formula One industry's incredibly good at is turning those challenges and potential hurdles into opportunities to excel and even to improve performance.

Much of the scientific study going on at the time at which we began really taking this seriously at McLaren was around how we could keep a driver's heart rate closer to the optimum level for every situation they faced whilst behind the wheel. We began using our own R & D and data analysis departments to measure and interpret biometric markers whilst they were in and out of the car. Tracking respiratory patterns and heartbeats in real time led us down a path of greater understanding that not only helped the race drivers to better results, but eventually played a significant role in overcoming weaknesses in our team that, firstly, we didn't even realise we had and, secondly, helped us to a first world title in almost a decade.

The biggest takeaway I took from this time was that although the body's responding in a perfectly reasonable and natural way, given our evolution and the threat it sees ahead, just like the brain, that response can be hacked into and manipulated to our advantage.

When we face a threatening scenario, like a lion wandering into our cave thousands of years ago, or another F1 car spinning on the track in front of us as a modern-day racer, the body's automatic response is typically a sharp intake of breath. It's not a conscious thought we have, it's not a decision we make, the body just does it almost instantly and we have very little control over it.

What's interesting to note and what we were able to back up with our research findings at the team is that this sharp inhalation then triggers a series of other automated reactions from our bodies.

Our autonomic nervous system has what's called the

sympathetic nervous system, which controls our fight or flight responses, and the parasympathetic nervous system, which is largely responsible for our rest and relaxation, feeding and digestive states, mainly conserving energy for use later.

The sharp intake of breath reflex we experience in the panicky moments of life activates the sympathetic nervous system which then automates the kinds of reactions I talked about earlier. It immediately increases the heart rate to prioritise blood flow to our limbs and prepare the body to take flight or fight back. So those stressful, anxious feelings we experience are all exacerbated because the body's limiting blood flow to the brain, which would normally help us with clarity of thought and a measured, calm response, in favour of stimulating muscles and blood pressure for the imminent fight for our life.

That sharp intake of breath is linked to an increase in heart rate, whereas what we were able to confirm through our findings with our McLaren drivers was that a longer, slow exhale is fundamentally paired with lowering the pulse rate and the activation of the parasympathetic nervous system.

Anyone who wears a fitness band or sleep tracker might be familiar with the term Heart Rate Variability, or HRV. It's the measurement of time, in milliseconds, between each adjacent beat of the heart and is a key metric in human performance and general fitness and well-being analytics. Athletes, including F1 drivers, monitor this during training as a gauge of general activity and recovery levels.

You'd be forgiven for assuming that if your heart rate was sixty beats per minute, the heart is beating exactly once every second, but it isn't. The amount it varies may be small, but when we zoom in, and that's exactly what highly sensitive fitness wearables do, we can see that it actually fluctuates. The fluctuation's a reflection of the body's ability to constantly and instantly react to its surroundings in the ways I've already described by increasing or decreasing heart rate. Higher HRV numbers are generally seen as a good thing as it means the body can adapt its responses more readily when needed.

In a healthy person, like an F1 driver, heart rate should typically increase momentarily as they inhale and then decrease momentarily as they exhale. Knowing this and appreciating that a lower heart rate is associated with better cognitive function in the heat of a Grand Prix, we began to explore ways in which we might be able to manipulate the phenomenon to our advantage.

Once we began to fully understand the direct links between effects on the body and mind in stressful situations and an increased heart rate, we started to look into training methods that might counteract it. There was a lot to learn.

The general state of either underlying anxiety or baseline relaxation in a person can partly determine how quickly these reactional effects take hold during a high-pressure moment. So whilst we clearly didn't have total control of the personal lives of our drivers, what we could control was the environment they operated within over a Grand Prix weekend. As such we began thinking more about their daily routines, their commitments outside of the car, like sponsorship and marketing engagements, etc., and trying to reduce their need to worry about anything other than actually driving. Their hotels improved, as did their transport; they got personal assistants, their own private rooms built into the garages and motorhomes in which they could relax. It was all designed to deliberately lighten their mental load and schedule so their baseline state when they finally got into the car was as calm as it could be. It was probably a pretty good time to be an F1 driver.

It didn't take long to appreciate that the benefits of thinking more about general health and well-being, together with a consideration for a person's state of relaxation, weren't just applicable to athletes and F1 drivers, and the team began to investigate ways in which it could help all of us achieve some of the same advantages.

What I learnt through this fascinating period was that being in a generally calm condition for most of the time, and certainly in the build-up to events, was a great way to minimise the negative effects of stress. Working on relaxation didn't necessarily eradicate any stress-related reflexes, but it did both delay the onset – meaning I was far more likely to remain in control in lower-intensity situations – and also lessen the severity of any negative impacts it did have on my performance.

More than that, though, I realised that breathing was one of the most readily accessible and key tools for being able to instigate a more relaxed state at will.

Hacking our biological triggers through taking intentional control of our breathing is free, available to everyone and relatively easy to achieve with a little practice. David Coulthard had been using various relaxation breathing techniques whilst he sat in the car waiting to drive out of the garage onto the track and he swore he found it helpful. Later, other drivers at McLaren began using a focus on breath as part of their training away from the racetrack, ingraining the process into their routines to be called upon when required. We, at the team, soon started doing the same things, with breathwork becoming part of the physical training regime many of us were now embracing in our bid to maximise our abilities.

I spent some time with Nordic breathwork coaches on a number of our team training weeks away between F1 seasons, and they taught me some basic techniques for breathing in the most effective ways. Things like placing one hand on my chest and one hand on my stomach, then taking a deep breath inwards from low in my abdomen, ensuring that the hand on my stomach moves outwards more than the hand on my chest as I did so. This means the diaphragm is moving the lungs from underneath, opening up the chest cavity and increasing capacity, and we're not breathing more shallowly from the shoulders. It feels unnatural at first, but that's largely because we've evolved to breathe less effectively in modern life.

We looked at slowing the breathing down, which promotes relaxation. Reducing our heart rate, through specific breathing exercises, helps to convince the body and mind that we're in a safe, relaxed environment, facing no immediate threat, and the reduction in stress that goes with it can be really significant.

There are many different methods, protocols and practices for intentional breathing exercises, all of which can offer benefits when mastered. Box breathing is an easy and commonly taught technique for regulating breath and you can alter the frequency to slow things down more and more as you become more adept. It simply involves visualising an imaginary square in front of you and as you inhale through the nose, count to four. As you count, imagine moving along the top horizontal line of your square from left to right. When you reach the end of that first line, hold your breath to the count of four as you imagine moving down the vertical line of the box. Then begin exhaling and move along the bottom horizontal line as you count to four at the same pace. Hold for the remaining upward leg of your virtual polygonic journey. Repeat the process over and over as you travel around the perimeter of your imaginary box, breathing in for four, holding for four, out for four, then holding for four. Within a minute or two your breathing's regulated and slowed and your heartbeat follows. If you can do it with closed eyes, even better, as this removes a visual layer of distraction and can heighten the relaxing effect.

One variation of the technique is to turn the square into a rectangle.

If, as we discussed earlier, we appreciate that the outward breath is a trigger for slowing the heart rate when we zoom right in and start understanding HRV more, it therefore makes some sense to extend the exhalation period to be longer than that of the inhalation if we're trying to lower the pulse. With that in mind, you can see where the rectangular box breathing visualisation comes from. I began by using four seconds and six seconds as this was what some of our F1 drivers were doing before climbing into their cars at the time. For them it gave all the benefits of delaying and mitigating the onset of the stress responses we talked about should they face a triggering moment out on track, but also gave them some moments of valuable undistracted focus. As the practice became more natural, the idea of moving around the imaginary box was replaced with repeating positive affirmations, mantras, or even instructions from the engineering team that they needed to remember. Because time was scarce, as it always is over a busy F1 weekend, the drivers used the few spare moments they had to adapt and develop a basic technique to suit their specific requirements and prepare them for heading into high-pressure and potentially high-stress situations.

As time went on, I found breathwork more and more useful, both in and outside of my job. I'd focus my breathing ahead of a pitstop, for example. I'd sit in the garage, adorned in my full fireproof race suit, balaclava, gloves and helmet, anonymous to the watching world as well as under a veil of privacy from some of my not-so-open-minded teammates. Whilst the race played out in front of us, I'd often close my eyes inside the helmet and zone in on my own breathing. Part of what makes breathing so central to meditation is that, because our minds are only able to truly focus on one thing at a time, by choosing to prioritise being aware of our breath, we inadvertently block out any other distracting thoughts. Occasionally I'd find myself in such a deep state of relaxation, I'd be amazed that the race was still going on with such devastating, bone-shaking noise just a few metres outside our garage, yet it was like I hadn't heard any of it for five minutes.

The result was that my baseline heart rate became way lower than it otherwise would have been and my mind became clearer. I was ready and in control for whenever we got the call to burst out into the pitlane for a stop.

I've found the same breathing-control techniques have helped me when I'm hit by an unpredictable blow. The sort of thing that you don't see coming, but which immediately puts you into a state of panic. And I'm not alone: many F1 drivers and other elite sportsmen and -women use their own version of the same thing to help them through the really tough moments. They do it because it works.

When you build practices that slow and regulate good quality breathing into your daily or weekly routines, it becomes part of your physiological habits. That means that over time it can grow into something that the body and mind can recall at short notice and consequently reap the rewards of.

Because I've been doing this for many years, I can now trigger my own response mechanisms in a fraction of the time that I used to. But we can all do it right now.

Imagine a highly stressful situation. The boss has just dumped an enormous and urgent task on your plate and you already feel overwhelmed with the workload you have. The children are playing up at the end of a long and tiring day and they start fighting with each other. You open a letter which has a bill inside that you weren't expecting and can't afford. Any of these are highly likely to immediately raise your heart rate; your temperature goes up, along with blood pressure; your breathing becomes rapid and shallow. These effects on your body draw all your attention to them, you become hyper-aware of how stressed you feel and it leaves no mental capacity to think straight or allow a measured response. These are often the moments where we blow our top. We slam the laptop closed. We shout at the kids. We feel like we can't cope and this leads to poor decision-making and negative feelings that can escalate to more serious mental challenges.

One potential response we can try and create, at least the one that helps me enormously in these difficult times, is to activate an instant version of the breathing practices I've learnt over the years. This doesn't deal with the problem you might be facing, but it can dramatically help you deal with it in a more useful way.

Once the initial shock of what's just happened recedes even a tiny bit, I take the biggest, deepest breath in through the nose that I can. As I do so, I vividly imagine my lungs filling up with air and expanding in my chest, visualising it in as much vibrant detail as I can. I then hold it for a few seconds, then release that big breath as slowly and controlled as possible. I allow my shoulders to drop and relax all the muscles I'm able to. Extending the exhale through tightly pursed lips so it makes a sound that I can focus my attention on helps me to block out external distraction. If possible I'll close my eyes too. The trick is to be super intentional about each stage, putting all your focus on it whilst it's happening to the exclusion of everything else. Go all in on those few moments.

When we feel under extreme pressure, often what we need most is to make a calm, sensible decision on what to do next, yet our stress responses conspire to prevent us doing just that. Taking a breath can go some way to bringing everything back under control, allowing us to think more clearly about how we should react. I've found it useful to stay calm for an unexpected emergency pitstop when the race car suddenly dives unannounced into the pitlane during a Grand Prix. I've found it useful as a father and as a husband on the many occasions in normal life when difficult situations get heated at home. It's been useful to remain calm on the road, when another driver unexpectedly cuts me up or even causes a collision, and it's certainly been very useful in the early days of my public speaking and television broadcasting career to keep me controlled and composed in the seconds before going live.

As the work of Dr Andrew Huberman, a professor of Neurobiology and Ophthalmology at Stanford University, has shown, even in situations that aren't necessarily stressful you should feel a substantial change in the way you feel after that one big, controlled and specific breath technique. With practice the effects get even more powerful, even to the point of inducing an almost semi-meditative state in just a few seconds. I find it so useful today. As it turns out, although I wasn't aware of this until my research for this book, it's actually a variation of a technique discovered in the 1930s, called the Physiological Sigh, and is even recommended to citizens on the UK Government website.

As a result of doing this regularly, or practising it, I now call on this particular skill in any moment where I recognise the signs of stress appearing. You can do the same. Not only does it almost instantly improve the way you feel, but it also resets many of the effects of stress on our body and mind that in most modern-day situations are almost entirely unhelpful.

Make pressure your ally

As I suggested earlier on, feeling pressure doesn't have to be negative. Personally, there are many situations where being put under pressure's helped me to achieve things. In fact, writing this very book has been a real struggle for me at times. The struggle was continually motivating myself to get it done in amongst the many other aspects of my life and business that take up time. That was until I placed myself, voluntarily, under substantial pressure. As I had already written a bestselling Formula One book, my publishers, I suspect, trusted me to just go ahead and write this one without too much trouble and, as a result, left the timeframe and subject largely open-ended. With very little pressure to deliver by a certain date, I found it incredibly easy to continuously put off the writing process. And that's exactly what I did. Fortunately I had the self-awareness, ironically after painstakingly slowly writing parts of this very chapter, to step in and save myself by begging Penguin Random House to give me a delivery date for the manuscript. The pressure I now felt to go on and finish the book was real and exactly what I needed to kickstart the process and move it up my priority list. So pressure can be great for motivation, to drive progress and innovation and to dig yourself out of trouble when it hits.

The key of course is learning to develop self-belief and resilience and to manage your stress responses when the pressure ramps up. Today my early morning routine involves meditation and breathing exercises; it incorporates music, reading, exercise and journalling, all of which are very deliberately intended to, amongst other benefits, relax me and lower my baseline stress levels. I spend at least an hour, often more, every morning practising these things, but if you want to give it a try, you can begin by spending just five or ten minutes on some simple breathing exercises like I described earlier. That, in itself, will have a significant effect on how you feel, but if you pair that with some positive affirmations about yourself and what you're capable of or a meditation whilst practising the breathwork, the impact could be even more far-reaching.

So what are you waiting for? It's just one breath. Why not try it now?

PITLANE LESSONS

- Pressure and stress are not the same thing. Both can be helpful or unhelpful depending on the situation.
- My early F1 pitstops were almost ruined by my inability to manage my own stress responses in a new environment, so becoming aware of what yours are and what triggers them is a key step.
- Find and practise techniques that work for you to improve your baseline relaxation levels. Starting from a lower point when stress kicks in gives you more chance to manage it.
- Practise reframing the high-pressure moments from terrifying to exciting. The excitement of a pitstop put me into a positive state which prepared me to do well as opposed to being petrified it was likely to go wrong through fear.
- The best high performers, including F1 drivers, use pressure as a positive motivating force. Work on building

your own self-confidence through internal conversations, and once you believe you're good enough, harness the power of high pressure to go and deliver.

• You will succumb to stress, you will find the pressure on you too much at times, but each situation is a step towards leaning how to improve.

4.

CELEBRATING SUCCESS FEELS AMAZING, SO DO IT MORE OFTEN
Why You Shouldn't Only Celebrate When You Win

Imagine this scenario.

A top F1 team creates and develops a car worthy of a world title. They employ two drivers: both are championship contenders. They get to a Grand Prix and do everything right. They lead the race with both drivers at different stages. Pitstops are great. They split their race strategies and it puts both cars on separate paths to ultimate success for one or the other of them. But . . .

The weather's all over the place and unpredictable, with torrential downpours descending at little notice. Rival teams crash and spin and cause multiple safety car appearances which turns the race on its head, but still our team navigates it brilliantly! Eventually, just after making their final pitstop with one driver, which puts him temporarily down to fourth, but on course for almost certain victory once those in front inevitably come into the pits for their scheduled stops, the race is ended early by officials after two more enormous crashes. Devastatingly, victory's snatched away by the premature finish not allowing the full strategy to play out. Heartbreaking for that side of the team's garage.

But all's not lost as their other driver *is* crowned victorious having found himself leading the race with a pitstop still to make just before the red flag came out. A brilliantly executed weekend, in really tough conditions, brings that coveted top step of the podium celebration they've all craved so much . . .

Only what if this happened? Days later the result bizarrely gets overturned following a protest and investigation, as officials eventually realise they got it wrong and that, because of the red flag, the final result should be taken from the end of the previous full lap of green flag racing and at that point the team's 'winning' driver was actually only second. More heartbreak.

If you guessed it, well done: that was the real-life scenario of the Brazilian Grand Prix of 2003.

At McLaren we were excellent that weekend, arguably better than anybody else as a team. We prepared well and worked together superbly – and the cars and drivers performed perfectly. Yet we didn't win.

The reasons we didn't win that race were largely unrelated to us and our actions. Events beyond our control combined to mean that even the very best people, with the very best car and the very best plan, executed in the very best way, didn't come out on top that day. That's not shirking responsibility, or taking anything away from Renault and Giancarlo Fisichella, who were the eventual rightful winners, but it does illustrate an important point.

Whilst there are always things to improve upon with the enlightening benefit of hindsight, in the pressurised moments of that chaotic GP we were pretty damn awesome. On another day, with the same performance, we'd have won the race comfortably and extended our championship lead even further. So was that race something we should have celebrated?

Is winning really everything?

Formula One's famous for those iconic moments on the podium immediately after the chequered flag's fallen at the end of a Grand Prix. The winner and two runners-up, plus a representative from the victorious team, get presented with the trophies, they respect the national anthems of the winning driver and constructor and then . . . THE CHAMPAAAAAAGNE! (For the last few years they've actually sprayed around sparkling wine from a sponsor, but that definitely doesn't sound as good!)

The biggest names in the history of motor racing have stood atop the podiums of the world's best racetracks and revelled triumphantly in a tradition almost as old as the sport itself. It's a privilege reserved only for the best of the best in this elite industry and has come to represent not only victory at the highest level, but also the glitz, glamour and outright extravagance of Formula One.

In my own F1 career I've been enormously fortunate to be able to stand under those podium celebrations on many occasions, staring up at my driver, joyfully sharing in the elation of having outraced the best teams and drivers on the planet. I can tell you, it feels amazing. Remember that, we'll come back to it: celebrating success feels amazing.

In the year 2000, when I arrived at McLaren, the team had won championships for the previous two seasons. Mika Häkkinen, our driver, was the current World Champion and had the iconic and celebratory Number One on the car. We were winners and the whole organisation was built on a winning mentality. It was an amazing place to start my F1 career, surrounded by hundreds of people who truly believed they were the best in the business. We went into every event with an expectation of challenging for the ultimate prize.

But, of course, we couldn't win races every weekend. At the time Ferrari, our biggest rivals with their lead driver Michael Schumacher, were of a similar mindset and had a great team of people who expected the same thing as us. If we ended up second, we'd still be under the podium to support our driver, but listening to the Italian national anthem being played for Ferrari as the winning team always hurt. It hurt because we were naturally competitive people, but it really hurt because that was how Ron Dennis, our genius, visionary CEO and Team Principal, made us feel.

Although he was innovative and disruptive in so many ways within the industry, at heart Ron was an old-school racer, with some old-school beliefs that took time to evolve. When it came to celebrating, he knew how to do it well and I've been part of some epic moments and parties instigated by Ron himself, but when I first joined the team it was pretty clear there was only one thing worthy of celebration.

Winning was everything. Second place in a Grand Prix or a championship was little more than the first of the losers at Ron's McLaren.

He hated losing more than anyone I've ever met, and losing to Ferrari was especially painful given the long-standing, often bitter, rivalry that extended beyond just the racetrack and into F1's political arena in which the team principals were so deeply entrenched.

The most inspirational and rousing team talks I've had from him over the years have either been straight off the back of beating Ferrari, or straight off the back of being beaten by Ferrari. Both driven by sheer unadulterated passion and often through fiercely gritted teeth.

So we were a group of highly competitive individuals who

existed with a sole purpose: to win. As much as it hurt Ron to lose, we all felt the same. Whatever the mitigating circumstances, no matter how well we'd done on the day, the bald truth was that we hadn't won in Brazil. Therefore it wasn't the sort of thing that the team celebrated.

Ron Dennis's methods generated a passionate team of people who collectively believed they were the best in the business. It wasn't unfounded arrogance, but belief based on past evidence as well as a culture of excellence in the organisation. It was McLaren versus the world and we did things our way.

That culture drove us on. We saw ourselves as winners. We thought and behaved like winners. Every loss hurt, but it also fired us up. The shared frustration pulled us together as a team and drove us on to come back stronger.

The reason we had so much confidence in ourselves was that we knew we were winners. We were part of one of Formula One's most successful teams in the history of the sport. The record books proved it. Personally I felt privileged to wear the McLaren uniform, knowing I followed in the footsteps of greats who'd worn it before me. Senna, Prost, Fittipaldi, Lauda, Hunt, let alone the mighty Bruce McLaren and of course a series of brilliant engineers alongside them all. I'd seen the pictures and films: they'd all celebrated being winners and now we were the latest generation. Counterparts from other teams, journalists, fans, all congratulated us when we won. On the occasions when we came in a close second, they still applauded us on a great fight. The world of F1 gave us incredible respect for who we were. We were putting on a show, keeping the battles alive and entertaining people. We were McLaren – it was only natural that we'd always be fighting at the front.

Until, that is, we weren't.

The wrong story

The 2003 season had started well, with David Coulthard winning the opening race in Australia, followed up two weeks later with Kimi Räikkönen taking his maiden F1 win at the Malaysian GP. But that was it. We only won two races in a season of sixteen rounds. Not very impressive when looked at through our unforgiving lens.

Those two wins and the celebrations that followed remained fresh in our minds. They'd brought us together and made us believe we were good enough to win again. We wanted to recapture that wonderful feeling; it served as a dangling carrot of motivation to achieve more. And yet each subsequent race was a let-down. As the winless streak grew, that confidence was dented. By the end of the season the parties and champagne of the first two races were distant memories. Our work rate and commitment had, if anything, gone up in the pursuit of the dream, yet we continually failed to achieve it. We were working longer hours and finding great improvements to the car and team, but still, there was nothing to celebrate as a result. It would be easy to think of it as a pretty poor year.

But that only tells a tiny part of the story. Kimi finished second seven times, with another two third-place finishes. DC, meanwhile, was on the podium twice. So, McLaren actually appeared under the winners' rostrum twelve times in the sixteen races, a pretty remarkable set of results up against the best in the world. This meant that we remained contenders in the championship fight until the final day of the season, when we finally lost out on the coveted world title by just two points to Michael Schumacher . . . and Ferrari.

We had, in fact, performed brilliantly. It was the first year in which our new car crew and Kimi, a young, inexperienced driver, had worked together. Unusually, we were using the previous year's car, which at times was fragile and let us down, but as a group we excelled. We'd done it through some innovative engineering to keep our ageing car competitive, a massive amount of commitment and determination and some truly inspirational teamwork.

We started extremely well and, as the season progressed, we got better, improving in most areas with each race. It's just that our main rivals that year ultimately did an even better job than we did. Still, we'd run the mighty Ferrari and the most successful driver in F1 history at the time all the way to the wire.

At McLaren, the underlying expectation was to see a season like that as a failure, and most people in that garage felt only loss and disappointment. Yet secretly, all I wanted to do was shout from the rooftops about what we'd just done. I wanted to spray champagne and party for days off the back of a year I personally felt had gone pretty well.

As the 2004 season rolled around, we fully expected to continue where we left off and make the tiny improvements we needed to go that vital one step further. There was never ever a question of 'Are we good enough to win?' We *knew* we were; it was just a few tiny margins on certain days that enabled the Italians to come out on top that year. There was no self-doubt, no crisis, just more confidence and a mindset of doing whatever it took to beat Ferrari. We had a revolutionary new car on the way in the MP4-19, which everyone was excited about. This was going to be our year . . .

But nothing turned out like we'd imagined it would in 2004. We struggled. In the early races, whilst we waited for the delayed yet innovative and game-changing MP4-19 to be ready, we felt the need to push the performance of the old car so much that reliability became our Achilles heel. In the first seven rounds, one or both of our two drivers failed to get to the chequered flag eight times and scored just five points between them. For a team of winners, that's pretty poor.

All of a sudden, instead of being part of Formula One's success story, we became a story for very different reasons. The headlines about us weren't celebratory; they were derogatory. Our counterparts no longer congratulated us; they commiserated with us. Journalists and fans no longer applauded us; they questioned us. We tried harder and harder to get the results we felt we deserved, but nothing seemed to work.

By round ten we hadn't even come close to getting onto the podium.

For most of the teams on the grid, these were pretty standard results, nothing to be concerned about and, for some, even pleasing. But for us, they were out of the ordinary and as the world began to question what on earth was going on at McLaren, so did we.

You see, one of the key effects of celebrating success is that it cements the moment, or the achievement, into the minds of those celebrating. Every time we'd punched the air as our driver took the chequered flag, hugged each other on the pitwall or sprayed champagne at the podium, it created important psychological markers in our brains. Markers we'd subconsciously refer back to whenever we needed to reinforce our belief about who we were or what we could achieve. By midway through the 2004 season our supply of recent celebratory memories was beginning to fade.

Our belief began to waver. On the surface we were still defiant. If you'd asked me or most of my colleagues at the time, we'd have likely portrayed an air of confidence, telling you that this was merely a series of unfortunate circumstances coming together to hinder our normal progress. Inside, though, a very different story was beginning to form.

The word 'story' is an important one.

In Chapter 3 I talked about how our brains often form their responses to a situation based upon whatever previous evidence they have of the most likely outcome. So, if you've had a hugely embarrassing moment when your mind went blank and you seemingly forgot how to speak in front of a prospective employer in the past, that might be the evidence your brain relies on to predict what's about to happen in your next interview. These pieces of historical evidence form a story in your mind about the probabilities of what's about to occur in an upcoming situation. If the 'evidence' was in some way interpreted as negative in the mind, the story will be too.

At the end of the 2003 F1 season the story in our minds was still that we were winners and that nothing short of winning the world title would do. That story was etched into our subconscious by multiple mini celebrations during the season and perpetuated by the plaudits and adulation of fans, media and even established competitors within the elite world of Formula One. Even Ron, hurting inside from what was ultimately another loss to Ferrari, did his best to celebrate our achievements and told us how this was the beginning of something special and that we should all be immensely proud of what we'd done together. In a passionate end-of-season speech, he told us 2004 would be the year in which we would take back the title.

Through the early struggles of 2004 the story we held in our heads didn't change. We saw each setback as a blip and convinced ourselves that everything would be back to normal soon. But as time moved on and the struggles continued, the lack of anything to celebrate began to take its toll.

Without the podium moments, the punching the air and

the pats on the back, the continuous hard slog of trying to dig ourselves out of trouble began to get monotonous and eventually a bit depressing. I don't expect the violins to come out in sympathy here; I fully appreciate the 'spoilt' nature of what I'm saying – going for just over half a season without winning a Grand Prix is barely a hardship compared to the life that many in the sport face every year. But satisfaction and indeed often happiness in any walk of life is essentially a factor of the results you end up with versus the expectation you had.

Many studies show an intrinsic link between life or job satisfaction, together with general happiness, and a person or team's self-belief. The self-belief comes from a confidence that life is likely to meet or exceed your expectations, which is clearly a positive outlook for the future. When you're winning, in Fı or life, it's obviously much easier to see a future involving more winning and that belief goes a long way to guiding the behaviours and decisions that inevitably lead towards those outcomes. If, every couple of weeks, you get to leap around hugging and spraying champagne and have the world congratulate you, it's easy to feel like a winner.

If, on the other hand, the expectation is that you'll be cheering and celebrating every week, but the reality is you have to endure others doing it instead of you, the opposite effect, as we discovered in those short few months, can kick in pretty quickly.

We tried to tell ourselves that we were still the best in the business. McLaren had such a long history of success, combined with recent achievements, that the stories we believed about ourselves were easy to hold on to for a while. But without the regular champagne moments that cemented those beliefs in place, our own questions began to arise. Are we kidding ourselves? Do we look silly walking around with chests puffed out with pride and yet with these results? Do we have a right to any confidence? Should we be resetting our targets? Is everyone laughing at us?

By the halfway point of that season, life remained miserable at McLaren. Some of our poor results were because we still didn't have a reliable or fast car, but our failures were also the consequence of the mood in the camp. With confidence low, I'm sure we were all secretly terrified of making mistakes. No one wanted to make things worse by trying something new or gambling on a risky strategy that might fail again. We weren't ourselves. We were terrified of what the world was saying about us. A prominent journalist at British newspaper the *Daily Express*, Bob McKenzie, even told his readers that McLaren were so bad that if they were, by some miracle, to somehow win a race during this disastrous season, he'd gladly run naked around Silverstone's Grand Prix track! The headlines were all for the wrong reasons and no one wanted to contribute to that, so subconsciously we didn't want to stand out.

From a psychological perspective these are all perfectly reasonable reactions to the situation we were in at the time. We've all been there, whether at work, at school, or amongst friends, when confidence is low and all we want to do is keep our heads down and stay hidden, protecting ourselves from whatever impending disaster we believe might come our way if we don't. It's an inbuilt self-defence mechanism to serve our survival instincts.

The problem is that, when sustained, those behaviours in life are less likely to lead to extraordinary results. And if you're competing in F1 or trying to succeed in business, extraordinary is exactly what you need to be.

A football or soccer analogy might be an attacking midfield player with the ball at their feet and a choice of making an intricate threaded pass between defenders into space for their striker to run onto, creating a chance on goal . . . or playing the safe option and passing back to their own defenders or goalkeeper to allow the attack to build again. A confident player and team are far more likely to play the risky ball into space, knowing it could get intercepted and the attack breaks down, but also that if the striker does get to it, there's a chance of scoring a great goal. A player struggling for confidence, one who's tried a few times and failed recently, is much more inclined not to put themselves at risk and so turns back towards their own defence. Without a series of recent successful outcomes to build evidence that there's a good chance their risky pass could work, self-belief is low.

The good news is that we did manage to dig ourselves out of the hole we'd found ourselves in, even if the real lessons only came some time afterwards, once we'd had a chance to reflect and learn, and we certainly learnt a lot that year.

The power of champagne

At the French Grand Prix we finally introduced a new car. We'd reluctantly cut our losses with the much delayed and ultimately ill-fated MP4-19 and pushed through an entirely fresh design around mid-season, the MP4-19B. It was immediately better, although some way from being fully optimised, with David Coulthard qualifying in third place on its first outing. Although we still only finished sixth and seventh at that race, that gave us a glimmer of hope. It was a very brief moment, on Saturday afternoon at least, of gently punching the air again.

At the next round, the British Grand Prix, in front of our own equally disillusioned fans, we surprised everyone, including ourselves, when Kimi finished second. Despite our forcefully ingrained understanding that second was just first of the losers, on that day it was a moment to celebrate, albeit with restraint.

It's a good thing we didn't get too carried away, because Kimi's car failed to finish the next two rounds. The difference between these failures and those that preceded them was that these were technical failures of our new and still somewhat fragile car. Because we'd managed to get back to the front, even if only briefly, we knew we could again. Confidence in our ability had begun to creep back.

One race later and we finally got one of the biggest champagne moments of my career. Kimi Räikkönen winning the Belgian Grand Prix from tenth on the grid changed everything.

When Kimi finally crossed the line after an hour and a half of racing and took the chequered flag just three seconds ahead of the pair of chasing Ferraris, an emotional volcano erupted within the team. I remember going crazy. We kicked chairs over in the garage. We screamed. We jumped. We hugged. We ran.

I grabbed the lens of a TV camera and shouted profanities into it at the top of my voice, telling the world that we were back (fortunately there's no way it was broadcastable, so I escaped any repercussions).

We sprinted to the podium, high-fiving and leaping all over each other on the way there. We drank and sprayed champagne and cheered together as a team, harder than with any previous victory because this one meant more. It ended a drought. It gave us reason to celebrate again.

That celebration was huge. Not in terms of the scale of the partying that followed (we were miles from a city in the middle of the Belgian Ardennes Forest), but in terms of its significance. All the fading memories of the past came vividly back to life. Lifting the trophy when it came back to the garage felt so natural. Other teams congratulating us, rather than the other way around, seemed like a return to normality. The media and photographers gathering around the team was just part of the fabric of life in the fast lane and like they'd never been away. We were back.

We remembered why 'celebrating success feels amazing'. It boosted the mood in the camp to levels not seen for many months and made us feel good about ourselves. Although any hope of bigger championship success was long gone by that stage in the season, it did bring confidence back into the team.

(There were other benefits, too. Ron's not one to forget someone disparaging our team. So you can imagine the pleasure he took in making all the necessary arrangements almost a year later to ensure that the *Daily Express*'s F1 writer, Bob McKenzie, did indeed strip naked and run a lap of the Silverstone racetrack in front of the enormous British Grand Prix crowd of 2005. A sporran and some McLaren-inspired body paint, together with a pair of trainers, the only concessions Ron was gracious enough to allow. In terms of celebrations, I suspect this was one of his best.)

After that victorious race we had a faster car than earlier in the year, but what was also clear was that with our rejuvenated belief and confidence in the team we behaved differently in the weeks and months that followed. Our decision-making and process-management in the races that followed were notably better. Though none of us had suddenly become fitter or stronger, we were faster with pitstops. We made big calls on race strategy and even when they didn't work out, we continued to make them afterwards instead of shying away from potential ridicule.

Our performance changed because we believed we were winners. And because we behaved like winners, more impressive results and podiums followed. The perpetual cycle continued and 'normal service' was resumed in the team, with the following season in 2005 being our most successful with Kimi, again taking the championship fight to the wire.

We managed to turn the slipping results and the mood of the team around through a combination of the new car and a series of unplanned yet accidentally powerful actions. Neither of these things was the result of the kind of meticulous consideration you might expect me to rave about here. But our mentality was always to ask ourselves what these happy accidents could teach us.

At the end of 2004 we had a series of meetings to look at what we could learn from a pretty disastrous year.

We had a huge number of technical failures, the most significant being the revolutionary yet highly flawed MP4-19 car. Having committed time, resources and all of our hopes to this machine, it let us down in a number of different ways, but at least its flaws were clear to see: they were easily quantifiable. If a part breaks, make it stronger. If a car's too heavy, make it lighter. In engineering terms, when the failure mode's measurable, the solution's normally measurable too.

As F1 teams traditionally did back in the day, in the post-season winter of 2004, we focused most of our resources on trying to engineer our way back to successful times by creating the best technology to make the car go faster in 2005. It was what we knew how to do best.

But many of our weaknesses that year weren't technical or measurable in the traditional sense. We'd let ourselves down on many occasions throughout the season through operational or human-performance-based failures. Our job over the winter was to get to the bottom of what those failures were, why they happened and of course what the big-picture solutions might be.

It was around this time that we were just beginning to explore a curiosity for new and innovative ways to improve our team as a whole. Money was almost never a restricting factor back then; it was simply about finding advantages by doing things differently and better and I feel proud to say that McLaren were often leading the way.

Ron had already raised eyebrows when he commissioned a Canadian specialist engineering company, Med-Eng Systems Inc., in partnership with Hugo Boss, to create a groundbreaking pitstop suit incorporating similar technology to that certified for use on Nasa's Space Shuttle. The futuristic gear had integrated cooling pipework and a backpack mounted pump system that circulated chilled fluid around our bodies in an attempt to maintain optimum core temperatures and therefore mitigate the effects of heat stress, like loss of concentration and fatigue. It looked futuristic and the thinking behind it was of the same ilk.

No one in Formula One had ever thought along these lines before and despite, in the end, the suits ultimately not working out as well as we'd hoped, it showed our unlimited desire to push boundaries in areas that other teams weren't prepared to go anywhere near.

This wasn't just about a particular idea like the spaceman-inspired pitstop suits; it was quickly becoming part of organisational culture. Ron led by example and was sometimes mocked in the media and the wider pitlane for it, but I took great inspiration from seeing him truly live the values he wanted to instil in all of us. When it came to that winter after the disappointing 2004 season, many of us had begun to fully embrace the ethos of being open-minded to almost anything, especially something no one else was doing, if it had even the slightest chance it might lead us to new success. I began to go out of my way to try and learn everything I could from the many brilliant minds I was surrounded by at the team. We were on a recruitment drive, from some of the brightest engineers in the world to management and finance specialists, and that now extended to a range of people tasked with harnessing human performance across the board. We were pioneering in the realms of data analytics and new technologies, but also physical trainers were starting to come in and not just to work with drivers. Sports and organisational psychologists, therapists, medical professionals and well-being practitioners were all now on the team's radar. And it was this area that sparked my latest fascination.

The circle of success

Within the pitlanes of Formula One, I can count a very small number of special people who've directly changed the course of my life for the better and for ever. Ron Dennis is one, Dr Aki Hintsa, our team doctor and dear friend to me and many others, was another. His inspirational life was ended way too early in 2016 by cancer at the age of fifty-eight, but the lives he affected in positive ways continue around the world in a better place than he found them. That's quite some legacy. I still miss him.

For someone to profoundly change the way another person thinks about everything in life, a few critical factors need to be established between those two people in advance. A deep trust and total respect are two of the most important and Aki and I had those without question. In fact, I suspect one of his greatest superpowers was that he had that with many of the people who knew him, such was his warm, empathetic nature, combined with his unparalleled experience both in sport and medicine. He knew things about human performance that I hadn't even heard of, let alone even begun to understand. Things he'd learnt working with some of the world's greatest athletes in Olympic teams, or the world's best long-distance runners from his years spent in Ethiopia.

What often impressed me most, though, was his ability to listen. Far from a preacher of his beliefs, he was more than happy just to sit and listen, to try and understand a situation he'd happily admit to not being an expert in. He had his own philosophy for getting the best out of people, but was open to finding new ways to apply that philosophy if the situation he was in required it.

That philosophy, encapsulated in a diagram he sketched out for me one evening when I asked for his counsel regarding our poor 2004 performance, he called The Circle of Success. Around the circumference of the circle he'd write six areas of focus that, when improved upon simultaneously, he believed could lead to exactly that, 'a more successful life'.

1. Physical Activity
2. Nutrition
3. Sleep/Recovery
4. Biomechanics
5. Mental Energy
6. General Health

Then he posed an interesting question.

'Which of these has significantly changed?' he said.

Immediately, he opened up a new line of thinking, which he was so often able to do. The conversation that followed ebbed and flowed, Aki always allowing me to share my thoughts and ask my own questions, with him sharing his own in his usual thought-provoking manner. He talked about how, in his model, significantly improving any single area, a combination of them, or all of the six areas, could contribute to a more successful life for the beneficiary. But, conversely, if one or more drops away or deteriorates, the negative impact can show up in all sorts of ways.

At that stage many of McLaren's employees were hardly a picture of perfect health. The nature of our travelling and hectic lifestyle, if left unchecked, which it had been for some, meant we slipped into bad habits and neglected our bodies. Our nutrition and sleep patterns were often all over the place. But crucially there was nothing new here; little about our general well-being had changed between 2003, when we were flying high, and 2004 when our world fell apart somewhat. The exception on his list was number five.

The mood in the team had deteriorated sharply, which affected the energy we felt and consequently gave off.

Aki and I talked about this for some time. We discussed the difference between the team's psychological states in 2003 and early 2004. One of the hypotheses I drew from the conversation, which in subsequent years I've studied further in my encounters with the corporate world, was that the absence of celebration contributes significantly to the negative self-story and lack of self-belief of those afflicted by it.

A key factor here is the importance of the word celebration. It might be easy to surmise that winning breeds confidence and that perpetuates a winning mentality and subsequent actions that are consistent with winners. All of that is largely true, but a number of studies have shown that to maximise the positive effect, or to harness a similar energy even when you may not be winning, using the power of the celebration is crucial.

In the first half of 2004 it seemed McLaren had nothing at all to celebrate. A series of failures and unfamiliar poor results stripped the team of any positive mental energy. The resulting negative energy led to low self-esteem, low confidence and a gradual rewriting of our own self-story in which we unwittingly morphed from winners to losers. The effect of the collective mindset shift meant we hesitated to make decisions, and those we did take tended to be risk-averse. Whilst we looked for safe options when it came to strategy and engineering choices, our competitors were being bold and brave, looking for, and grasping, every opportunity. We were the footballer continually passing back to the goalkeeper and so it's little wonder we didn't score goals.

At the Belgian GP we won the race, but it's the celebration that still sticks in the mind all these years later. It was visceral. I remember the sights, the sounds of the screams, the smell of the champagne. I remember the feeling inside that every one of us shared together.

By celebrating as a team in that garage and under the podium at the Spa-Francorchamps circuit, we collectively rewrote the stories in our minds. The win was part of it, but the memorable nature of the celebration afterwards, the synchronised release of dopamine we all shared, the outpouring of collective emotion, the physical contact, the photos, the powerful effects of these actions, made those stories easier to recall in the future.

When Aki pointed out to me that it was the Mental Energy in the team that was the only real thing that seemed to have changed for the worse, it soon became clear that when that mental energy improved, so did our behaviours and subsequently our results.

This prompted another question: what happens if we don't manage to get that one great result that breaks the negative cycle and helps turn things around like we did in Belgium 2004? How do we celebrate and get the positive effects of celebrating if there's no win to celebrate in the first place?

What helped was that at least some of the answers were hiding in plain sight just a bit further down the Fɪ pitlane.

You don't only celebrate when you win

In reality, in most seasons there are no more than around three or four teams that realistically have a chance of winning races. Even fewer can hope to be in the championship fight beyond the halfway point. So if those people outside of the top few were only motivated by winning, they'd be in a perennial state of disappointment and disillusionment, because they had nothing to celebrate.

How on earth did those teams and their thousands of employees stay motivated and driven to do what we all did? Every one of us gave everything and more to our teams. We sacrificed a 'normal life', with our friends and family and time at home, to commit almost all our time (oh, so much time) and energy to taking on the best in the world at this game of Formula One.

So why weren't they in exactly the same situation as us? Why weren't they in a continuous negative feedback loop? Why did their confidence and self-belief not crater too?

The reason, of course, is down to the expectations they set themselves.

If you, like McLaren did back then, base your value or worth only upon achieving the perfect end result, like winning a Grand Prix or World Championship, there will be few opportunities to celebrate.

One of the topics that continually arose in our meetings was the apparent dichotomy between our belief that winning was the only thing we should be striving for and the new appreciation that we needed to be able to celebrate on a regular basis . . . even if we weren't winning. Ron was predictably resolute early on that 'rewarding mediocrity', as I remember him putting it, was just not the McLaren way. His argument was understandable from his perspective. He'd built this organisation into a group of world-renowned technology companies, as well as one of the most successful F1 teams of all time, and he'd done it by never ever settling for second best.

I think it took Aki, someone he'd put an awful lot of trust and belief in, more so than any of our new psychologists and experts in the field, to gradually open his mind to the new philosophy. Aki was rarely ever forceful with opinions, often just calmly posing questions that made everyone think about what he'd just said. There weren't many people who could have that effect on Ron, but Aki was one and I remember it standing out as a rarity that Ron didn't seem to have an immediate comeback to some of his questions. In truth it was the same for all of us though. Less about not having a direct retort to a question posed, and more that we were all beginning to think a little deeper about everything. Our experts presented external studies and data around the effects of the brain's release of a potent neurotransmitter, dopamine, and explained what it all meant when it came to motivation and mood and even how that positively influenced the actions people took. But it was often Aki who made it make sense to us. We tried not to jump to obvious or existing conclusions and we strove to be open to the possibility of new ones, no matter how different or unusual they appeared at first.

Over time, as the world evolved in its thinking, and particularly as we at McLaren began to study and understand human behavioural traits in our pursuit of ultimate performance, the idea of only ever being able to celebrate finishing a race in first place seemed more and more counter-intuitive.

We grew to further appreciate that an F1 Grand Prix is a

complex event with many variables, most of which would always be beyond our control.

Some of those uncontrollable variables, like weather and most notably the actions of the other teams and their drivers, would often drastically shape the outcome of a race weekend and yet there might be little to nothing that we could do about them. So that meant that no matter how good we were on any given day, there were elements outside of our own performance that could determine whether we won or lost.

The same is true outside F1. Every one of us, every business, team, or individual, can only control what we can control. We can only ever do our best; nobody in the world can do more than that. So whatever goals we choose to set for ourselves, the overarching caveat should always be to understand that. And if we do succeed in that often tough mission to achieve our best performance possible, whatever the actual result – like that near miss at the Brazilian Grand Prix of 2003 – my goodness I believe we should celebrate it.

Only ever celebrating the outright victory has inherent problems in our modern understanding of human performance.

What we began to realise over time after working with team psychologists and behavioural scientists such as Dr Hintsa was that whilst the more traditional view that many of us had grown up with *can* work in some scenarios as a motivational driving force, it can also be pretty demotivating in others. One interesting study in 2022 from the Department of Psychology at the University of Groningen in the Netherlands looked at whether, in the context of a sports match, the goal of winning is really the most important goal to have. They looked at a mixed sample of 647 Dutch competitive korfball players and had them fill out tailored questionnaires to create data sets. Part of their conclusion was that whilst aiming high and celebrating a big win has a host of positive effects on the winner, like we've discussed, the practice of only aiming for that also comes with detrimental side effects.

Victory in any sport is often determined by factors outside the participants' control. They can lose, even after executing a 'perfect' operation, something that in any other walk of life would be celebrated. The need to focus on a rival's performance at the same time as their own can detract from the 100 per cent focused approach required by elite sport. As the study says, 'Such thoughts typically undermine performance attainment, and in the longer term make athletes vulnerable to structural frustration, chronic fear of failure, and burnout.' All of which can clearly get in the way of achieving the one thing that allows a team or athlete to celebrate . . . winning. Essentially, it can lead to long spells of disappointment forming that detrimental negative feedback loop.

The teams further back on the grid, the ones scrapping week in, week out, over an often elusive single point or two, just had different expectations to us. That point, a manageable target, was their big win and it was achievable, sometimes even by just finishing the race. That point was the reason they got out of bed in the morning and made all the same significant sacrifices we did in pursuit of our goals. Whatever their goals were – scoring a point, beating a rival, finishing the race in a better position than they started it, or even just getting to the chequered flag in one piece – when they managed it, that was their champagne moment.

Adjusting what you're aiming at to reflect your current situation, like we touched on in the first chapter, is one way to create more confidence-boosting opportunities to celebrate. I suspect that had anyone suggested to Ron Dennis at the beginning of that tough time that we reset our expectations until we find our way back to the top, he'd have blown a gasket. His argument, I imagine, would've been that if we begin to think like a midfield team, then that's exactly what we'll be. And from a winners' mentality perspective, he could be right.

A team that only strives for fifth place is probably less likely to take the kind of calculated gambles and risks that winners take. It's likely to only ever subconsciously do enough to finish fifth. Winners think like winners and the rest think slightly differently. But Ron's insistence that we should keep believing we were the best team in the business was undermined by the lack of the champagne necessary to corroborate that belief. It was harder and harder to sustain as time went on.

So what we came to deduce, with the benefit of time and reflection, was that if celebrations were what gave us the psychological boosts we needed to keep operating in the right zone, then we needed to find reasons to celebrate, even if we weren't winning races. We assessed our performances not just on the eventual outcome, but on the way we got there. If we executed everything brilliantly and got the best result we could in the circumstances, even if not the one we'd ideally love to have come away with, that was something to recognise. This is one of the biggest lessons I hope you take away from this chapter, because it's one of the biggest I've learnt and still actively benefit from today.

The other answer we came up with, without diluting our overarching mission of standing back on the top step of the podium regularly, was to celebrate the smaller wins. In the words of author Paulo Coelho, 'The great victory, which appears so simple today, was the result of a series of small victories that went unnoticed.'

Celebrating the small victories along the way can give a number of regular boosts of dopamine, the brain's feel-good chemical. Dopamine acts as a neurotransmitter, sending signals to other parts of the brain that generate a pleasurable reward; and when that happens, our brains pay attention to what we did to cause the lovely feeling and calculates what we need to do to repeat the success, leading to a higher probability of us achieving our goals.

At McLaren we never removed our ultimate goal of getting back to the top, but we also made a point of celebrating the kinds of things we'd previously taken for granted.

So we tried to identify as many small, previously unappreciated 'wins' as we could during our everyday processes and practices. The active change was to encourage everyone to be deliberately conscious about doing it all the time, something we'd overlooked because of the previous sole focus on the grand prize.

It started at the top, where executives recognised small achievements that previously went quietly by unnoticed. Senior leadership then expressed the importance of middle management doing the same with their smaller teams and the practice cascaded.

Hitting a budget or timeframe target became reason for celebration. Bringing a tenth of a second of lap time improvement to the car, irrespective of where the car finished a race, was a small victory and was recognised. We did the same for acts of great teamwork, a successful pitstop practice, a well-presented car or garage, or good decision-making during a race weekend.

The celebrations may not have been as explosive as those for the coveted race win, but they soon started to impact people's mood, and because we found reason for lots of them, the cumulative effect over time became surprisingly powerful. It could be as simple as a high five or a fist bump to my corner crew after a good pitstop, or as big as having someone called out personally in front of the entire organisation at the company-wide post-race debrief in the factory.

By acknowledging the great things people achieved every day, even tiny things, through team meetings in front of their peers or publicly through press releases and media interviews, we brought back some positive mental energy into the team. We gave everyone opportunities to experience those small dopamine hits as often as possible and it helped to complete what my good friend Aki would call The Circle of Success. And it did bring some success. In 2005, the mood was better, the mindset was better, the car was better and the results were better too. We went to the podium twelve times from the eighteen races we took part in that year, winning seven of them. I don't believe for a second that there isn't a very strong relationship between those results and our new approach to celebrating success.

You can put this into practice in your own life with exactly the same philosophy as I've tried to do ever since.

Most of us go through our days achieving some remarkable things that go entirely unnoticed by our conscious minds. Things that don't just happen by accident, but through a series of often small but critical decisions that we take without ever appreciating them. That's life: we take those small but remarkable achievements for granted without realising just how consequential they actually are.

MARGINAL GAIN

One really easy way to start recognising what we're doing, and rewarding ourselves, is to follow the procedure I talked about in Chapter 1. A job list of simple things you can tick off as the day goes on. The key is to start off by making the list as achievable as you can and then celebrating each one as you manage to get through it. You can think of all manner of work or personal goals to put on the list, but if they're small enough or achievable enough the feeling of completing them and then getting to the end of the day with a finished list can deliver quite a powerful dopamine shot that makes you feel like a winner. You set out to achieve something and did it, you were successful, and you will be sure to remember: 'celebrating success feels amazing'.

The continual feeling of 'winning' that those small internal celebrations give you breeds a belief that you can achieve more. Bigger wins are more likely to follow. The important part here is the conscious celebration. It's easy to dismiss a tiny achievement as insignificant, but just like the tiny technical marginal gains coming together over time to improve the lap time of our F1 car, our positive mental energy builds in the same way.

I've tried to encourage my children to adopt a simple version of the same strategy. Before bedtime when they were younger I often asked them to write down up to three things they'd like to achieve the next day. We kept it simple, like making the bed, or doing their five-minute Duolingo app lesson, and we made sure they ticked them off by the time they went to bed the next night. It gave them a sense of achievement, which I hope had a small but positive effect over time in making them feel like winners.

The other way I've found that helps me to get a similar feeling is to write a journal entry every day. I've now been doing this for years and find it incredibly therapeutic for a number of reasons. One of the methods I find most powerful is to note down either an achievement itself from the day, or a comment or reflection on something I've achieved. Reminding myself of the good things I've done that day provokes a little internal celebration. But the act of writing them down also helps to commit them to memory, making it easier to recall them when I'm looking for evidence to convince myself that I can achieve something similar in the future. I have mini celebrations each evening once I've made my entry into the book and again when I complete a week of journal entries. The effect continues, until hopefully the book gets completed at the end of the year and I celebrate and start again.

Have a think about the things, small or otherwise, you can celebrate in your life, but also how you can celebrate others around you. It's proven that both the celebrator and the 'celebratee' get positive effects, so if you run a team at work, find ways to celebrate them. If you're a parent, celebrating your children in their most formative years can literally change their lives. Relationships thrive when actively celebrated.

Just like in F1, one celebration leads to both the desire for another and, at the same time, the likelihood that another will happen. So go and find, or create, your own champagne moments.

PITLANE LESSONS

- When you strike gold in your life, make the celebration memorable and go big. It'll pay you back later when your brain needs reminding you're a champion.
- Don't limit celebrating to only the enormous wins in your life; they're not the only things you deserve that winning feeling for.

- Learn to find, but also to generate if necessary, smaller moments in your life to celebrate. Each one, no matter how tiny, adds to the feeling of being a successful person. The more you repeatedly feel like a winner, the more likely you are to make decisions that lead to winning outcomes.

5.

TALENT CAN WIN RACES, BUT TEAMWORK WINS TITLES
How and Why You Build a Winning Team

F1 is perhaps the biggest team sport in the world. Although the drivers get almost all the public's attention and focus, no driver has ever won a world title on their own. The largest teams have well over a thousand people, and even the smallest players in the game consist of hundreds and hundreds of team members. It's also a world of precision and accuracy, of extreme pressure, big prizes for big success and huge consequences when things don't go well, so those hundreds and thousands of people have to be extremely good at what they do.

Those people design the individual parts for the cars; they manufacture components; test them; research and develop cutting-edge materials and substances; assemble the cars; drive them; improve them; operate them; analyse them; paint them; transport them; simulate them; finance them; strip and rebuild them; they manage the people that do all these things; they feed those people; train them; look after them; develop them; pay them; clothe them . . . the list of roles and responsibilities goes on and on. It's a huge operation just to get two cars onto the starting grid on a Sunday afternoon.

If you want to succeed in F1, you need the very best people available from anywhere around the world in your team in every single one of those disciplines. Which means that the ranks of the biggest teams are stacked with the most highly skilled, experienced, super-intelligent, best-in-class individuals wearing their colours in a bid to win the ultimate prize.

But even a thousand of the world's most elite individuals, albeit dressed in the same uniform, don't necessarily always make the world's most elite team.

Because assembling a group of brilliant people is only part of the challenge; getting them to work well together can be entirely another. Choose the wrong ones or put them in the wrong environment and, no matter how brilliant each is as an individual, the team dynamic, and therefore the team's output, could easily suffer as a result.

F1's littered with examples of the most brilliant teamwork. Races and even World Championships have been won by teams who didn't necessarily always have the fastest car or the biggest budget, but who utilised incredible teamwork to create an advantage over sometimes technically stronger competitors.

The dramatic conclusion of the 2021 F1 season in Abu Dhabi will always be remembered for the controversial and ultimately incorrect application of the rules which allowed a grateful Max Verstappen to overtake Lewis Hamilton on fresher tyres on the last lap of the race to take victory and the title. People will argue over the details of that for the remainder of time. But overshadowed now in the same race, a few laps earlier, was a moment of great teamwork from the other Red Bull Racing driver, Sergio Pérez. He was asked by his team to sacrifice the result of his own race in order to help Max to achieve the big prize. By running a sub-optimal strategy – staying out on track way longer than ideal instead of making the obvious required pitstop for new tyres – he was able to drive super-defensively and effectively hold up Lewis Hamilton's charge for the front. That stopped Hamilton from building a lead big enough to make a free pitstop should a safety car come out towards the end of the race. When that fateful crash happened a few laps from the end and the safety car was indeed deployed to slow and close up the field behind him, Lewis could've dived into the pits, got new tyres and zipped back out again before they all bunched up in his rear-view mirrors. Lewis would've almost certainly been an eight-times World Champion instead of seven. That moment of Red Bull teamwork brought Max back into contention on a day where there's no doubt that Hamilton's Mercedes was the faster car at that track.

And I have lost count of the number of times at McLaren when, on the Friday before the Australian Grand Prix, the first race of the season, we reached the end of the day having struggled to get our new car to work effectively in the practice sessions. In the evening we'd sit down with the drivers and comb through the data for solutions, desperate to improve the car for the all-important qualifying session on Saturday. We'd draw our best conclusions and come up with a plan before finally climbing into bed exasperated, unsure that we'd be able to turn things around in the short time we had left.

On almost every occasion I'd wake up to great news. The team back in the UK, our factory-based colleagues, had worked through our night with an exact copy of our car on a hydraulic seven-post test rig, rapidly and accurately learning to predict how the car would behave dynamically once our proposed changes had been applied. Many of them were ex-race-team engineers and technicians, so they knew exactly what we needed and how to help. The UK data analysis group would run thousands upon thousands of digital simulations for hours on end to ascertain how tyres would wear or race strategy might be affected with a new car set-up.

On the opposite side of the planet our teammates put in the hard graft whilst we slept, and found mechanical tweaks or strategic plans to help the team on the ground. It was team-work at its best, hundreds of people, thousands of miles apart, in radically different time zones, but all working together, for each other, towards a collective outcome.

Utilising the right members of your team at the right times and in the right areas to make best use of those resources takes thought and consideration, as well as coordination.

But if you're able to tap into the power generated when a number of highly talented people work towards the same goal and create free-flowing channels where ideas, suggestions, expertise and experience can move to the right areas at the right times, you level up your capabilities as a team by an order of magnitude.

Talent can't always get you over the line, but teamwork often can.

So I know what the best teamwork looks like. My decade in Formula One's pitlane with McLaren also had me witness some of the worst. As with most failures in life, studying the lowest moments we go through and the decisions and actions that got us there can often offer the biggest lessons and the most valuable guide on how to become better and succeed in the future. And some of my most valuable learnings in that area were imposed on me in the cruellest and most painful of ways in 2007.

Fernando Alonso and Lewis Hamilton, two of the undis-puted greatest Formula One drivers of all time, were brought together as teammates that year. On paper it looked like a dream line-up, yet turned out to be a nightmare that was dis-solved after just one disastrous season because the two simply couldn't work together, which had a destructive impact on the wider team.

Winning the F1 World Championship's an indescribably difficult thing to do. There are so many elements you need to get right, over such an extended period, and always whilst under constant and immense pressure. To achieve it, any F1 team needs to have found all of the right pieces of the puzzle at the right time. I often use the analogy of baking a cake. To create a successful cake, one needs ALL of the right ingredients. If just one is missing or wrongly measured, any one, the cake won't taste right, or won't look right. It simply won't be a success. Being successful in F1 is much the same.

Although clearly simplifying the process to some extent, the main ingredients for winning the coveted title in F1, for baking the perfect F1 cake if you will, are a great car, great drivers, the right finance and a great team working together.

At the beginning of 2007, we at McLaren believed we had pretty much all of the dream elements required to challenge for the elusive world title in Formula One. It was exciting, because these 'perfect storm' moments in sport, as in life, come around rarely.

We'd designed and produced a car for that year inside our factory that, from very early on in pre-season testing, was clearly fast, highly competitive and reliable. The team was working well with systems and procedures behind the scenes that were highly developed and largely efficient and we were in a confident position internally.

We'd recovered and rebuilt after a difficult 2006 season in which we'd learnt a lot that was now in place to be better for 2007. Amongst the many changes to the way our team worked were two significant and very public ones, our racing drivers. McLaren had lost our highly talented Finnish driver, Kimi Räikkönen, to rivals Ferrari, and Columbian Juan Pablo Montoya had left the team to race in the American Nascar series, but both of their replacements turned out to be the world-class drivers of the 2007 field.

Fernando Alonso was a double World Champion, *the* current World Champion. He was universally recognised throughout the sport as being one of the greats, even at his relatively young age . . . and he was now part of our McLaren team. We were excited, expectations were high and, with the car we'd produced over the winter, we went into that season almost giddy at the prospect of getting back to the kind of sustained winning ways that can put you firmly into the mix for the sport's biggest prize.

On the other side of the garage came another new face to the race team, Lewis Hamilton. This was a surprise to many people, not because he wasn't talented or fast in a car, but because it was a very un-McLaren thing to do, to take a complete F1 rookie and put them into one of our coveted race seats.

Still, we all started off with the same wholesome goals in mind: we wanted to win races, hopefully win the championship and be the best team we could be over the course of the season.

This isn't unusual. In almost every case study of team failures I've looked at, across sport, business and personal or social groups, they start their journeys with the best intentions. In public cases, like ours, press releases and interviews from those early days all portray a united front, a shared vision, 'Us against the world'. Behind the scenes, though, often deep in the subconscious or at least in the unspoken thoughts of those involved, lay hidden clues, tell-tale signs that the road ahead might not be as idyllic as many might have believed.

Lewis was young and inexperienced in comparison to Alonso, and as a result many people in the team, whilst not begrudging him the opportunity, had all their hopes for success very firmly planted with Fernando. There was a desperate scramble to be assigned to the de facto 'Number 1' car and a vociferous desire not to end up working on one that was almost certain to spend much of its time in gravel traps and bringing up the rear at the hands of a new driver learning the ropes at their expense. They wanted to work with the driver they were convinced would bring them the best chance of personal glory. They didn't have the team's interests at heart; they had their own.

These signs of personal agendas, self-serving goals that weren't necessarily in line with the overall mission of the team, were an early indication of some of the cracks in the organisation that, as the 2007 season went on, began to gradually rip the team, together with any hopes of our success together, wildly apart.

All of this was heightened by a peculiarity in F1, which has implications for the way any team works together. There are two different competitions at stake, the Drivers' World Championship and the Constructors', or team's, World Championship, which means that different people's priorities can occasionally come into conflict with each other.

Personal egos, firstly those of the drivers, but then of wider team members, got in the way of the team's accomplishments that year. As the season unfolded, the relationship between Fernando and Lewis broke down further and further, moving from teammates to arch enemies, and as it did so the team gradually broke apart too. Mechanics and engineers took sides, forming a giant split down the middle of the team's garage, effectively creating two opposing small teams within McLaren.

By the time we'd got just a few races into the campaign, it became clear that Lewis was just as fast as Fernando. That gave him, and his side of the garage, the welcome, yet largely unexpected, hope that they could also fight for the big prizes. Hamilton moved quickly from young apprentice to title rival and was hungry for it. The other side of the team were taken aback. This wasn't the way they'd envisioned the plan working out and they naturally felt they had to fight back. It became a battle for supremacy.

Feelings of animosity grew quickly and spread from just the drivers to their wider crews of people. Mechanics and engineers on both sides gathered around their guy as they each became more desperate to overpower the other.

Team debriefs became guarded affairs, with no one willing to share the entirety of what they'd learnt that day for fear of handing the same advantages to their rival in the same room. Information was held back for private discussions later rather than opening up to the wider group so we could all learn more together. The very essence of teamwork was being eroded in favour of personal gain.

Over the course of the season both sides began using the media in a war of words to garner support. The British media backed Lewis and the Spanish did the same for their man, but it was the team that unquestionably lost out. We were in one of those rare years where it was all there for the taking, yet we were somehow snatching defeat from the jaws of victory.

Things got worse as the season went on. There's a now infamous incident from the Hungarian GP pitlane when the fighting in the team boiled over onto the racetrack. Fernando deliberately refused to leave the box after a pitstop to change tyres in qualifying in order to hold up Lewis, who was waiting in his car behind him, and in doing so prevented him getting round an entire lap before the chequered flag was waved to end the session. It left Alonso on pole. The calculated move was in response to Lewis ignoring team protocols that should've allowed Fernando to leave the garage first at the beginning of qualifying as it was his turn to benefit from the early run and clear track.

The whole woeful saga kickstarted a chain reaction of events that destroyed any form of meaningful teamwork inside McLaren's garage. We'd ruined one of those vital key ingredients required to win and as a result . . . Ferrari picked up the prize.

Make no mistake, we had a great collection of people at McLaren, but in that year we proved that great people alone are not enough; it's imperative they operate in a coordinated, cohesive way, working together towards a shared goal or outcome. But even more than that, people in a team, even great ones, who end up actively working against each other with opposing motivations, can be one of the most destructive dynamics any group can face.

Life, like F1, is a team sport. Parental partnerships; romantic relationships; families; siblings; friend groups; classmates; colleagues; neighbourhoods; sports teams; communities; hobbyists; social media followings; political or economic groups – these can all be considered teams in some sense, and in need of *teamwork* to maximise anyone's benefit from being part of them.

There were many reasons why McLaren went on to win the 2008 Formula One World Championship, just a year after we seemed to have reached our nadir, but one of them is that we found ways which helped us radically improve our team environment.

I've tried to distil what our team learnt from those difficult twelve months into six principles for effective teamwork, which form the basis of the rest of this chapter. These are what I talk about when I go into businesses to help them reach their potential, and I have high hopes that I might just be able to share something you can benefit from too. If you want to achieve more, reach remarkable levels of accomplishment and smash through the goals you've set yourself, then doing it with a great team around you is a proven benefit, so let's go.

1. Remember that we're tribal creatures

What my time in F1 taught me, often with brutal force, is that simply assembling a group of talented people doesn't really make a team. They only become that when they learn to work together effectively.

We're tribal creatures, designed to work together as a collective, or group, to survive and thrive. Many thousands of years ago our tribe's purpose was survival: without the help and support of those around us, we'd die. We'd get eaten by animals, we'd be attacked by rival tribes, we'd starve to death or suffer rapid demise from poor health or injury. The very existence of the group as a whole relied on the well-orchestrated teamwork of its members to sustain itself and grow. There was no room for ego getting in the way.

Thousands of years later it's easy to think we live in a different world, have different needs and face different threats and so need a different approach. But how different is it really?

In business, life and Formula One we face threats every single day; most won't pose mortal risk to us personally, but our companies and teams face regular challenges from competitors whose goal it is to impose their dominance over us, to steal our market share or position on a leaderboard and move into our territory. In the worst cases, if we fail to work as a team and make the wrong decisions, our businesses die.

Families need to look after each other with parents supporting children's development alongside schools. We provide food and shelter for each other and one or more people in that little team needs to go out and gather the money to bring home and pay for it. We try our best to protect each other from harm, keep each other safe and healthy, and provide nurture and comfort when a member of that team's sick or struggling.

Friend groups can play a similar role in supporting their members through tough times in school or life in general. Sports teams face rival tribes each week in competitions where there's often only one winner. Political parties rally reinforcement in the form of voters and come together to fight off opposition and champion their causes.

We have the same needs of our tribes. They offer just as much value and make us similarly stronger as they did thousands of years ago . . . yet we regularly fail to appreciate this. We often actively choose not to work together because our modern-day egos or personal desires have evolved to become more important to so many of us.

The earliest days of mankind might on the surface seem almost totally divorced from the sleek, high-tech world of F1, but when we took a step back, we realised that some truths endure. Humans are built to connect with each other, to share with, and fight for, our tribes. Each of us possesses different skills, characteristics, talents, beliefs, strengths and of course weaknesses, and only when we combine and work together as a team can we ever hope to utilise the power of all those positives and minimise the impact our 'negatives' have on our performance.

For us at McLaren, recognising this was one of the first important steps we needed to take to rebuild our team spirit.

2. Get rid of egos

In 2007 at McLaren we should've absolutely won both F1 World Titles, yet we won neither. There were a number of profound failures, but the biggest obstacle was ego. The desire to win personal battles and be proven 'right' became more powerful than the collective desire to be the best Formula One team. In the end no one at McLaren won because, as the egos grew stronger, the team became weaker. You, like we did, can learn from our mistakes. You're welcome.

Have you ever blagged your way through a meeting or presentation, when a junior member of the team might have been better placed to respond to the questions you faced? Have you told an employee how *you* want them to do something, rather than ask them how *they* would do it? How many parents blindly dismiss a child who's questioning something they've said or done? None of these examples are using the strengths of the team in the best way, so if these things are obvious, then why do so many people and businesses fail to get them right so regularly?

Vast quantities of research show us that the most common reason is the human ego. Jim Collins, in his book, *How the Mighty Fall*, talks extensively about the ways in which ego can negatively impact team performance. He concludes that it largely comes down to not sharing opportunities and credit across the team's members, together with being quick to apportion blame when something goes wrong to protect an individual ego:

'I can't let the receptionist get credit for an idea – I'm the Creative.'

'That meeting was an opportunity for me to put myself into a room with the big boss, I couldn't miss that chance!'

'They're my employees: they do things my way!'

'They're kids, they have to follow instructions, and I don't have time for silly questions!'

Ego.

In these situations we must go right back to the beginning and ask what is the purpose of our team? Why does it exist? What are we trying to achieve? Whatever the specific answer, it's almost always the case that we can get closer to it, more efficiently, if we work together. That's as true in F1 as anywhere else. The team exists to collectively try and achieve our sport's

biggest accolade, and whilst fans outside may see global super-
stars behind the wheels of our cars, to those inside the team
the driver's simply another member of the group, nothing
more, nothing less. Sergio Pérez was willing to sacrifice his own
chances in a race because he knew that helping Max Verstappen
win would benefit the team as a whole.

And so, if those 'superstar drivers' start to display signs of
their egos getting in the way of us all working together, I prom-
ise you they'll be quickly brought back down to earth by those
around them today as that won't win us a championship.

Something like this happened with Lewis in his first year at
McLaren. As he navigated the massive shift in his entire life and
career I suspect he may've been poorly advised. He was just
trying to deal with a set of extreme pressures never encountered before and fight his corner, but through inexperience I
believe he chose the wrong course of action, often using the
media to try to protect his own interests. Occasionally he criti-
cised the team publicly, suggesting he hadn't been treated fairly,
which ended up pissing off the people who were supposed to
be helping him. As a senior member of the team by then, I had
more than one frank conversation with his trainer, Adam, one
of his closest confidants at the time, pointing out that he was
in danger of alienating the people around him when he needed
them most. I knew the message would be passed on.

When you're trying to address an issue like this, you don't
have to be confrontational, but you do need to be clear that the
team always comes first, and that personal egos have no place.

3. Build deep bonds

The stronger the connections between every member of a
team, the more likely they are to be able to put their egos to

one side. But these strong connections can have benefits that go way beyond even that.

When I first joined McLaren and got my dream job as a Test Team Mechanic back in 2000, I remember going to my first-ever test in Barcelona with the team. I didn't know anybody. I was crippled with imposter syndrome, nervous and awestruck in equal measure. At the end of my first day at the track, I walked across the paddock to have dinner in the team hospitality area and had that terrifying moment I'm sure many of us have experienced as a 'newbie' at school or work, where I had my plate of food, but then had to turn around and find a table to sit at. Everyone else seemed like best friends on tables that were full, like cliques, none of which I fitted into yet. The other mechanics I'd been working with that day were at a table with no spare chairs and so I had little choice but to sit on my own at an empty one. I felt like an outsider and a long way from being part of the team.

After a few painfully long moments someone came and sat next to me and, as I looked up, I was astonished to find it was none other than international superstar F1 driver, David Coulthard. This was a guy I'd been watching and admiring on TV from home until just a week ago, a guy I idolised and looked up to and here he was choosing to sit with me, someone he'd never even met yet. It took me a while to get over my initial nerves.

We chatted for some time, him like the suave and sophisticated gent that he was, me like a teenage superfan having just won a backstage pass at a One Direction gig, but whilst I had so many questions I really wanted to ask him about racing, it was him quizzing me most of the time. He asked how my first day at the track had been, he asked about my family, about my hobbies, my pets, my friends, music, football. We barely spoke about F1. After a while, once I'd got myself under control again,

I said, 'David, I hope you don't mind me asking, but you know everyone here well, your engineers and trainer are over there on that table, your mechanics are over there, yet you chose to come and sit next to me, someone you've never met before . . . why?' I've never forgotten his response to that question. He said 'That's exactly why I came and sat with you. I don't know you, yet you're part of this team . . . we're teammates. I need to know who you are and what you're about and I want you to understand the same about me. If we want to get the best out of each other, and that's exactly what we need to do here, we need to get to know each other.'

David Coulthard saying we were 'teammates' was singularly powerful in helping me to overcome the anxieties I'd felt all day, but the very thought of teammates understanding exactly who the people in their team really were was a thought-provoking concept I've gone on to study in much more depth as the years rolled on. In that example, me knowing that DC was willing to go to the greatest lengths to not just drive the car, but to drive the team into the best place he could, was of course inspirational, but from his perspective he needed to know that the car he was being asked to risk his life in at over 200mph was being designed, created, put together and operated by a team of people who had his back, who cared and had the same goals and determination as he did.

On the flip side, the team of hundreds of dedicated people, being asked to give their all, sacrifice time at home, being asked to *live* for this team, not just *work* for it, needed to know that the guy they were doing it all for, the guy who'd take their machine into battle, was willing to go to the same remarkable lengths.

You can see something similar at work when you consider the staggering capabilities of a Formula One pitstop crew, who work together in a highly efficient and coordinated way, under unbelievably challenging circumstances. There's the sensory overload of standing in a pitlane as a heavy, sharp, angry, hot and ferociously impatient F1 car races towards you at motorway speeds, hoping it'll screech to a halt centimetres away from you. If that wasn't scary enough, the thought of millions of people watching, desperately relying on you to get their driver back into the race trouble-free and ahead of their rivals adds to the experience. Your competition might be doing the same thing, at the same time as you, just a few metres further down the pitlane. The operations that have to happen are complex and require absolute precision from everyone involved and it all needs to be completed as close as possible to two seconds flat. The only way that happens is through some of the greatest teamwork in the world.

That small group of people need to be individually excellent, but importantly they need to have complete trust and belief in the people around them to operate as a great team. Each person needs to truly believe they're the best at what they do, but also that they're surrounded by others of a similarly elite standard and that they can 100 per cent trust those teammates to deliver and have their back when necessary. That trust comes from getting to know each other on a far deeper level than just as colleagues in the same uniform.

A team that really knows and understands each other, not just professionally, but knows the people behind the job titles, can learn to help each other achieve their collective and individual goals much more effectively. In a corporate structure that's something I try and encourage more and more in the work I do today with my leadership teams, but you don't have to have a managerial position to embrace the idea . . .

My twelve-year-old daughter plays football for the local under-thirteens team. The group of girls came together three years ago, with most of them having never even kicked a ball before and only a few of them knowing each other from one or two school connections. Many of them, including my own daughter, had to be persuaded to give it a try for the first time.

Over three seasons, the shared experience of learning the game together, with the coaches centring the whole process around fun, combined with some inspirational role models emerging across the women's professional game, has brought the girls together in the most incredible way. They've been on a journey and are now the best of friends. They've also become one of the best examples of a high-performing team I can think of.

They've been beaten 6–0 together in the pouring rain, yet come off the cold, muddy pitch with smiles. They've fallen together, but helped each other up together and have never given up. They got to know each other inside out by hanging out away from football. They trust each other. They hug each other if they score a goal, but also if they concede one. Today they're winning leagues and trophies, which is great to see and thoroughly deserved, but far more impressive is the way they work for each other, look out for each other, stand up for each other . . . love each other. They've developed a bond so tight that I believe they would do literally anything to help each other, should they need to. That, right there, is the Holy Grail of teamwork.

The best F1 teams put considerable time and effort into building deep relationships between the pitstop crew members for exactly this reason. Trust in any walk of life comes from having a real understanding of who it is you're dealing with in any situation. In the highest-pressure moments of a pitstop, especially where the stakes are greatest, like on the final day of a season when there's a championship on the line, even half a doubt about someone in your team can affect your performance.

Doubt, or a lack of confidence in team members, creates distraction that can cost you focus on your role. We might be talking about less than 1 per cent of your attention being dragged from where it needs to be – you might be worrying about whether someone else is doing their bit – but that can be enough in this elite environment to change the outcome. The pitstops that help win races and championships are the ones where everyone's seamlessly operating in 100 per cent synchronicity with each other.

So, creating that crucial bond and trust is a priority for the best F1 teams. That means taking active steps to make it happen.

One of the byproducts of the way F1 operates as an industry is the fact that it's populated by some of the highest performers in the world in every role across the board. That naturally helps to create an environment of mutual respect and increased trust straight away, just by knowing the general calibre of the workforce. It's also a world in which team members don't just turn up for work each day, do their jobs and go home again. We literally travel the globe together for most of the year, facing the extreme pressures of the competition, but then live together in hotels, go for dinner together, have breakfast together and almost everything in between. There's a natural impact of that lifestyle on everyone involved in that, as you can imagine, we all get to know each other far better than most co-workers ever get the chance to. But if a team is looking for an advantage over their competition, and they all are, this form of bonding is not enough because it's what everyone in this sport does.

At McLaren we chose to take things a step further. We wanted to build the kind of bonds that meant we knew each other so well and trusted each other so much that we'd do almost anything to support each other when it mattered. We looked at military training exercises designed to push teams to rely on each other to survive and used them for inspiration. Our version of this took us to extreme environments outside of our comfort zones and into places we'd never usually find ourselves in between F1 seasons.

One that stood out for me was when we went on a training camp inside the Arctic Circle, where there were only about three or four hours of daylight each day. We were set challenges to find our way through vast snow-covered landscapes, devoid of reference points, and trek our way to a location. No one completed the challenge until everyone completed the challenge, so we had to work together, supporting those that struggled. Phones stopped working in temperatures as low as −20 degrees, as did parts of our bodies. Our safety net of technology was gone. Light disappeared quickly as full darkness set in somewhere between 2 and 3pm, disorienting everyone. We couldn't split up, it was too dangerous, so we worked together. At times we literally had to cuddle each other to share body heat, but we found a way and everyone contributed something.

On the same trip we were encouraged to chainsaw a hole in a two-foot-thick ice-covered lake and take it in turns to help to dunk each other into the water. There was real risk of death had we not taken care of each other and literally held hands to lower each other into the water before pulling our colleague back out again. From there it was straight into a hot tub and then repeat the process. It was hugely uncomfortable to do, but the sense of collective achievement was immense at the end of the adventure. And that was the point. We got to know each other's strengths but also our weaknesses as they were all there on display for everyone to see. No one got left behind or left out of anything as the only way we were ever going to get through the activities was by pulling together. It pushed us into some of our most vulnerable places and relied on the entire team to support each other knowing it could be them suffering next. We weren't going to war, but it felt like it and we were certainly going to be going into battle in our own way once the season got underway.

We built our team by going through shared experiences as a group and, in the process, developing a deeper understanding of who we all were. I found out a lot about myself on those trips, we tend to when facing fears or uncomfortable situations, but I also found out who I had around me as we embarked on another journey around the globe up against the best in the world at what we do. In some cases it was like discovering new members of the team, even though we'd known each other for years. I learnt that one or two people who were generally the loud ones on tour, those full of bravado in the garage, had a sensitive side I'd never seen before. At first we'd made light-hearted jokes about them buckling when things got tough as we were lost in a dark forest or on an expansive frozen lake, like we'd always do in the familiarity and comfort of our pitlane environment. But the situation there was different, very different. None of us could be confident enough to be that bold for long. Our years of experience, or a successful record in F1, counted for very little whilst we were facing a challenge this unusual. We were unceremoniously levelled as a group and having to fall back on our inherent skills and characters, and importantly on each other, to get through it. We had to become a better team quickly.

Quiet team members proved they were analytical, crucial in that environment. We found out who was really calm when things went wrong, not because they'd been doing a particular job for years and had experience to lean on, but because that characteristic was in their make-up. Likewise, leaders emerged, creative thinkers, those with extraordinary stamina or even unlikely empathy. The process drew out traits that were sometimes buried or restrained in our usual world and it allowed us all to see those around us differently. On one hand we'd been forced to lay ourselves bare in front of each other, which meant that we had to drop any pretences and have our vulnerabilities on show, and on the other it meant we were witness to the same from our teammates.

(In actual fact on day one of the trip we did at the end of 2006 – the very first time we'd all really got to know our new driver for the following season, a young rookie called Lewis Hamilton – we truly did lay ourselves bare as events ended with the entire pit crew squashed naked into a sauna that wasn't quite big enough to fit us all in!)

You don't need to go to the extremes we did to see positive results. Even having fun at an office party or a company 'off-site' can have a positive impact. Group holidays, school trips, volunteering or taking on a challenge with your children or partner all have the ability to create memories that no one but those there at the time share, and from some of those experiences come the bonds that are the foundations of great teams.

My experience as a witness to multiple corporate team-bonding events is that the more emotionally or physically engaging an activity is, the more it will help forge those all-important connections. When teams are pushed to, and even beyond, their usual limits, or are forced to dig deep together to overcome something that in other circumstances would have been beyond them as individuals, then they'll know a lot more about the people they did it with once they've come out the other side. If that experience becomes emotional, either because it was stressful, extremely mentally or physically demanding, celebratory, or because it uncovered truths about the team that weren't obvious before, the group are far more likely to connect deeply and share that unique moment in time together.

These processes might uncover members of the team who

either don't fit or want to truly be there and that's also fine. If you want to build a strong, high-performing team, that's one of the most important discoveries you can make early on.

MARGINAL GAIN

The strength of a team lies in its diversity. It's a collection of people who all have different, complementary things to offer. But just as we may actually have goals in life, but don't make the most of them because we don't write them down, we can also remain frustratingly unaware of the strengths and weaknesses of those in the team around us, because we don't pay conscious attention to them. It means that we might miss some of the unique skills that those who work beside us bring, or opportunities to help support those who need it. I think it's always worth taking the time to conduct a silent audit of the people in your team. Make an effort to think hard about the things they do best. Are you making the most of their abilities? Are you maximising their strengths? Conversely, are they being asked to do tasks that don't match the gifts they have? I find this a great way of tapping into unrealised potential and making sure that square pegs aren't being forced into round holes.

4. Establish shared values

Part of the reason it's so important to forge those strong connections with your team members is that it's one of the first steps you can take to help create the right kind of team culture.

As McLaren discovered in 2007, good teamwork isn't just a question of having the right people; the environment in which those people are expected to operate can have a significant bearing on how well the team works.

Teams are made up of different people, with different characters and personalities, strengths and weaknesses, skills and experiences. The most effective teams are often the ones that find a way to embrace and harness as many of those differences as possible.

Some of the best team cultures I've experienced and studied are based around flexibility and adaptability, but with a firm, non-negotiable set of values underpinning the whole thing. The values a team holds dear are its core beliefs in how they exist, and generally people joining that team need to fit in with that. That means the people who form that team ideally need to have values aligned to the team, but the team itself needs to be able to accommodate the individual needs of its people as much as possible. For startup companies, their values are normally one of the first things to get set in stone. What do they stand for? What are their own parameters when it comes to playing the game they're in? What are they going to be prepared to do and what are they not going to be prepared to do to succeed? In established businesses, their values might have evolved over time, but having people in the team who align with them remains important when it comes to the collective effort.

At the McLaren I joined in the year 2000, I don't think we'd actually documented team values anywhere official, but we almost didn't need to: they were everywhere you looked. Under Ron Dennis we knew that only one thing mattered and that was winning, and the way McLaren went about achieving that was through attention to detail at an order of magnitude greater than any of our competition were prepared to go to.

The problem comes when these core values ossify and start to inhibit members of the team.

When Adrian Newey, F1's most decorated car designer and technical chief, was lured away from the mighty and historic McLaren in early 2006 to join a new, disruptive young startup team owned by an energy drinks company, Red Bull, many thought he must be mad. Behind the scenes, though, he'd been sold the dream of building something huge from scratch, where his quirky nature and desire to diversify into other areas of design was embraced, not quashed. Red Bull placed greater value on being creative and being open to doing things differently to the ways of the established teams.

McLaren had been relatively set in its ways for many years. It expected members of its team to conform to the McLaren way of doing things, sometimes even down to their hairstyle. For many people, that was too restrictive and created frustration. Adrian, being a creative force, needed the freedom to work in whichever way gave him the most creativity and focus in the high-pressure world he lived in. Red Bull Racing gave him that freedom and it unlocked even more potential and drive than McLaren had managed to get out of him previously. It took him a few years, but leading a team of designers his way, rather than Ron's, created a culture that produced championship-winning cars for six Constructors' Titles and eight Drivers' Titles before he finally moved on in 2025.

When a team has an inclusive culture that embraces diversity of thought, rather than constricting it, it spreads throughout the people in that team and is perpetuated at all levels. That could be a line manager in an office giving staff the freedom to be flexible with their hours because they know they're struggling to manage children at home, for example. Perhaps a small thing to the company, but something that could make a huge difference to the individual and, as a result, transform both their productivity and their willingness to give that same flexibility back to the team when required. People who are given this sort of accommodation are then far more likely to treat others around them with the same empathy and understanding, supporting them when necessary. If, over time, they progress through the business, the culture is sustained.

5. Keep everyone's goals aligned

Think about the teams you're involved with. How closely are your unspoken internal personal goals and agendas aligned to those of the team you're part of?

Now do it again and be really honest . . . Is what you think is best for you also what's best for your team?

One of the things about having two separate championships being fought over in a season is that a racing driver will always, almost without exception, strive to perform in a way that serves themselves before thinking about how that impacts the team. They rarely set out to actually harm the team's chances and are occasionally even seen to sacrifice a result to help a teammate or the team itself, but this is rare and nearly always only once the race or championship has developed in such a way that they no longer have a chance of victory themselves. They're selfish, but they need to be to get to the top of the game, because of the way the game's structured.

Despite this, it's rarely a problem that most F1 teams encounter, because usually an organic pecking order develops: one driver will be naturally faster than the other and so the two don't often end up competing for the same positions over a season. When I joined McLaren we'd experienced years of relative calm and driver stability. Mika Häkkinen and David Coulthard were teammates for several years, but Mika was clearly the more successful, picking up two world titles. The dynamic was repeated when Kimi Räikkönen replaced Mika. It was only ever Kimi who found himself in with a shot at the big prize.

Occasionally, though, a team is thrust into a 'perfect storm', where the quality of the cars and both drivers creates a situation where teammates are left fighting each other for the top spots in each race. And that's exactly where we found ourselves in 2007. It was unfamiliar territory.

Our problem wasn't necessarily that we had the wrong drivers; both were excellent in their own right; in fact, they were the two most complete F1 drivers I ever had the privilege to work with. Our biggest problems that year stemmed from the situation those drivers found themselves in, that is, fighting against each other for the biggest prize in Formula One. Poor communication and mismanagement inside the team then led to some serious relationship breakdowns.

I'll deal with the lessons we can learn about relationships and communication more specifically in other chapters – here I want to look at how a team sets targets or goals and then goes about collectively chasing after them.

Every team needs a mission. In all of the examples of teams in life I gave earlier, each works best when they have a clear reason for being: a purpose, something their members are striving for together. In 2007, our mission as a team was very clear: we intended to win the sport's biggest prizes. We'd secured enormous financial backing and showed our intent by poaching the current World Champion away from the team he'd just won that accolade with. We meant business and everyone, inside and outside the team, knew it.

What we failed to clarify inside our organisation was how

we were going to go about it with regard to our new driver pairing. Our strategy.

There could've been a number of different paths we might've taken, from openly choosing to operate with a more formalised system of preference between the two drivers, something other teams had done and had success with, to declaring a level playing field and equal opportunity between the two and letting them fight it out on track. Both plans are fraught with their own complications, but they were at least plans. Something our fateful season lacked entirely.

There was a pre-assumed pecking order, but never one that was communicated or agreed upon by those involved. This led to Fernando Alonso feeling that as the clear leader he was 'in charge', and that he was owed preferential treatment. In the early days, the young rookie driver, Lewis Hamilton, had no real personal expectations of being valued equally to the current World Champion and so he initially settled into the role of being just grateful to be there and learning from the best in the business. He subconsciously, albeit temporarily, accepted the unspoken label of 'Number 2 Driver'.

Pretty quickly, though, the dynamic between the two changed. Lewis began showing signs of matching his more experienced teammate, even on occasion out-performing him. So naturally his own sense of self-worth increased. Inside the team we also sat up and took notice of what our young rookie had to offer. I've already described how this all went horrendously wrong.

There were many failures to learn from that year, but the lesson I want to focus on here is one of deciding on a clear path of action to achieve a team's mission, something we can all benefit from. Think about two people moving a heavy sofa. The mission is fairly clear. The sofa needs moving from location

A to location B. But how that mission should be executed is more open to interpretation. If each party involved interprets it differently, the process could become messy. Who's going to lift which end? Will one walk forwards and one backwards, or will they carry it sideways so both can see where they're going? Which route will they take? Has the pathway been cleared? Will one take charge and count them into the lift?

Answering these basic questions in advance can enable the team to operate smoothly and efficiently and achieve the mission more seamlessly. Whatever our goals in life, whether they be small or large, having a plan discussed and agreed on ahead of time can be a huge advantage whereas, conversely, failing to do so can seriously hamper progress further down the line. Although it would've been very difficult to predict just how quickly Lewis would level up to Fernando's high standards in that year, we certainly should've come up with a functional plan. We put so much time and effort into multiple race strategies each week, yet we failed to do the same in the wider operational context.

Today McLaren do things differently. In 2024 and 2025 they find themselves back racing at the front, challenging for titles where each driver's biggest rival is back on the other side of their own garage. But this time they have a plan. They've had open conversations with the drivers, Lando Norris and Oscar Piastri, about how they'll work together as a team and give both equal opportunities for as long as they can. But it comes with the caveat that if there's a decision to be made in the greater interests of the team, even if it consequently favours one driver over the other on that day, they'll go ahead and make it. The drivers race under 'Papaya Rules', a term seized upon by the media, but essentially meaning they race for McLaren and the McLaren fans and partners, before they race for themselves, with 'Papaya' referring to the team's colours. It also states that they must never crash into their teammate in the heat of battle. The team comes first.

6. Find your team's story

Sometimes the environment or situation a group find themselves in can bring them together in such a way that they form team-like bonds. Disaster survivors, friends who experience major trauma together, families or even companies that feel they've suffered an injustice, all have a shared reason to feel united.

When McLaren were fined $100m and thrown out of the World Constructors' Championship of 2007 after the controversial Spygate affair, in which the team were found guilty of industrial espionage, we experienced a similar feeling. But this time it wasn't just down to a set of circumstances beyond our control that had happened to us; it was in part a conscious strategy from our CEO to create a story powerful enough to bring the whole team together in the most extraordinary way.

We were hit with what, to this day, remains the largest financial penalty ever given out in any sport. But the part of the punishment that hurt my colleagues and me at the team, much more than any monetary penance could, was being disqualified from the teams', or Constructors', World Championship of that year. That was painful. If I'm honest, it still hurts all these years later.

As a team we could've easily interpreted these events, together with the resulting punishments, as a self-inflicted failure by our management, which to a large extent it was. We could've turned on our own leadership and lost faith in our boss. But we didn't and here's why.

The various elements of the entire Spygate saga, from start to finish, form the basis of a story. That story, like most in our lives, whether personal or professional, can be recalled and narrated in a number of different ways and the way we tell it, to ourselves and others, can change the impact it has profoundly.

In our case, our CEO, Ron Dennis, chose to tell the story, which could easily have contributed to his and the team's downfall, in a way that instead galvanised the team around him. He emphasised elements, maybe exaggerated others, that portrayed us, the team, as victims of a self-serving and misguided former employee and a political witch hunt from the powers that ran the sport.

He told us how we'd been unfairly treated, despite being the ones who'd been open enough to bring the breach to the FIA's attention as soon as we'd learnt of it entering the organisation. He talked about us cooperating to an extraordinary level because, as a team, we had nothing to hide. He shared 'top secret' details from inside the court hearings to back up how he said the FIA and our arch enemy Ferrari had worked together to ensure McLaren suffered. He talked about how the unprecedented punishment was in no way reflective of the supposed crime and that it was all part of a wider political power play from deep within the sport. A power play designed to hurt Ron and McLaren, an act of personal vengeance inflicted by FIA President Max Mosely on his long-standing adversary. As Ron told us, though, in his rousing and remarkably inspirational company address, in the end it wasn't just him that had been hurt . . . it was every single one of us in that room proudly wearing the McLaren team uniform.

The message was clear. We'd all been targeted here. This was a coordinated attack on McLaren and WE ARE McLAREN, so we should all feel attacked. The prize we all deserved, the accolade we'd all sacrificed so much for, the title we'd all won together, reserved only for the best team on the planet . . . had been stolen from us unfairly. Our response, the only one fitting of the best team in Formula One, was to pull together, dig deep, work even harder than before and take on the rest of the world in what could be an unfair fight. We'd show them what *this* McLaren team was all about by winning the World Championship the following year . . . just let them try and stop us again!

Twelve months later we were World Champions with Lewis Hamilton.

The reason that story's so powerful lies in the way it was told. The facts were all accurate but curated in a way that provoked a powerful response. It was designed to not only deflect responsibility onto an outside entity, an enemy, but to give us a collectively shared emotional trauma to react to. Because *we* had all suffered in being disqualified from the teams' championship through no fault of our own, the story held true for us: it fitted perfectly as an explanation for our disappointment and therefore gave us someone to be angry at outside of our team, at a time when we all wanted to feel angry towards someone. The shared trauma, which ONLY members of the McLaren team could understand and empathise with each other over, brought us together and created unbreakable bonds. We put up barriers to the outside world, defences in the war we were facing, and focused on not letting anyone break in and steal the next one away from us. And it worked.

I know it worked, because I personally felt all those things. I stepped up and went above and beyond my normal responsibilities to find ways to make us stronger in 2008. My teammates did the same and I know for most of us this drive was fuelled by a strong feeling of having been deeply wounded by an enemy force the season before. Those feelings remained; fifteen years later I still feel strongly about it and know it's largely because of the power of the story and the collective mission it put us all on together.

The truth is there was a lot more to the story than Ron included in his speech that day, much of which I was even well aware of, but because of his storytelling skills, tapping into the rich, successful and proud history of the McLaren Formula One Team, it focused on the elements that he knew would resonate with us, that would inspire us and that would drive us together to achieve great things.

The example above may seem very specific and unique to our unusual circumstances that strange year, but it's really an example of the power of finding ways to bond a team together and give them a very clear reason to do what they do. If we accept a description of great teamwork to mean 'a well-coordinated and driven group can achieve more when working together than the individual can alone', it stands to reason that the *more* coordinated and driven the group is, the *more* effectively they might achieve their goals. By Ron turning what could've been a damaging and destructive story for the team into one that lit a collective fire underneath us and created a steely determination to 'show 'em what McLaren's made of!', we literally embodied that description of teamwork.

The lesson here's about finding whatever you can around you and your team to inspire or drive them all in the same direction. We created a shared enemy, an injustice that affected every person and therefore elicited a collective response to fight back. You might be able to do the same in your world. Has a business competitor used underhand tactics to get one up on you? Did they poach a key member of your team? Has a government ruling or new law disproportionately affected your business?

These are all stories that can be told in a number of ways, but the way you, as a leader, frame them can have a real bearing on the response they create within a team.

If you're 2–0 down at half-time in a football match, you can either accept the opposition are better, stronger, fitter, more aggressive and tactically more astute than you, or you create a story about why they're leading that gives your team reason to fight back. They're playing dirty. The goal was offside. You've just heard them laughing at us as they walked off. You could tell a story about a time in the past when you were in a similar position, but turned it around and went on to win the league, so if you want that amazing feeling again, it has to start here.

In a family setting, it might be centred around school exams and inspiring your children through storytelling to put the effort in to get the best results they can. Creating a powerful image that resonates with them of where they could end up if they do well, or how regretful they might feel if they know they didn't put as much effort in as they could and the results reflect that. If the story hits the right triggers it might just give the nudge in the right direction that tips them into a successful outcome and it could be operating as a family team that does it.

> Whatever the environment, the more powerful the *feeling* of being part of a team is, the more powerful the effectiveness of that team typically is.

The team needs to make us feel safe and supported. It needs to give us an identity bigger than our own. It should make us feel strong and connected to the talents and experience of others. It should make us feel resilient and protected from the outside world when we need it. It should give us more belief and allow us to set more ambitious goals. Ultimately it should, by its very nature, make us feel like we can achieve more than we otherwise could if we went alone. That's the power of effective teamwork.

PITLANE LESSONS

- Is your work being derailed by the ego of any of your team's members (including you)? What steps can you take to remind everybody that the team always comes first?
- What's motivating the team? Does everyone have their own individual reasons for being there or are you on a collective mission together? Are you pulling in the same direction and is everyone clear on what that direction is?
- How well bonded are you all? Have you been through shared emotional experiences together? If you have, do you ever talk about it or use it and, if not, could you make that happen?
- Can you create an emotional drive through storytelling and build up rivalries or challenges that you can ONLY overcome with the people around you working together?

6.

IN F1, LOSING'S AN ESSENTIAL PART OF WINNING
The Importance of Embracing Failure

At the end of 2016 I was given the opportunity to interview the sport's brand-new World Champion, Nico Rosberg. I was in Abu Dhabi for the final race of the season, in which Nico needed a podium finish to finally take his first F1 World Title after two consecutive years of his teammate at Mercedes, Lewis Hamilton, beating him. Up until that time Lewis was being talked about as an all-time great of the sport, already a triple World Champion, and Nico, as a good 'Number Two' driver.

As the chequered flag was waved late into the evening at the Yas Marina Circuit, Nico got his podium. He was, for the very first time, Formula One Champion of the World. It was a remarkable achievement.

The next day we all flew home and I spent a few hours with him in a 4x4 Merc as he drove me around the off-road course at Mercedes-Benz World in Surrey in the UK, asking him questions about what he'd just achieved.

At the time of the interview no one could have known, not even his own team, that just twenty-four hours later he'd announce his shock retirement from Formula One, one of the most surprising stories in the sport for years.

We talked about all sorts of things, including what it'd taken to finally overturn the mighty Hamilton. He said he'd given absolutely everything he had in his pursuit of the dream. He'd had to ask everything of his family too, a big part of the reason it turned out that he'd go on to announce the decision to retire as World Champion. His wife had taken the children for large parts of the year to allow him the space to focus, to the exclusion of all else, on maximising his performance. He wasn't prepared to ask that of them again and I respected that.

One thing that really stood out for me, though, was the way he viewed the years in which he'd failed to win the big prize beforehand.

He said he'd noticed other people, the media in particular, taking a very different view to him of the years in which he'd been beaten to the title by Lewis. They'd described Nico's previous two seasons as failures because he didn't win when the team had the dominant car.

He saw it very differently. He described those campaigns merely as the stepping stones he needed to climb over to become champion. In each one he talked about how he'd learnt something new about his rival, but importantly also about himself. Strengths and weaknesses that, once known and understood, could be used to formulate a plan to win. He said he didn't think he could've become FI World Champion without going through that process. But he also said that if, back at the start of 2014 when his team first began to excel, anyone had asked him, 'Would you go through two years of painful defeat and learning if it means you'll be the World Champion in 2016?', of course he'd say yes. So failure wasn't the word he used for those years: they were simply a part of the journey to becoming The Champ.

In the wider world, Rosberg's attitude to failure might seem eccentric. Because the majority of people don't think like that. In fact, the fear of failure is the biggest single thing holding most people and businesses back from their true potential . . .

We're told from an early age that failure's a terrible thing, something we should avoid at all costs and be ashamed of when it inevitably happens. In sport, which is often seen as fairly binary in terms of winning or losing, even more so.

The word itself has such negative connotations that it's even used as a derogatory term for someone who's under-achieved in life. The schooling system often teaches our children that failure's a disaster, ingraining into them at such a young, impressionable age that if they don't get a certain result, in a certain exam, on a certain day, they've failed. That's it. They leave school with that failure tag, in some cases, permanently attached.

If a relationship between two people breaks down, it's described as a 'failed relationship' and those involved are com-miserated. When an entrepreneur attempts to solve a problem through an innovative new business idea, if that startup runs out of money trying to find the solution, the business and its founder are tarnished as 'dismal failures'.

But it's also because trying something new, stepping into the unknown, genuinely does strike fear into people. From an evolutionary standpoint, it makes perfect sense: why would we wander into that unknown, terrifyingly mysterious cave when we have a known, safe one of our own? There might be something in there that'll eat you! The unfamiliar can be a scary place, so many people understandably have a reluctance to go there through either an inbuilt sense of self-preservation, or just the preservation of the much more comfortable and well-understood status quo.

For some people, remaining in the comfort and safety of their familiar surroundings works just fine. People happily never leave the village in which they grew up, or they work in the same job their entire careers, and I have total respect for that. At the end of the day, none of us has the right to tell others how to best live their lives. But what if you have a burning desire to grow into new areas and explore new limits?

Growing in life or business requires stepping into unknown territory. It means learning new skills, exploring new experiences, walking through doors that you, and sometimes those before you, have never walked through. Unnerving though that can be, it's an unavoidable requirement for those who want to innovate, excel and set new standards.

And yet history's littered with people who, as their time on this planet draws to a close, talk about the regrets they have from the life they've lived. Overwhelmingly the vast majority of those regrets stem from the things they *didn't* do, rather than the things they did. For many, their fear of failure was more powerful than any ambition or desire.

But in Formula One teams, the greatest fear is not moving forward and it's a philosophy ingrained into my own make-up today. I'm OK with leaping into the unknown; in fact, it excites me. Not through some masochistic desire or lack of self-preservation, but because I know if I push myself into uncomfortable circumstances, I'll end up moving forward in my life or career.

> I'm cool with failure. In fact, I know I can't move forwards at the pace I want to without it.

When I get to the latter stages of my own life I won't look back and regret the many decisions I took that went wrong. In fact when I zoom out on my performance graph of life as I get towards the end, I won't even notice the tiny spikes of ups and downs along the way from every choice I had to make. I hope I'll only be interested in the big picture, the overall trend of that graph, and I'm confident, partly because of my Formula One upbringing, that it'll show an upward trajectory, one that has me moving forward because I was always willing to fail to get to where I wanted to be.

So although Nico Rosberg's philosophy on failure might seem outlandish in the wider world, in F1 it's merely an encapsulation of the way we feel about it. For us, failure, or a failure to succeed at something, can be merely a comma in a story, rather than the full stop it's so often seen as. The failure's a chance to pause, reflect and then keep going with the task, leaving the ending open. With each comma, we give ourselves the space to learn something that might help us to improve and edge closer to the outcome we want.

The subtle art of always having a go

In simple terms there are two ways to find your route to success, whether in F1, business, or just in life.

You can set about a process of learning as much as possible about your chosen subject. Gather data, conduct research, read, watch videos, etc. But in a world of endlessly accessible and exponential information growth, the reality is that we can go on doing this forever, continuously learning more as time goes by. So if our target's simply to be perfectly prepared, or even just as prepared as possible, it's a target that can never truly be reached unless we add in another factor: time.

The factor of time's a crucial one, but it can be introduced into the decision-making equation in a number of ways; how that's done can determine whether it's a hindrance or a help.

Many big decisions in life or business have a predetermined, immovable timeline attached, like the beginning of a Grand Prix. No one's delaying the beginning of a race whilst you make up your mind which tyres you're going to start on. We simply have to formulate our decision-making process around the factor of time. In business it might look something like 'Here's our offer of investment into your company; we need a decision by the end of the week,' . . . so you'd better make your mind up by the end of the week or the offer disappears.

In this type of scenario you can't put the decision off, so you still want to be as prepared as you can and have as much information to hand as possible to help you make that call, but you can only gather that information until the point that the timeline dictates. When that point arrives, despite understanding that further valuable information will undoubtedly be out there, or will become available, you simply have to decide based on what you have in front of you there and then.

In F1, with these types of decision, knowing the timeline's fixed, we focus our resources on collecting as much data as possible, in the most efficient way possible, and on analysing what data we have in the most productive way possible. That means that by the time the decision of which tyres we want to start the race on, or which strategy we're going to deploy, comes around, we're in the best place we can be within the set limitations of our timeline. In this case, no matter what the outcome, failure or otherwise, we can be confident we made the best decision based on the best knowledge we had at the time the decision had to be made. So our aim's to make sure we do indeed have the best knowledge possible.

When asked about how he made the really big, life or death type decisions, the former American president Barack Obama gave an answer that I always try and refer back to in my own life. He said that if he had to decide whether or not to send troops into battle, to take his country to war, surely one of the most difficult and consequential decisions anyone could be asked to make, he asked two questions of advisors. Firstly, can we delay the decision in order to gather more information and be more informed? If the answer to that was a firm no, the timeline was fixed and critical, then the next question was this. What's the best and most up-to-date intelligence we have right now?

He said that when faced with a choice like that, one that could affect the lives of many people, he did it with the knowledge that all he was able to do was draw the best conclusion he could, with the information he had, in the time available. He said he was able to sleep at night, even if further information later came to light which, had it been available at the time, might've informed a different opinion, with the belief that he did his best with what he had. No one can do better than that. Whatever the eventual consequences of that decision, even if it resulted in tragedy, could it really ever be seen as a failure of Obama's leadership if he made the best choice based on the best information available?

So time as a deadline can help us to focus our efforts, give us an end-point by which we need to reach a conclusion and hopefully it's one that leads to great outcomes. But when the opposite applies, when there is no definitive deadline on the horizon, time can become your enemy.

It's this open-ended timeline, together with an innate fear of failure, that stops millions of people and many companies from taking the decisions that could ultimately lead them down a path towards success. In helping big organisations to overcome their challenges with an F1 mindset and approach, I regularly see well-known brands and businesses stuck because they're waiting for 'the right time' to launch a new product, service or process. Some can't bring themselves to take a leap into the relative unknown and try something new through fear of not getting it right, and others just appear trapped in a continuous treadmill of external surveys and market research or internal meetings and conversations.

Of course, gathering more and more information ahead of a new venture can be a sensible approach, but like many things there's a line that, when crossed, can turn it from helpful to unhelpful. Firstly, the appetite for more knowledge is infinite, so there's a temptation to keep going forever through a fear of not ever being quite fully prepared. Secondly, it can easily be used as an excuse to mask the terror facing those tasked with making decisions, a reason to push the big scary moment further down the line, so to speak.

In F1 we have a significant advantage in that respect: the risks of not pushing ourselves off the deep end outweigh those of simply opting for the safest option.

We can't let perfection become the enemy of progress.

We exist in a highly competitive industry in which we don't have the luxury of being able to continuously wait for the 'perfect time' to try something new, or fine-tune our ideas forever in the background whilst continually putting off 'launching' until we're 100 per cent ready. We have to get on with it or, quite frankly, someone else will and our advantage will be lost.

Make no mistake, it's almost always scary the first time you put a brand-new big update on the car and wait to find out if it performs as you hope. The component might've just rolled off the production line the night before and have only been dreamt up by the designers the night before that. It's untested in the real world and now it's doing 200mph in a Grand Prix weekend with millions watching. The same applies to making a spur-of-the-moment bold strategy call mid-race. There may be no precedent for it, it might not be an obvious decision, but one thing's for sure: once the call's made, we're about to find out if it fails or not.

Whilst I was at McLaren, we regularly took decisions that resulted in failure.

With regard to our engines, in partnership with Mercedes-Benz, in the early 2000s, we continually chose to push the extreme boundaries with exotic materials and innovative technologies in the constant pursuit of outright performance. We ended up with engines in our cars that were enormously powerful, that had tools available to the driver to make them more usable and drivable, and that were class-leading in terms of their compact, lightweight construction, all helping the overall performance of the car. We won many races with this philosophy and continued to develop at an astonishing rate, bringing new, updated engines to most races of a season, as was allowed back then.

But as well as winning many races and challenging for world titles in some of our epic season-long battles with Ferrari and other teams, we also lost many races and one or two championships because those cutting-edge, continually experimental engines blew up a lot.

At the time it was hugely frustrating, infuriating even, because winning was what we all existed to do. But when I think about why these failures happened, they were normally because we intentionally chose to push the limits of extreme engine engineering: it was only at that fine line of the highest possible performance that success was possible in a sport like F1. Our rivals were doing the same and, in those particular years I mentioned, it happened to be Ferrari and then Renault that experimented their way to the right answers first. But we got there too. Just a few seasons later, we were champions with our fast, reliable Mercedes engine in the back of our car. It's highly probable that we wouldn't have got there without exploring those limits and learning something valuable from every failure in the preceding years. Failure made our success possible.

What we were doing was indulging in the art of just having a go. It might sound a bit hit and miss for the precision-engineering-led Formula One mentality, but it's often one of the quickest routes to success, and in a world that's literally all about speed, it can prove a bit counter-intuitive when done the Fi way.

What we've found over time in many of the situations we face as an Fi team in this fiercely competitive industry is that first-mover advantage, as it's often known in the business world, can be significant. If the leap into the unknown turns out to be a good one, you get there ahead of your rivals and reap the early rewards whilst they play catch-up. But even if it doesn't work out, if the idea turns out to be a dud, the amount of learning you get from that real-world failure can far outstrip what others might be trying to figure out gradually in their theoretical, or virtual, worlds back at base.

A parallel example might be the Space Race between the USSR and USA in the fifties and sixties, which became highly politicised and competitive. No one could ever be 100 per cent sure it was perfectly safe to send humans into space, let alone to land on the moon and exit the relative security of the vehicle that got them there, before they actually did it for the very first time. Of course, they relied on the best science of the day to inform their decisions, but time was of the essence: no side wanted, or could afford, for the other to get there first. The fastest way to figure this stuff out was to try it. It was scary, terrifying even, and things went wrong . . . badly. But with each catastrophic, sometimes tragic failure came an unprecedented amount of knowledge that not even the most exhaustive research at the time could've uncovered, and on 20 July 1969, 650 million people watched around the world as the USA got there first.

If, for you, the end result's sufficiently important, then rapid experimentation and repeated failure, followed up by in-depth analysis (we'll come back to this later) is often the fastest way to learn. There's highly likely to be pain along the way and it's up to us to decide if the potential outcome justifies it, but if you really want to achieve something badly, if you have that burning desire inside to grow, sometimes biting the bullet and getting on with it is the best, maybe even the only, way.

The people who never start their own business, yet say they want to, are normally stuck, standing at the precipice, looking over the edge, terrified to take the leap. The same for those 'trapped' in a long-term relationship they want out of, or even businesses that know they need to evolve to survive, but can't. They're normally paralysed by the fear of the next step leading to failure, which more often than not boils down to the harsh reality that deep down they don't yet want the change badly enough.

When meeting people at the events I do, or in the many messages I receive online asking for advice, I hear versions of this assertion a lot . . . 'I can't wait to leave my job, I hate it, I really want to leave more than anything!' A small amount of questioning normally reveals a different reality. The truth is that, as the well-known quote says, 'Change often only happens when the pain of staying the same becomes greater than the pain of changing,' so the fear of failure has to become less than the fear of a future you already know you don't want.

MARGINAL GAIN

One knock-on effect from this attitude is that if you accept there'll be times when you fail, you prepare for those moments. At McLaren we always wanted to have a plan in place long before it happened.

Our mindset was: if failure's inevitable, it makes sense to try and be ready to make the best of it when it happens. In a twenty-four-race season, we might do up to a hundred competitive pitstops with our two cars. The statistics tell you it's highly improbable that all of them will go perfectly, despite any team's best efforts, so we have to accept that a number of them will have complications. Which means that we practise for failure too. In amongst our thousands of pitstop rehearsals we regularly and randomly throw in hundreds of examples of the most common failure modes. Maybe the car comes in with a puncture, where it might be squatted down on one side, preventing us from getting the front jack under the wing to lift the car. We have a plan for dealing with it. The same goes for the failure of a piece of equipment like a wheel gun or a jack. We don't want any of these things to happen and try constantly to mitigate against them, but we want to be as ready as we can if they do.

Accepting that failures happen also means you're far less likely to be derailed by their impact when they do. Ron Dennis used to encourage us to do our initial debrief and analyse what we could on Sunday night after a bad race, then use a specific point on Monday morning to reset and focus on the next opportunity. The learning continues, but the mood has to change. Finding a way to limit the negative impact of failure and switch into a positive mindset as quickly as possible is a key routine to build.

Your mental switching moment could be a specific time after the event or, through practice, linked to or piggy-backed off an already ingrained or scheduled habit like brushing your teeth or your regular Monday morning meeting. By thinking ahead about what you'll do in the event of something not working out or 'failing', not only do you prepare in a time of clarity, but importantly you build in an acceptance that failure's inevitable. 'It will happen at some point along my route to success, so let's make a plan for when it does, so we can emotionally move past it quickly.' It's never easy to think this way in the moments when disappointment happens; in fact, picking yourself up off the floor when you've been knocked down is actually one of the hardest things to do. But who said becoming a world champion was easy? It isn't, it's hard, which is also what makes it so special when anyone achieves it.

Never let a failure go to waste

Of course, you won't extract the true value from all those experiments if you don't take the time to analyse what happened, and what you could do differently in the future.

The trick's to try and take a moment of calm to zoom out. 'Failures' tend to come with emotion attached. If we didn't care about the result it wouldn't affect us, but if we do care, then it matters and we're often all in, emotions and all. When something triggers a big emotional response from us, either positive or negative, we tend to be zoomed all the way into that moment. Our field of vision's small and we're swept along with what's right in front of us at the time. That means the disappointment of losing or falling short of a target can easily seem like the end of the road, even the end of the world.

It can take time to be able to get out of that state, calm down and see the bigger picture. After the disasters of 2007 it took me weeks, maybe months if I'm honest, to let the disappointment of that season fade away enough to see that it could somehow be a blessing in disguise. Nico Rosberg had to get away from the FI circus and spend some time on his own before he could fully reflect each time he was beaten.

Once you've metabolised the fact of your failure, you can begin to make use of it.

As I've touched on already, 2007 could easily be seen as a total failure to succeed in our objectives at McLaren. We set out to win the world titles by trying to put all the correct pieces of the jigsaw puzzle in place – from drivers to engineers, processes to finances, to the car itself – and yet we came away without either of the sport's two big prizes. We 'failed', and in a number of different ways. But I now firmly believe that the many cock-ups and failures of that fateful season were a blessing in disguise. Those same failures became a key part of why we won the sport's biggest accolade just twelve months later.

At the end of that season we could have just wallowed in our misery – the mood in the McLaren camp was understandably low – but instead we initiated a series of leadership meetings to firstly analyse exactly what had gone wrong and then to identify and implement measures to make sure this could never happen again at the team.

We looked at data, at feedback from inside and outside of the team, we spoke to as many people as we could and looked back through the season's notes and debrief records and cross-referenced the whole lot with our on-track results and media stories of the time. It provided some interesting correlations, with insights into where things may have started to go wrong and missed opportunities where we might have been able to make corrections along the way.

Analysing things forensically is what we do in F1, but even for us back then, dissecting a major failure in this way was far less common than you might think. We often had the mentality of moving on and forgetting the bad days. There was sometimes an undertone of arrogance that went something like this: *we know where we got it wrong in that race, so let's not dwell on it and just get it right next time.*

But at the end of 2007 and into 2008 things were changing fast at the team and even across the sport as a whole. We were well into our own push for the pursuit of ultimate excellence in every area and this drove us to think about everything differently.

We knew we could raise our performance targets for the new 2008 car, but by then the major areas of the design were locked in place and manufacturing well underway. We could up the measurable targets we set for every development piece we brought to the car at each race weekend, meaning reducing lead times on new upgrades and increasing the amount of performance they brought. We could essentially try to do all the things we always did, but just better.

In reality, though, that's what every Formula One team always did: try to improve on what they'd done the year before. In our world that was a given, it was the norm, so if we wanted to increase our chances of coming out on top, we couldn't afford to just do what everyone else did and hope for the best. That wasn't the McLaren we were trying to create. We had to look for every opportunity we could find in every area and that meant searching in places we hadn't necessarily gone before.

There's a popular saying that goes 'Success leaves a trail of clues behind it', which we used to refer to a lot. Looking back at great results and understanding what led to them, looking at the decisions we'd made, the actions we took, etc., are all great ways to find the formula to your past successes in the hope you can repeat it in the future to get similar results. These 'clues' are there for all of us, and in the most part we tend to take note of lots of them without even thinking.

It's called a positive feedback loop and is a key mechanism for learning in life. We teach our young children by giving rewards when they do something well. They like the reward, so they try and remember what they did to get it and do it again. We do the same with training pets.

Of course the same applies in life with negative feedback loops. When we try a new food as an infant for the first time and don't like it, we screw our faces up and try to reject it. It leaves us with a negative sensation and so we remember we don't like that and do whatever we can to not eat it again. Another example's the way in which we might remove privileges for bad behaviour. It creates a negative feedback loop that hopefully 'corrects' or changes the future actions of whoever's on the end of it.

Both of these feedback loops are hugely valuable in life, but one's designed to take something away from the process and one to add something into the process. Because of this, as most of us grow older in a society that rewards growth in both business and personal achievement or attainment, we often tend to lean more into positive feedback loops than negative ones. We look more for what we can add, over what we should take away. On top of that, getting positive feedback feels like a nicer experience as opposed to the negative version, so generally we seek out one over the other.

All of this means that our general human bias is towards looking for clues to improve from our successes much more so than from our failures. At McLaren, and I'm sure Formula One as a whole, we were doing pretty much the same until the end of 2007.

The end of season review that year prompted a deep dive into the things that had gone wrong and cost us the title. It was almost certainly the biggest negative feedback loop we'd ever deliberately undertaken. It was also the most powerful.

Whilst we have an inbuilt recognition that when bad things happen we should probably avoid repeating those things for the sake of our safety and the general progression of the species, we also have a tendency to put them out of our memory as quickly as possible. Most people don't want to be reminded of what they see as their worst days in life and are much more content reflecting on the good ones. We were the same. But during the winter between 2007 and 2008 we took a conscious decision, uncomfortable though it might be, to analyse in forensic detail the most dismal aspects of our team's performance over the previous twelve months or so.

In true McLaren style, where attention to detail was everything, we weren't just going to find out what had happened, but pick it apart with a fine-toothed comb, dissect it, put it under the microscope and look for even the tiniest of clues in our failures that could help us get across the line first in 2008.

It made a lot of people feel awkward, having to not only relive the poor decisions made and actions taken, but being scrutinised by peers in the most excruciating detail, then having the findings shared amongst the wider group. In an elite environment like Formula One people pride themselves on being the best in the business, so acknowledging and then openly picking apart the areas we'd failed at was hard to take for lots of people. But we told ourselves that if we wanted to really be the best, this was an essential part of the process. Naturally some found it easier to buy into than others. If you were at the heart of a consequential poor decision earlier that season, firstly you already knew that, but secondly you'd probably moved on and firmly put it in the past. This disrupted all of that.

But I'm a firm believer that true greatness is never found down the easiest paths: it's always discovered as part of a difficult journey. We all came to the eventual conclusion, even those who stood to be scrutinised the most, that choosing the difficult path would ultimately lead to our eventual success . . . greatness in a sport of greats.

Obviously the first part of that painful, gut-wrenching process was identifying exactly what those failures were. Some were easy, obvious and of course very public, like the moment the feud between our two superstar drivers descended into the FI equivalent of school playground antics in Hungary during qualifying. When your drivers are screaming at each other over team radio, disobeying clear instructions . . . then clearly something's gone horribly wrong.

That was of course a huge failure, but it was also a symptom showing up because of earlier failures further upstream. Like a huge row erupting between you and your romantic partner, it's rarely just contained to the one situation you're rowing about – if it was, it's likely it could've been sorted out without the need for the big row. It's more likely a symptom emerging to highlight a bigger issue. Perhaps the same thing's happened before and it's annoyed you both but you never spoke about it? Perhaps the relationship's under pressure for any number of reasons and the argument is it all spilling over in frustration? Symptoms, like the ones that highlight problems with our own health at times, are there as warning mechanisms to let us know we need to address something.

In our case, events at the Hungarian Grand Prix were exactly that, alarm bells alerting us to major problems we hadn't dealt with. So in our post-season analysis we had to admit that not only had we fucked up, but we'd done it over and over again, blatantly ignoring the signs along the way.

There'd been some very early signals, as far back as the Monaco Grand Prix months before, perhaps even prior to that, that the relationship between our two drivers was starting to become strained. Up until then, on track, the team had been flying. We had a great car. We had the current World Champion in Fernando Alonso and a young rookie, Lewis Hamilton, showing all the signs that he was way better than even we'd predicted. Things were looking good for a fantastic season ahead. And yet, with the benefit of hindsight, which is exactly what delving into your failures gives you, there were perhaps some very early cracks beginning to form outside of the car.

When we went back over casual conversations that happened in the garage between the drivers and mechanics or engineers, even some of the post-session debriefs that took place at the end of each day, looking at them with the perspective of now knowing what followed, we could see signs of animosity between the two drivers beginning to form. Just small things that on their own at the time had appeared meaningless and insignificant, like one driver playfully belittling the other, or both 'joking' they were faster than their teammate. These were changes beginning to happen. Prior to this there seemed like nothing but genuine respect between the two, Lewis with lots to learn from the best in the business and Fernando happy to share his wealth of experience and knowledge.

No one was saying that we should've seen the signs that early, but it gave us all the appreciation that these might've been some of the precursors to the problems escalating.

The truth is that two drivers in an F1 team don't have to

be best friends, they don't even have to like each other at the end of the day, but they should have respect for each other and for the team. When that begins to break down it's a very early symptom that something might be starting to fail.

We could've dismissed the drivers' falling out as simply an inevitable personality clash – and that could well have been part of it, as even today Lewis and Fernando are unlikely to be going on holiday together – but because we were going deep in this investigation, we had to ask more questions of ourselves. Could this relationship breakdown be a symptom of something else that hadn't been addressed even earlier still?

To do that, we had to try and understand these particular failures from the individual points of view of the drivers themselves, why they might have turned against each other.

Lewis had come into the team with his big break. His whole life changed more than most people can comprehend in the space of a few weeks after being announced as our race driver for the 2007 season. I saw some of it happening in front of us, but of course I only saw part of it. The world's media, but especially the British media, went wild, pinning him up as the country's latest flag-bearer. A highly polished team of people, our team, suddenly did everything for him, from telling him what to wear, what to say, what to do, where to do it and at what time. He instantly became part of the huge McLaren machine, itself part of the even bigger FI machine. His star shone brightly in his home country even before he'd turned a competitive wheel in the car, with the narrative at least partly driven by the team's own media department. It was a great story, the young go-kart racer who'd approached Ron Dennis at an awards ceremony when he was just ten years old to tell him he wanted to drive for McLaren. Three years later, aged thirteen, he was signed to the team's young driver programme and now, finally, the story was entering the next exciting chapter. This was a tale Ron wanted to tell; understandably he was proud.

Expectations inside the team were that, in his first year, Lewis would learn from the master on the other side of the garage. He'd find his feet, make mistakes but gradually hone his craft, improving as he went. Trying to imagine it from Lewis's personal perspective, I'm sure he wanted to try and live up to the hype he was seeing around him, but even he'd have never imagined winning a title in his first year at that early stage of the season.

Very quickly, though, in a car that was arguably the class of the field, he realised he was a lot closer to the champ than anyone might've imagined and this changed the whole situation.

If you were Fernando Alonso back then you might imagine why this could ruffle a few feathers. The cheeky young upstart of a rookie, in the sport you're the current king of, turning up and, instead of sitting back and learning the ropes from you, quickly becoming a nuisance, even an actual threat, out on track. Perhaps even getting more attention? Neither of them handled it well.

When Ron had agreed the deal to bring Alonso to the team it was almost a year before he actually arrived. He was a single World Champion at that point, something he'd go on to double in his final season at Renault before joining us. He was the hot ticket in the pitlane, the guy that had finally toppled the long-standing unprecedented reign of Michael Schumacher. He was the very clear leader of the team at Renault, their Number One driver and his status in the sport would surely mean he could walk into any other team and command the same position.

At McLaren we famously had a policy of never contracting a Number One and Number Two driver in favour of always giving both fair and equal status, whilst some other teams openly put their support behind a 'team leader'. In recent history it hadn't ever really presented any issues for us, as one of our two drivers, despite both being treated equally, had always naturally ended up as the more dominant and so an unofficial hierarchy had just organically formed, keeping the two on slightly separate paths and to some extent out of the way of each other's ambitions.

As far as I'm aware in the initial conversations between Ron and Fernando, the topic was never really addressed. It was widely known that we'd never put any favourable circumstances for one driver over another into a contract and we'd always been publicly open about this, so why would Fernando, or his people, ever think it would be different for him?

Our most viable theory on why some of the issues that arose between the two halves of our team occurred is that, although there was no official or contractual conversation about our drivers' status within the team, there may've been an implied one.

It was SO obvious to all observers, including all of us in the team and Lewis and Fernando themselves, that the current and double World Champion heading into the 2007 season would be the natural leader of the two at McLaren. It was surely never in doubt that the team would naturally unite behind Alonso for any title challenge, so why would it matter that it wasn't written into contractual terms?

The real failing, we concluded in the wake of one of our most difficult, controversial and tumultuous seasons in history, was that at the heart of many of the eventual problems was a lack of transparency and clarity in setting out and managing expectations at multiple stages along the way. Because it *seemed* so obvious, no party was ever clear enough about what they expected to happen. It was effectively left to chance because no one doubted the outcome. From there the failures gradually, and then more quickly, escalated because, as we'd never identified the cause back then, we clearly never rectified it. Instead we tried more and more desperately to put 'Band-Aid' solutions over symptoms, instead of understanding and addressing the root of the problems.

So, one of our biggest lessons here was around communication. It turned out that we hadn't just failed in our communication between the drivers and team management, but in many areas of the organisation. It was a lesson we learnt only by delving deeper and deeper into the failures and continually asking what might have led to them in the first place.

But all of that pain would have been for nothing if we hadn't put our learnings into practice. We launched an investigation into our comms, systems and techniques and found plenty we were able to improve upon.

My own role changed at the team as a result and I was moved up into a newly created position with one of my main responsibilities being to ensure open and clear communication and working practices across the team. I was given a mandate to help develop more transparent systems for the technical front of the operation, so no one could be in any doubt as to the equal opportunities presented to either side of the team in terms of car developments like new upgrades as well as strategic opportunities. Meetings and debriefs had to become more open and honest with learnings shared, rather than kept to one side to create secret advantages, something else we found had presented problems during 2007. Even the building of the cars themselves had to change and I facilitated the two halves of the team to work together to ensure consistency from one side to the other. Tiny things like mechanics routing wiring harnesses around the chassis differently to each other, or following slightly different procedures in the garage had the potential to create conflict. But more importantly these inconsistencies had the ability to create differences that might either cause problems or give advantages, even by just a small amount.

My task was to help smooth out the whole operation, but that meant breaking habits we found had existed for a long time in many cases, but which had only reared their heads as problems in recent times.

So together with our Sporting Director, Dave Ryan, we agreed that a plan of failing fast and learning from it was the best way to develop our new strategies for moving forward.

We'd learnt so much from our individual failures. But maybe the biggest thing we learnt was that failure was something to be embraced, not feared.

With a new-found appreciation for the good that can come out of getting things wrong, I proposed it was better for us to immediately put plans in place for the very start of pre-season testing. I said I'd continually review them and learn from what went right and wrong, rather than hold off and spend weeks analysing and developing more considered systems before we implemented them. Essentially, we'd learn more and faster by just trying something new if we were open to continuously adapting as we went. Obviously we used all of the tools, data and feedback we could to ensure the best outcome before making changes, but with the knowledge that it could almost certainly be improved upon as we moved forward. To do this I needed the support of everyone in the team and that wasn't always easy to achieve.

Firstly, most of the human race are inherently reluctant to change; we're generally more comfortable in the well-known space of 'normality' and habit, even if they're often bad habits.

Secondly, as I mentioned right at the beginning of this chapter, we've been conditioned in our societies to avoid failure.

The reactions I got from different areas of the team varied. I had those who thought they were just fine doing things the way they'd always done them, and those who openly scoffed at the idea of heading blindly into a series of tests and experiments, as they saw them, that were most likely to produce more failures . . . something we'd all had enough of the year before.

I asked people to consider that if in ten months' time they were World Champions, would they accept a few small hiccups along the way if it was just part of the process to get there? Of course they would. The reality is no one gets to achieve great things without some ups and downs along the way, but those small failures, even the big ones like we'd had the year before, would become a distant memory during the celebrations of an eventual win. Even if 2008 wasn't to be our year, by failing fast and moving our team forward as a result of what we learnt, we'd get there in the end. Any of us would take that big prize, which would live with us forever, over the short-term pain of trying something that didn't work out first time around.

So we moved forward. If we were going to get some of our new methods wrong to start with, despite our best efforts, it had to be clear that we were all trying to move the team in the right direction. Everyone had both the responsibility, but also the opportunity, to shape the direction we went on everything. If something new wasn't working, they were to come up with a reason why and an idea to change it again and we would. If it failed, we'd understand why, learn and try again. If it failed again, the same thing applied and each time we'd get closer to a successful outcome by empowering the entire team to be part of the process.

I used the example of the drivers in practice sessions. They push more and more until they find the limit of grip in the car for that track and those conditions. The way they find that limit is normally by stepping over it and running wide or having a big understeer or oversteer moment. A small mistake, or 'failure', that ruins that lap time, but gives them valuable learning about how far they can push when it really matters in qualifying. Would we rather our drivers played it completely safe, made no mistakes, but never really found the limits of performance? Or are we happy for them to try different things as part of the process of learning how to get the best from the car, even if on occasion it ended in a practice day crash? We all knew the answer.

Over time we started to turn the tide and began to see results. The cars' build quality and consistency went up as the two sides of our garage worked together to find the best solutions to problems. Our meetings and debriefs became more productive, with less focus on who was right or wrong and more on what we could all learn. The drivers and their engineers worked together much more on set-up direction and the race team collaborated more closely than ever with the design team in the Drawing Office and factory as a whole. It certainly wasn't a seamless, linear progression if you zoomed in to the day-to-day, but zoom out and the trend was almost all upward as we learnt faster than ever before.

We won the 2008 F1 World Title with Lewis Hamilton in just his second year in the sport and it's an achievement I will forever be proud of. I honestly don't believe we'd have done so without the epic and painful failure that was 2007. Just like Nico Rosberg saw his World Title win in 2016 as a longer journey than just the twenty-one races of that season, our 2008 win with Lewis was exactly the same.

The concept of rapid idea experimentation can often be

a faster and more immersive route to eventual success. But it requires you to embrace failures as opportunities to learn.

One way to do this in your own life is to think about some of the big ambitions and life goals you've failed to hit yet. Imagine you're a Formula One team and go through your own version of a forensic post-season debrief like the one I described earlier. If that particular goal's still important to you, ask yourself why you haven't fulfilled it yet. The question shouldn't be 'Why didn't I ever get the job of my dreams?' which suggests the failure brought an end to the process, but 'Why haven't I got the job of my dreams yet?' It keeps the dream alive and if you go deep enough with your lines of questioning, you might just shed light on the answers that previous failures have thrown up, but that were perhaps overlooked. As much as success leaves a trail of clues, failure does the same if we're willing to uncover them.

PITLANE LESSONS

- Imagine the big wins you want in your life, the game-changing ones you're desperate for, then imagine achieving them, reaping the rewards, but in exchange for going through a few big failures and pain on the way to it. Would you still take the win?
- Try reframing 'failure' as 'learning'. If you're reading this then no 'failure' has ever truly beaten you so far in life. I bet every single one taught you something?
- The sooner you come to terms with the fact that failure will be a part of your journey, the sooner you'll be able to move past it when it happens.
- Preparing for failure isn't a defeatist attitude; it's smart and creates advantages over those who don't.

- Success leaves a trail of clues, but so does failure. Make sure you make the effort to learn lessons from every setback you encounter.
- Use the factor of time as a powerful tool in decision-making and learning from failure. If moving forward with something's the most important goal, don't let perfection get in the way of progress.

7.

EVERY DETAIL MATTERS, BUT SOME MATTER MORE THAN OTHERS
Why It's Important to Focus on the *Right* Details

Pre-season testing doesn't always go well. It can often be a frustrating nightmare. But 2007 was different. We'd rolled out a really good car and our performance was looking incredibly promising. We'd managed to avoid the firefighting and trouble-shooting that typically come with early tests. One of my colleagues turned to me: 'It's amazing. We've produced a car that's already operating at 90 per cent.' Then someone else butted in: 'The great thing about having a car that's 90 per cent ready, is that we're about halfway there!'

Cue silence in the garage.

At the time it took me a while to compute what they meant. Eventually, though, it clicked. The difference between a really good car and a great car was that final 10 per cent, and yet finding it involved way more than 10 per cent of the work. It needs a monumental effort to go from good to great, with anything in life; that's why so few truly achieve it. Very often, the difference between good and great can often come down to details. The kind that either most don't think deeply enough about to discover, or they aren't willing to put in the sizeable, often wildly disproportionate, effort required to make relatively small gains at the top end of performance.

It's fair to say that F1's a detail-orientated industry. We might

work with cars, but when it comes to complex industrial processes and the importance of attention to detail our world has
a far closer link to aerospace than it does to the automotive
industry.

When I think of how my time working for McLaren, perhaps F1's most detail-obsessed team, has changed the way I live
my life today, my mind's always drawn to the way that we constantly emphasised the overwhelming importance of the finer
details. Being forensic about certain aspects of what I do has
absolutely come about from a life in elite motorsport, especially F1 and even more especially at the McLaren Formula
One Team.

Ever since the arrival of a thirty-three-year-old entrepreneur called Ron Dennis on the international scene of Grand
Prix racing with McLaren in 1980, attention to detail has been
what makes them stand out from the crowd. A crowd, by the
way, which unanimously obsesses over attention to detail. Back
in 1980, though, the bar for standing out in that crowd was com-
paratively low and Ron saw an opportunity.

He took over the struggling McLaren team and reinvented
the way they approached almost everything. Upping standards,
professionalism, appearances, sponsors and, very soon, results.

He won his first GP with McLaren in 1981 and the F1 World
Championship just three years later.

Ron's life is governed by the kind of detail that most people
can't even comprehend. Legend has it, he used to get the gravel
on his own driveway at home collected up and cleaned before
being put back again at regular intervals! He doesn't see the
point in doing anything at all unless it's done as close to perfection as is physically possible. He believes that the attention to
detail you put into anything is reflective of everything else in
your life. If you don't dress well or take care of your appearance,

why should he believe you'd be any different in business or in a relationship? In fact, it goes deeper still, because he might suggest that the very *level* of detail you're willing to go to when it comes to how you project yourself might directly reflect the *level* of detail you'll go to in other areas of life. Do your socks match your tie? Is your hair well kept? Are your shoes polished, your shirt pressed, etc., etc? Whilst many would barely give a second thought to what deeper meaning may lie behind these things, Ron reads people and companies in exactly this way.

As a result, McLaren had to aim to be 'perfect'.

Not many people are like Ron Dennis. He seemed to have an infinite supply of energy to channel into what he was convinced was the right way to do things. There was never a day when he'd be shown something by an employee that was *pretty good* and accept it. *Pretty good* wasn't anywhere near good enough. It would make him angry that an idea of that lowly calibre had even made it as far up the chain as to be put in front of him. As a consequence, it rarely ever did.

The understanding and appreciation of Ron's expectations were built into the DNA of the organisation, so we all knew what was required and standards were very high, but in reality none of us had Ron's eye. So it was still a nervous moment when he was presented with something or even when we saw him coming our way in the factory. We tidied and cleaned the race bays furiously as he walked, often with VIP guests, towards where we assembled the cars. And I mean we tidied and cleaned an already operating-theatre-like race bay that looked like you could eat your food from the highly polished, gleaming Italian floor tiles. Half an hour later we'd invariably get a call to say that Ron had noticed a mark on a cupboard door or that someone's coffee cup was on the desk, even though in the midst of being consumed, and it looked untidy. It was frustrating and exhausting . . . but it would've felt exactly the same to Ron, I imagine.

The point is he knew what he wanted his company to look like, he was obsessive and consistent about it and so that *is* exactly what it ended up looking like. He was in a position to be able to dictate the standards, but he also lived them. The team and the wider McLaren Group, as it ended up becoming, grew as a detail-possessed extension of Ron himself.

I often asked myself whether the level of obsession Ron inflicted upon us was healthy or not. It often felt unhealthy from our perspective. The race bays *were* always spotless. Any guests or potential sponsors being shown around *were* jaw-droppingly impressed every single time we saw their reactions. Yet it never seemed good enough for Ron. That could feel demoralising, like we could never achieve the standards required, which affected our self-belief. Was that a healthy way to treat staff?

We, of course, had the choice of whether we wanted to be part of that environment. I saw many great people come and then go at McLaren over the years because they couldn't, or didn't want to, operate in that kind of forensic environment. The fact that I, and many of my colleagues, stayed for so long shows that at some level we appreciated what Ron was trying to build and wanted to be part of it. Although it was clearly infuri-ating at times, I grew to understand that, like most things in this world, mastering skills and mindsets, becoming the best at anything, comes at a cost. Ron's demands gave us the kind of infinite goals I've already discussed, which kept us continually striving to be better every day. With them came huge rewards. So somewhere down the line, quite early on in my case, I con-cluded that if this was the price I had to pay to not only become a World Champion, but to almost certainly enhance the rest of my life . . . I was willing to pay it. Over time I put more and more trust in Ron and McLaren and I became more and more McLaren-like.

From a personal perspective, I answered the question of whether or not the life of crazy attention to detail was unhealthy for me, by weighing up risk versus reward. I had, and still have, the utmost respect for him and what he's achieved. I will forever be grateful for the lessons he's taught me, intentionally or otherwise, and attribute much of my own success in life to being inspired to achieve previously unimaginable things whilst in his presence . . . but I didn't want to end up morphing into him. That was the risk as far as I was concerned. I needed to retain my personality, my character, my cheeky spark, the part of me that probably frustrated Ron the most. At the same time, I wanted to learn from him. I wanted to attain his desire to succeed and constantly improve, to up the level of everything I did now and forever more. I wanted to learn to think a bit more like him. That was the reward.

So it was a case of maintaining the right balance between fun and living a life I loved living and then, when I needed to, zoning in with laser focus to the kinds of fine details most people wouldn't even be aware existed. I think I managed, in the most part, to do that. I had enormous amounts of fun, travelling the world, experiencing some crazy things most twenty-somethings couldn't even dream up. In many of those extra-curricular moments I was far from laser-focused. If there *was* any attention to detail, it wouldn't be on the kind of details Ron would've approved of.

For almost ten years I woke up, proudly put on my McLaren uniform and spent my working days in the unending pursuit of looking for any detail, no matter how small, that might make us better. In the many years since, I now carry much of that same obsession in my personal and business lives, but if I'm honest, it's only since leaving the team that I've learnt to under-stand how best to apply it.

Ron believed that if you choose not to pay attention to something, then you're opening yourself to chance, so you need to be comfortable with that. There wasn't much in his life, and certainly not in the business of F1, where Ron was happy keeping his fingers crossed and hoping it would work out. I see things a little bit differently.

I can still focus in on, and notice around me, details others don't see or care about. I get called into companies to help them grow and attain greater success than they currently have because I'm able to think like Ron would about the details that matter to them, the ones that, when we pay attention to them, can help improve outcomes and create advantages.

But then I can go home and not care that the gravel on my driveway isn't perfectly clean. I want order, organisation and tidiness in my life, but I'm not going to be obsessive about it in the areas where I don't see it as a requirement for a competi-tive advantage in something I really care about. Balance. In my mind at least, it's that conscious balance that keeps my atten-tion to detail on the right side of the healthy/unhealthy line: being unconditionally non-negotiable about certain elements, yet frivolously relaxed about others.

Because getting the details right in anything we do is always a balancing act. At the uniquely narrow and wall-lined Monaco Grand Prix, an F1 team will put less focus on experimenting and fine-tuning the car into some perfect set-up window for the twisty street track around Monte Carlo and much more time into getting the driver into as good a headspace as pos-sible. Whereas at most tracks the team spends most of the practice sessions understanding which details of the car's per-formance they can improve, in Monaco it's a bit different.

The biggest opportunity for more performance comes from building a driver's confidence to thread the car at high speed between the tight barriers, which comes from more time in the car and less time in the garage making mechanical changes and looking through data. It's the same level of attention to detail, just different details.

My years in this sport have given me an appreciation of the value of going into more detail than your competition to create advantages, and that's as true of F1 as it is in business and life. What I want to do in this chapter is explain that the key to generating as many of the right outcomes as possible is knowing which details to put your energy into and which ones to relax on a bit. Doing that involves thought, and can mean asking yourself tough questions (and coming up with honest answers), but that's what I'm here to help you with.

The details YOU choose matter

Choosing to be selective about which details you focus on puts you in good company. Formula One's drivers have a variety of differing levels of attention to detail. They also, like the rest of us mere mortals, vary wildly in the way they apply them.

Of those I was lucky enough to work with at McLaren, Mika Häkkinen stood out as one of the first I noticed being super-focused when it came to maximising his performance behind the wheel of a car. His main rival outside of our own team, Michael Schumacher of Ferrari, had come into the sport years earlier and changed what it was to be an F1 driver with regard to fitness and preparation. Mika had to step up his own game to compete. I remember him being obsessed with extracting whatever he could from the car – in testing or practice, he'd try different racing lines or steering wheel switch positions and come back to relay, incredibly accurately, what he'd found and it almost always matched what we saw in the data exactly.

He was also aware that although at McLaren we never officially had a 'number one' driver, the preferred strategy calls in a race, for example, always went to whichever driver had the best chance of winning or was ahead in the championship . . . so Mika just set out to make sure that was mostly him. He was generally quicker than teammate David Coulthard, but went into some detail to make absolutely sure it was the case.

I only found this out years later, but it turns out that on many occasions he used to go out in practice and, once he had the car set up to his liking, of the three sectors each track's split up into for official timing purposes, he'd maximise two and back off slightly in one. On the next run he'd go flat out in a different two sectors and ease off by a couple of tenths in the other. He knew by adding his fastest sectors together just how fast he *could* go, but the overall lap time on the timing screens never showed it. His time gave DC a target to aim for . . . but it wasn't one that mattered. Then, in qualifying, Mika pushed in all three sectors of the lap and took two or three tenths off David's best, which left him scratching his head for answers.

David Coulthard took a different, broader approach to which details he utilised to his advantage. DC did many of the things that Mika did, but was less 'old school' about his role. He appreciated the importance of the other aspects to his position as an F1 driver. He needed to be a leader and role model in the team, so he worked on that and put a lot of time into building relationships in the hope it might help. He gave his full attention to the brands he represented as a team ambassador. As a result they loved him, and I'm sure in some cases it helped to renew big money deals that enabled our team to keep fighting in the astronomically expensive F1 development race, and of course that helped to give DC the car he wanted to drive.

Lewis Hamilton took all those traits to a whole new level and added new ones. His unprecedented results behind the wheel didn't come by accident. He took control of as much as he could because it was his life's work. He had a powerful driving force motivating him, part of which was down to so many people in his early life telling him and his dad they could never make it. He wanted to prove them wrong and his way of doing that was by harnessing as much detail as he could. He stayed later at the track than anyone else looking through data; he got himself into better physical and mental shape than anyone else; he built a personal brand that far exceeded anything else the sport had ever seen before. This all helped him achieve better results in almost every area of his life than any other F1 driver.

Fernando Alonso put a lot of focus on finding ways to create advantages for himself within the team environment, often through what seemed like quite political methods. I've talked about some of these many times before, but it became another string to his bow; sometimes it worked, sometimes it didn't, but he was often willing to go to extraordinary lengths to get what he wanted.

Kimi Räikkönen was completely different to all the afore-mentioned drivers, but no less detail-focused in his own way. In the car he was blindingly quick and had total belief in his own ability. But unlike much of the growing philosophy of the time, where technology was allowing us to go to greater depths of detail in data and simulation techniques to find even the tiniest areas to improve on the car, he always had a very clear but simple focus. He was much less interested in spending time chasing a fix to fine-tune the car to handle a specific bump on the exit of turn three, for example, and all about solving the car's one biggest issue. Fix the car's more general braking stability everywhere, he'd say, and I'll do the rest. And he did. He tended to focus on the car's biggest problem and making that better, the macro detail, and not worry too much about the micro details he saw as less influential to his lap time. He also had a rare, but important, appreciation for the details in his life *away* from F1. It seems like a strange thing to say, but being a Formula One driver was never the most important thing in his life. His friends and family were. I'm sure it's a big part of the reason he's been able to walk away from the sport at the end of his long career and not miss it to the point of being desperate to come back.

Four out of the five of my drivers I mentioned above achieved World Champion status, the best of the best. Three of those four were champions multiple times. From the outside it looks like they're all on the same mission – to win more races and score more points than the other drivers – yet they all did it by amplifying the very different but very specific details they saw as most important to their particular journey.

In that is a simple lesson for all of us. The modern world, and especially the social media portal into it that many of us use, will have us believe we should all be hitting the gym at 5am, in the office by 6am with a green smoothie in hand, looking down upon anyone not willing to grind and seize the day in the same way. For some people that's absolutely part of a route to success, but not for everyone. Others can quite happily achieve what they want by sleeping in until 10am and approaching the day differently. It's a personal solution to a personal challenge and if F1 drivers can reach the pinnacle of elite competition in a variety of ways, by focusing on a variety of details, then we should all take heart that we can do our own version of the same thing.

> What you focus your attention on, and how much of it you want to give, is up to you.

If you're looking to excel in something, improve your outcomes, learn or develop skills or build habits that support any of your goals, the best way to do that is through paying attention to the right details, the things that are going to work best for you. But, of course, we don't have infinite resources. You can't always, like Ron, focus on *every* detail.

So how do you decide where to focus?

The power of first-principle thinking

When I'm looking to focus my attention on the details I think will help me get the edge in life, I almost always fall back to First-Principle Thinking. The method, which originates from Ancient Greek philosophy, involves questioning everything you think you know about something, then once you've answered those questions, questioning them again . . . and again. In simple terms it's a way of challenging our assumptions and inherent biases. By consciously and continually questioning the validity of an idea, we end up breaking it down to the simplest elements that we know, or at least think we know, to be true.

From there, using those known 'first principles', we can reason back up the chain and, in doing so, often find new ways to solve problems and reach very different answers to the instinctive ones we might have given initially. It's a great way to innovate, but also to distinguish what's true for *us*.

In F1 we use this method a lot. When a new set of technical or sporting regulations comes out, the teams need to think carefully about how best to exploit the new rules to their advantage. A new set of regulations can provide a whole raft of challenges, but also a world of opportunity. A seasoned car designer would find it easy to base their response on the years of experience that've gone before, the many iterations of previous cars that've evolved during the last period of rules. Assumptions can be formed subconsciously about how to solve certain problems.

If they evolved their thinking from one regulation cycle to the next, the ideas for something like a new floor would be intricate, creative, accurate, even innovative, all lavished with the kind of winning levels of attention to detail F1's known for. But if they'd failed to put the same level of attention to detail into their first-principle reasoning before they started, they may well miss a glaring opportunity buried somewhere in the new rules that others could exploit. And that could be costly.

To avoid that, we're taught to question everything. We question each other and encourage an open culture of embracing that. It wasn't uncommon at McLaren for anyone to quiz anyone else about why they'd done something a certain way. Whilst at first it can feel awkward or even threatening, it soon felt quite normal because it was so commonplace in the team. I ended up regularly visiting the Drawing Office to ask, for instance, why something had been designed in a certain way that made it hard to fit to a car. No one got upset with that. More often than not, I got a perfectly reasonable explanation that made total sense: perhaps they'd had to work within certain parameters I wasn't aware of and they'd done a great job. But very occasionally conversations like that nudged someone to go back and take another look at the problem in a different way. It might've taken someone from another part of the team's operations entirely to point it out, or just to raise the question, but if it sparked focus into a new set of details that might just create some kind of advantage, it was worth it. That's teamwork.

We can do exactly the same outside F1. We begin by asking ourselves: what are the problems or challenges we're solving for? What is it we want to achieve or get better at? Once we've figured out those details, naturally most of us jump to some kind of instinctive conclusion about how best to get there. Of course, sometimes our instincts can be really helpful. If we face time pressures and need to act immediately on something, trusting our gut can be a great way to utilise the experience and knowledge we already possess. But if we've decided this is one of those things that really matters to us, that we want to focus our attention to detail on, going back to first principles is a valuable process to go through.

Let's say you want to improve your health and fitness and lose some weight.

Instinct might tell you that the obvious solutions are to join a gym and go on a diet. These things may well work for some people, but the chances are that you're either not already doing them, or if you are, they aren't the solution for you, otherwise you'd already be achieving your goals. So if this is something you care about and are driven to achieve, let's look at it like an F1 team might look at it.

If you're clear about those targets, what exactly do they mean? Why do you want to improve health and fitness and lose weight?

First of all, let's hypothesise that you've stumbled across the realisation that you're now deep into middle age, a little heavier, with young children, a busy life, and want to have more energy and mobility to be able to keep up with it all. (I can neither confirm nor deny if this hypothetical case study could be based in any way on my own experiences.)

An F1 team would look at the dilemma and continually ask: what are the most basic facts that we know to be true? Then work up from that base-level knowledge looking at the simplest solutions first. In a case like this the challenge is that you have a busy life with lots of important elements to it, many of which you either can't or don't want to give up.

- What's actually stopping you from achieving these goals right now?
  - A great place to start. Why can't you just go and do it? Is there really something in the way?

- Of the twenty-four hours in your day, how many do you spend doing things that can't realistically be eliminated or reduced? Can you plan your time better?
  - That question itself has to be continually revisited, each time being more and more honest with oneself. There'll be sub-questions prompted by those answers . . . and so on.

- What is your order of priorities with the waking hours you have each day / week / month?
  - What most people say is important to them doesn't always align with their behaviours. So break that down and get really honest. If scrolling social media isn't one of your highest priorities, how can you justify spending two precious hours of a day doing it?

- What can you do to maximise the quality and restorative function of your sleeping hours?
  - Making slight changes to the way you spend your waking hours can make a big difference to how you sleep and getting better sleep, as opposed to just more sleep, can affect your energy during the day.

- What's your diet like?
  - Making the right inputs into your body helps to get the right outputs from it, from general health to mood and energy levels.

- Do you get enough exercise?
  - Moving your body has many benefits, but maintaining physical mobility is particularly relevant here. If you stop using it, you'll begin losing it. Ask what you can do to increase your daily movement.

- What do the voices in your head tell you about you?
  - This is more important than people realise, but most people struggle to be honest here.

These questions are far from exhaustive and each one is only the beginning of a line of self-interrogation, but once you get down to the most basic level, the first principles of truth for you, it provides the most amazing platform to rebuild your belief system in each area. It requires honesty, the kind that you rarely see in the fantastical online world, but the kind that's necessary if you deem the potential outcome worth it.

If you answer the fundamental question about why you want to lose weight in the first place and say it's because you want more energy and mobility to continue playing with your children long into the future, you have to know that's 100 per cent true. Continually questioning that answer with brutal honesty might eventually reveal that it's not actually about that. First-principle analysis might show you that, in reality, you feel pressure to look a certain way for the summer because your friends all work out. In which case, if the six-pack is in fact your biggest priority, either accept that and build a detailed strategy to achieve it, or go back and ask if that's a healthy and sensible priority to be focusing on and start a new line of questioning.

All of this might prove uncomfortable, but you'll find that at the end of it you're focusing on the right details.

Always look under the bonnet

One of the reasons I believe first-principle thinking, and using it to continually check in with yourself to make sure you really are focusing on the things that are most important, is so valuable is that sometimes, quite understandably, we can lose sight of the details that actually matter.

It can be easy, too easy, to focus on the extreme finer details like those Ron Dennis and the F1 world make look so impressive. They absolutely are impressive, staggeringly so sometimes, and like many elements of the kind of elite-level environments we tend to use as case studies in this context, they can often make the difference between winning or not.

Underneath all of this, though, are the more basic, fundamental details needed to prop it all up.

Like a house, we're often wowed by the beautiful decor and elegant design, the finishing touches, but rarely do we ever appreciate the value of what lies beneath the building, the foundations. The foundations aren't seen as attractive; once built over they're never seen again. No one posts pictures on Instagram of their foundations, nor do they ever feature in glossy magazines, yet without some serious consideration and attention to detail being put into them before the building even rises out of the ground for others to admire, the whole thing could collapse.

I visit lots of big companies where they ask me to implement a strategy incorporating F1 levels of attention to detail into their organisations. Typically what they mean is they want their client offerings to be polished to perfection, or their new offices designed like McLaren's Technology Centre. They want to focus on the tiny details that will mark them as a cut above the rest and signal value to customers they didn't even know they needed yet. They're often looking to finesse what they have, searching for what they see as that final 10 per cent that might make them champions. Yet whilst, as we've discussed, there're significant opportunities in this space for almost everybody and every business, if they haven't yet got the basic details, their solid foundations, right yet, it's effort that'll never be fully rewarded and could even cost them dearly down the line.

When I approached Ron Dennis and his deputy, Martin Whitmarsh, midway through my decade at McLaren, to give them some harsh truths about some major failings I'd seen emerging within the organisation, it was a terrifyingly bold move. I was genuinely scared, having made my appointment to see them, as a 'lowly mechanic' they barcly kncw, delivering news I had no idea how they would take.

From my position at the time on the 'shop floor', in amongst the hundreds and hundreds of other McLaren workers going about their business every day, I'd become indoctrinated into the McLaren way. The belief that the tiniest, almost invisible, details could sometimes be the most important in gaining an advantage over our rivals had been well and truly instilled in me by then. I saw things that weren't perfectly straight or that were slightly out of place that I'd have never noticed just a few years earlier and I put an inordinate amount of time and effort into getting things 'just right', because that's how it had to be at McLaren. No one else did detail like we did.

What I'd begun to notice was that all was not quite as glitzy and shiny at McLaren as it should've been, or indeed as it appeared to the outside world.

Large parts of the workforce, the lifeblood of the organisation, were not happy. We gave the impression of a slick, efficient, precisely organised operation, made up of the best people in every department, with the best resources and the best technology at our disposal. Everything you could see, looking in at McLaren from the outside, suggested that if it wasn't quite perfection, we were pretty bloody close. Of course that's exactly the image Ron had designed, but in truth it was an image that reflected Ron himself and yet, from what I could see from the inner sanctum, not necessarily a reflection of my daily reality.

It dawned on me that we were spending a huge amount of time polishing things and curating a vision for others to see, yet very little time on making sure that vision was backed up with real substance. As I said to Ron, it was a bit like we'd spent our entire budget on making the car look good, with shiny surfaces covered in sponsor logos and fancy aerodynamics, yet completely neglected the engine underneath, which had gradually been left underpowered and unreliable. We could never really win without the entire package. I'm not sure he liked the analogy, but it demonstrated my point.

Essentially, the people of McLaren, our foundations, weren't solid. Some felt unheard, unloved, unappreciated; some felt restricted and frustrated; and most felt inherently disconnected from the one thing they should've been most proud of . . . being part of one of the most historic and successful Formula One teams in history.

As I began to move up in the organisation, leading teams of my own, I realised this wasn't something that had just happened. It had been deteriorating gradually, snowballing in its severity and appeared to have a roughly inverse linear correlation to McLaren's increasing focus on the way the company was perceived by others. I concluded that, although the company clearly had class-leading, even revolutionary, levels of attention to detail, we were sometimes prioritising the wrong details.

I knew enough through my own leadership experience, and many books I'd read on the subject, that a team of people need to feel like they're all important parts of the process and that every single one of them can make a difference to the end product. In our case, whether you were designing the car, building it, or working in finance, hospitality or anywhere else in the organisation, you needed to believe you were making a difference to the outcome of one of the world's biggest sporting events, as well as creating the next chapter in the long-running, inspiring McLaren story. These were critical details that had been overlooked for too long and the result was that we were in danger of spawning a toxicity from the inside that had the potential to destroy us. I strongly believed we needed the same levels of attention to detail, the superpower we had over everyone else in the sport, but focused in a different way. And this was how I found myself nervously sitting across a desk from Ron and Martin trying not to get fired by explaining where they were going wrong . . .

Luckily for me they were both hugely appreciative of what I had to say. Martin seemed immediately impressed. I know Ron was too – I just think he struggled to accept the reality of failings in the moment and perhaps needed to reflect on it later. They'd had no idea of the mood within their own camp, which was obviously a failing in itself, but it was a reflection of the culture that had been allowed to inadvertently develop that no one felt able to put their hand up and say something felt wrong.

They gave me the freedom to lead the change we all eventually agreed we needed and I treated the 'project' like anything else we did in our detail-focused world. I thought about it in the same way I would think about trying to make the car go faster. I spoke to hundreds of people, built data sets from questionnaires around things like satisfaction and happiness, metrics that had never been measured before, and produced reports that shared my findings all the way through. I set up channels for people to offer up ideas for improvement in every area and made sure we actioned the best of them. I tried to look at even the smallest of details about the way we operated as a team and the way the people in the team felt about what they were doing and then searched for ways to improve them. Importantly, I gave members of every department a voice in the process and allowed them to feel heard. They led the change they wanted to see – I just facilitated it with the support of Ron and the management team.

MARGINAL GAIN

When you give your attention to details that had previously been neglected, you're opening up an enormous opportunity to improve. We had a huge area of untapped potential. People had been frustrated, and what they could achieve had been inhibited, but all of a sudden it was like the door had been opened to a new avenue to improved performance. Of course that avenue was actually always there – it wasn't really new – we'd just never looked at it in the level of detail it required. It'd been overlooked as not being as important as the outside-facing, shiny, impressive details that Ron prided himself upon.

So we began to apply our world-beating focus on detail into the core functionality of the business. It took time and I was only one small part of the process, but we made game-changing inroads, many of which I've talked about in other chapters, towards making people feel like they were connected to the very special end product we had. That is, competing on a global stage at the pinnacle of our chosen sector, under the inspirational and legacy-generating name of the McLaren Formula One Team. Just like when we improve the car, or a pitstop, it came from many small improvements in every area, making everything we did a little better, by sometimes just the tiniest of margins.

Think hard about the details you share with the world

One of the most common reasons any of us lose sight of maintaining the basic, intrinsic details of our lives, in favour of focusing on the showy, extrinsically motivated, Instagram-worthy versions, is that we've been conditioned to think there's more value in what other people see of us, over what we ourselves feel. Perhaps that's what happened to us at McLaren.

But of course the truth is more nuanced than that. And after years working under Ron Dennis, I'm never going to turn around and say that the appearance we project doesn't matter. I think it can be hugely important. We like to say, 'Don't judge a book by its cover', but in reality that's exactly what every single one of us does. We make snap judgements, rightly or wrongly, from the second we lay eyes on another person of interest to us, and it's the same when it comes to brands and businesses.

We can use our public-facing image to our advantage if we get the details right. This is what McLaren and other F1 teams have done successfully for decades – bringing in big-money sponsors and performance-enhancing technical partners to help them succeed. F1's an expensive industry to compete in, especially back then, and so big sponsors and partners were a must just to survive, let alone have any chance of winning. We needed hundreds and hundreds of millions of dollars just to be at the right end of the grid every year.

In a world where social media's become almost inescapable, your Insta or Facebook presence is often the first touchpoint people see of you and it can be important in a number of contexts to make sure it sends the right message about you. I'm not just talking about getting more likes or followers (although that can be a business-shaping metric to apply detail to). It's also likely that meetings in the 'real world' like job interviews, dates or live events will all be inevitably followed up with some 'virtual world' research. What's found in that digital exploration can, and will, inform the opinions of those real people that might make decisions that affect your real future.

Because of Ron's positioning of our brand as a detail-focused, ultra-high-end and hyper-professional organisation, he didn't want McLaren to partner with just anyone. I could never have imagined us with a car sporting the familiar golden arch logo of McDonald's, for example. Not because they aren't a hugely successful company; they clearly are. Not because they couldn't afford the staggering price tag of a title partnership with a leading F1 team; they clearly could. But because Ron wouldn't see their image – as a low-cost, fast-food outlet for the masses – as aligning with ours. He'd see that it might devalue our brand perception by joining forces with theirs. Some might say that's arrogant; others would say it demonstrates an impressively consistent level of attention to detail. Ron felt we needed upmarket blue-chip companies on our car, so that's what we got. Executive car manufacturers, luxury clothing and watch brands, fine diamond producers and so on.

Ron was very clear about what and who we were as a team and he was then incredibly intentional about making sure our public persona reflected those details. From his perspective it all made perfect sense: McLaren's image was an extension of his own – he literally lived the values he insisted the company lived by too. So I suspect if he'd asked himself 'Will what people see align with who I am and what I feel inside?', he'd genuinely have been able to answer with a confident and proud yes.

The problem for us was that this was only part of the story. Ron's focus on these superficial details had blinded him, and others, to what was going on elsewhere in the company. That's why it's so important to be aware, both when it comes to yourself and others, about the motivation and reasoning behind whatever thought goes into that public-facing image.

From a motivational perspective, the simple questions are why do you feel a need to deliberately curate an image of yourself for others to see, and what exactly are you hoping that image will say about you? They should be pretty easy things to answer, as long as you're truly honest.

When it comes to reasoning how you create that image, for me one of the most fundamental questions to ask is the one mentioned above: 'Will what people eventually see align with who I am and what I feel inside?'

If we're honest, how many of us paint a picture online of ourselves that looks nothing like the everyday reality? I bet most of us do to varying degrees. In itself it's nothing new, the medium through which we do it may have evolved, but for generations we've 'dolled' ourselves up for dates, put on a posh 'telephone voice', or exaggerated our abilities in job interviews.

I'm sure even old telegrams and wax-sealed, calligraphic letters were enhancing the truth about their creators back in the day.

I'm guilty of using a little creative licence to describe myself at times too, but I've come to the conclusion that it's a tool we can use effectively if we're aware of it. Our first point of contact with someone, online or otherwise, is often the moment when they make a small, instinctive decision, more often than not subconsciously, about whether or not they'd like to find out more about us. It's our shop window display, there to grab attention and entice people in off the street, so to speak. Once they make the choice to step inside, of course it's up to us to ensure they're not disappointed and let down. And that's where we can easily find ourselves going down the wrong path.

Just like at McLaren, if there's a substantial disparity between the details that go into the outward-facing image and the detail on the inside, at our core, things can become increasingly toxic if left unchecked.

> Portraying yourself as someone you're not because that's what you think the world expects of you is a sure-fire way to waste valuable energy and gradually eat away at your own confidence and self-belief when you find you can't live up to the external expectations you've set for yourself.

You can tell everyone you're this perfect image of yourself and possibly even get affirming admiration for it in the short term, but if that isn't the real life you see when you put your phone down and look around, it's going to get you down very quickly.

The other side of the coin is that, just like a customer liking what they see in the shop window and deciding to step inside the store, they need to have their needs and expectations met once they walk through the door. If you put a substantial amount of attention to detail into creating an online dating profile for yourself that portrays an unbelievable fantasy image of yourself for others to see, you're likely to get lots of positive swipes in the app, making you feel good in the short term, yet unlikely to find much long-term success in meeting the right people. The people that do like what they see, that appreciate the detail you've gone to online, are not looking for someone like you; they're looking for someone like the character you've created. Then because of that, if you ever get as far as going on an actual date and meeting these people, they're likely to be hugely disappointed to find that you're not who they thought you were. You might even be able to keep up the pretence for a while, to add the details from your online presence into your real-world encounters, but not forever.

That's what it felt like at McLaren at that time, like we were telling the world we were the best of the best, yet struggling to keep up with that persona in some areas inside the walls of our own factory.

There are of course two ways to correct the discrepancy. We have to look at ourselves with true honesty and ask, 'Are we living a life true to our core values, or are we pretending to be someone we'll never truly be able to live up to?'

The first response to that question could be to change the details we're broadcasting to the world to make them more aligned with who we really are. Aligning the details you focus on in life can literally be a game-changer.

The second option could be to emulate what we did at McLaren. There wasn't a problem with the image; it was the way we were operating on the inside. We'd neglected the basic details of maintaining who we were as a team, letting some of our standards slip as a result and it was that which needed correcting. In our case our image *was* exactly what we all believed it should be. We wanted to operate in that way and wanted to be proud of it – we just weren't giving it enough attention deep inside the business. By acknowledging this and refocusing our efforts into becoming the McLaren we all knew we should be and wanted to be part of, we were able to realign the details on the outside with those on the inside and exploit our enormous potential. Over the next couple of years we became Formula One World Champions again and I can assure you we were just as much champions on the inside as the trophy and title showed us to be on the outside.

PITLANE LESSONS

- As the example of multiple F1 World Champions shows us, there's more than one way to be successful. Find the details that matter to you, and work for you, and focus on them.
- Whatever challenge you want to overcome or excel at, think about looking at it through the lens of First-Principle Thinking.
- Don't double down on the finer details until you have the basics under control.
- Regularly check in with yourself to make sure you're not being distracted by a focus on the wrong details.

8.

GOOD LUCK IS HARD WORK IN DISGUISE
How You Can Learn to Get Lucky

I want to take you back to the Brazilian Grand Prix of 2008, the final race weekend of that intense season. The championship had gone down to the wire, but McLaren were in a strong position: going into the GP Lewis Hamilton was seven points clear of Ferrari and Brazil's Felipe Massa at the top of the title standings. Felipe had only a narrow chance of victory, as he needed to win the race and hope that Lewis finished outside the top five. We were favourites, and yet we'd been in a similar position twelve months earlier at the same track and for a variety of reasons, mostly of our own doing, we'd managed to throw away the title on the final day. As a result, defending a seven-point lead felt far from straightforward. We were also hoping desperately for a clean, uncomplicated, boring, processional Grand Prix where we could just bring the car and the championship home. We got nothing of the sort.

It rained heavily just before the start, which delayed the race. This heightened the tension we all felt: suddenly we'd moved away from the more normal, dry-race-ingrained procedures. Then, when the race finally began, it was immediately clear that the Ferrari was way faster than us on the now drying track. Massa established a lead of several seconds. The conditions were volatile, changing from wet to dry and back again quickly. Teams and drivers were forced to frantically react, trying to ensure they were on the right type of tyre to cope with rapidly evolving grip levels. Ferrari appeared to be managing better than most; they maintained their lead, which soon began to look unassailable. Still, the big prize was still in our hands. If we finished fifth or higher, we'd be champions.

In the closing laps of an incredibly tricky race, rain began to fall again onto a dry track. We made yet another frustrating and very high-pressure pitstop to switch from dry back to wet tyres. The problem then was that at first there just wasn't the quantity of rain to make the circuit wet enough for our new tyres to work. To anybody watching it must have looked like we'd made a huge mistake. All the more so when, largely unnoticed by many people, a relative back marker, Timo Glock in his Toyota, had decided he had very little to lose so would buck the trend, gamble and stay out on slick, dry tyres.

Initially it looked like his roll of the dice might work. Because, unlike those around him, he hadn't made an extra pitstop, he suddenly found himself in an unfamiliar position inside the top five. Whilst we, struggling to find grip on wet-weather tyres that were not well suited to the barely damp track, found ourselves back in sixth place. Worse still, the laps were running out fast. It seemed the title was slipping away from us.

But then, in true São Paulo style, the heavens opened. A torrential downpour crashed down onto the track and all of a sudden we were now on the perfect rubber for the moment. Massa crossed the line to win the race. His enormous home crowd went wild, thinking he'd done enough to become champion. I remember hearing the roar whilst I focused intently on the screens in front of me in the garage, my desperation mounting with every second.

Then, just a few unforgettable moments later, in the final corner, of the final lap, of the final race of a long, tough season, we overtook a now desperately struggling Timo Glock – still on his dry tyres, he was now tiptoeing his way towards the chequered flag, like Bambi on ice – and we made up the one final position we needed to secure just enough points to win the Formula One World Title.

It was one of the biggest days of my career. I'll never forget the outpouring of emotion in that moment, but just as significant was its afterlife: that victory shaped how people view me today. Positioning myself in the business world as someone who was part of a World Championship-winning F1 team, as opposed to *just* an F1 team, has helped build extra credibility in almost everything I've gone on to do since. So the question is, were we just lucky? Have I been dining out on something that was actually decided by the gods?

Here's another question. Do *you* feel like a lucky person or an unlucky person?

Most of us swing back and forth in flux across a spectrum between these two states at different phases of life, as we reflect on the outcomes of various moments in time. In the same way, F1 fans will no doubt all have stories about how their driver or team was plagued with misfortune over a season they didn't win, or how someone else just seemed to get all the luck on their way to victory. It's an age-old response and gives us what seems like a perfectly reasonable explanation for something that happened 'beyond our control'.

But is luck really beyond our control? That's the question that's long fascinated philosophers, scientists, F1 teams and both the 'lucky' and the 'unlucky'.

We can turn to the *Concise Oxford English Dictionary* definition of luck.

luck
/lʌk/
noun

1.   Success or failure apparently brought by chance rather than through one's own actions. 'It was just luck that the first kick went in.'

But it doesn't really answer the question; note how it drops in the word 'apparently' as an academic get-out-of-jail-free card. So, as with everything else in this book, I'll try and turn to the wonderful world of Formula One and my experience within it, to see if I can offer some helpful clues to help you to draw your own conclusions.

A fast, reliable car, a talented team and driver line-up, vast resources and a relentless push from over a thousand people all year round are all essential if you want to win the F1 World Championship. But nobody in history has ever lifted the trophy without an additional helping of good fortune along the way.

If I think back to successes I was directly involved in, there are countless moments along the way where it could be argued that both good and bad luck played their part. There are moments you'll never be aware of, small things behind the scenes that frequently shaped the outcomes of race weekends, the kinds of micro events we all experience every day of our lives and barely notice. But there were also bigger, more significant occurrences, many of which seemed way beyond our control, like the rain at the Brazilian Grand Prix that both helped and hindered us in our pursuit of F1's greatest accolade.

It's absolutely true that had the rain not fallen to the degree it did that day in São Paulo, in that exact location and at exactly that point in time, we might've never caught and passed Timo

Glock in those final few hundred metres of the race and the outcome of the championship, that chapter of history, might've been different. It's also true that we had zero control over the timing or intensity of the rain, likewise the decisions of other players in the game. But there are holes, big ones, in the idea that all of this was simply a question of the gods deciding to swing things in our favour.

Our success was not created in those final moments of the race. We'd put ourselves in the position to fight for the title on the final day with some outstanding work all the way through that season. In fact, our hard work had begun long before the season started, because we were trying to respond to the major failures from the campaign before. Many of those elements were firmly in our control.

And if we zoom in to that inclement afternoon in Brazil, it becomes clear that we utilised the experience, skills and technology we had available to us to make the best of the continuously changeable situation we faced.

We'd been in a similar predicament the year before at the same track. We had the chance to win that championship, but came away empty-handed after a series of errors combined with technical malfunctions on the car and the fact that other people did a better job in the circumstances. That gave us experience to draw on and some powerful motivation. It was brutal, but we often learn far more from our failures than our successes and so we were able to lean on that twelve months later.

We had the right team of people, most of whom had been through the trauma of 2007 together and as a result were better equipped for the pressure and uncertainty of that history-making season finale than any other team on the grid.

We were also able to tap into our own accurate weather

predictions. We'd employed our own dedicated team meteorologist, in our own sophisticated van packed full of the latest satellite and radar technology, strategically nestled up in the hills surrounding the São Paulo circuit. It meant that whilst we had no control over the weather, we could meticulously predict many of the important details about how and exactly when it would affect us. More so than other teams that hadn't gone to those lengths. So, whilst fans were screaming at their TV sets thinking McLaren had made a terrible mistake by changing to full wet tyres in only very light rain, inside the team we knew the downpour was coming.

We had a pitstop crew better prepared than anyone else after the game-changing work of Dr Aki Hintsa and the McLaren Lab, with their focus on the kind of human-performance fine details that we knew no other crews were interested in at the time. That meant that when that final pitstop decision did come late in the race, we were never going to buckle under the immense pressure and delivered exactly what we needed to.

Lewis himself had the harrowing task of desperately trying to make up the vital points positions we needed on a treacherously low-grip but constantly changing track, yet he didn't throw it away. He pushed right up to the limits, but no further. The rookie Lewis Hamilton from a year earlier may easily have lost focus and spun out trying too hard.

So whilst luck very clearly played a part in helping us to win that season, we also very intentionally put ourselves in the best position to make use of it.

Which means that I'd like to propose a different definition of good 'luck': 'The moment when great opportunity meets great preparation.' We can't always predict when the chance might come along, like those pivotal moments we took advantage of in Brazil, but we can make sure we're always ready for it if it does.

You might well ask, 'How do I know *what* to be ready for?' if you're preparing for a chance opportunity that hasn't come along yet, and the answer is 'As much as possible.'

This is the argument that people like James Clear, author of the global bestseller *Atomic Habits*, make too. Life's constantly preparing us with every experience we have: with each event we witness we become more aware of what the world could potentially throw at us and this gives us an evolving perspective through which to view it. But we can also take our own conscious steps to improve our readiness for anything that comes our way and F1 teams like mine realise how important this can be.

Fail to prepare, prepare to fail

Perhaps the most obvious, but certainly the most important, is to look after our own health and well-being. It's the single most fundamental pillar holding up literally everything else we do in life, yet most of us don't treat it as such. If you lost your health tomorrow, no matter what kind of unbelievably amazing opportunity landed on your doorstep, a lottery win, the job you've always dreamt of, meeting your soulmate, whatever it was, you'd be unable to take advantage of it. When the opportunity came, you'd be unprepared, so it wouldn't feel like much in the way of good luck. You'd undoubtedly trade in all the money, the job or the person in a heartbeat to have your health back, I guarantee it. So the number-one step we should all take is to do whatever we can to improve or preserve our health. It'll increase your chances of being 'lucky' in almost every scenario possible.

The McLaren Lab was our version of ensuring that the bodies

and minds of every member of the team would always be in the best place they could be to take advantage of any opportunities, or face any challenges, that came our way. We took the health, well-being, and physical and mental fitness of the people in our team seriously. Partly because we appreciated how improving those things could literally help us to be better at our high-performance roles, but also because we clearly understood that if any of us lost even one of those things, McLaren would lose that person from the collective effort of the team. Physically conditioning the pitstop crew would help to make us prepared, with the right people in the best shape, to take advantage when a chance to make a big difference came our way.

After that, there's an endless carousel of ways in which we ready ourselves for when opportunity knocks; the chapters of this book catalogue many of them and most can be broadly applied to all of us. From acquiring knowledge we might later need or benefit from, to learning skills, forming relationships, testing ourselves or those around us, building resilience, determination, self-confidence and so much more. Because an F1 team has pretty specific goals in mind – to win races and eventually world titles – we can optimise for that with a targeted version of what I've described above.

In the wider world it's not really that different. We tend to at least have an idea of what a day full of lucky breaks might look like. It could be being awarded a last-minute penalty in a big football match, getting a phone call to say you've got the dream job interview you had your fingers crossed for, or bumping into the investor that could fund your latest business venture whilst in an elevator. If these 'lucky' moments lead to a big success, you're highly likely to look back on them. Yet you'll only ever remember them as 'lucky' moments if you were able to make the most of them and that comes largely down to preparation.

When we take steps to practise the skills we need for life, we're almost always helping to ensure that we'll cope better when fate throws one of its curveballs at us.

That mindset is summed up in the words of the South African golfer Gary Player, who's credited with first uttering the words, 'The more I practise, the luckier I get.' It's a quote I refer to in my own life a lot, but for me it could have more than one meaning.

On one level he was talking about how the more time he spent out on the putting greens, the more often he began to hole those difficult shots that others might sink only on the rarest of occasions. He was building technique and muscle memory; he was literally getting better at the thing he was doing because he practised the thing he was doing over and over again. The idea of him getting 'luckier' was really only a sarcastic reference to the way other people saw the game. If you don't practise, or don't practise enough to get to the level you want to achieve, the most tricky and unlikely shots in the game will be left somewhat to chance. You might have to be 'lucky' to get them in once in a while and, when you do, there'll be a shock intake of breath, a startled look on your face as you and others proclaim it to be your 'lucky day'. Whereas, if you're dedicated and put in the practice hours, if you keep going when others go home, you improve, as does your threshold of what might be seen as a really tough shot to you. What others see as luck doesn't surprise you anywhere near as much because that's exactly why you practised.

In F1 teams we do exactly the same when it comes to things like pitstops. We practise thousands of stops in a bid to build technique and muscle memory, so when we smash out a sub-two-second pitstop in a race, it's not quite the same wow moment it might be for those looking on.

But fine-tuning the technical aspects of a sport like golf or F1 pitstops to help you become more 'lucky' is only one side of what I take Player's quote to mean. In exactly the same vein, rehearsing your daily practices – the small, less easily quantifiable elements of your life – can be just as beneficial in the pursuit of luck.

I'm talking about things like the way you show up for work, the way you treat others, the way you speak to people, the way you treat and speak to yourself. They affect the way others tend to treat you in return. People respond to actions and behaviours, both good and bad, with actions and behaviours of their own that may well affect you, so if you have the power to influence that in your favour, it makes sense to, doesn't it? These and many other daily details of life can all be practised and worked upon until you get better, or 'luckier', at them. It's really the same thing I was trying to achieve by improving the way McLaren treated staff at the team. I knew that if we empowered people, making them feel valuable and their experience and expertise respected, they'd react by going to greater lengths to make a positive difference and as a result the team might just get a bit 'luckier' in everything we did.

A step into the unknown

Much of the above relates to the sorts of events that you might reasonably expect to encounter. Rain is a regular occurrence in São Paulo. But sometimes you're presented with implausible surprises that appear to emerge from absolutely nowhere.

Many years ago, I had such a moment at McLaren, one that caught me by surprise and that for a long time I regretted not being ready for, because it could have shifted the trajectory of my whole future career.

I was still a Number Two Mechanic then, which in the typical F1 team structure is some way down the organisational hierarchy. But I'd been making waves with management by taking it upon myself to point out what I thought were some fairly major problems in the company and trying my best to help the team find solutions. It was all with a view to helping us, in whatever way I could, to win. Clearly, from the surprised reaction of almost everyone else at the time, it was unusual for someone in my position to be motivated enough to improve things at a corporate level, even less likely for them to go directly to Ron Dennis and Martin Whitmarsh, our two most senior figures. But as time progressed I began working more and more in this space, looking to focus on human performance across the business, attempting to begin the repair process of what I'd seen as years of neglect of our company's biggest asset, its people. Before long I began to feel that McLaren's executive team had started to appreciate what I was doing. Ron took more of an interest in what I was trying to accomplish and became more and more supportive. I ended up working closely on the project with Martin Whitmarsh, who'd been promoted from Managing Director to Chief Operating Officer, and I was in his office on a regular basis giving updates on what I was learning along the way. Importantly, I never arrived at a meeting bearing only problems. I spent time preparing, making sure I had answers to the questions I was likely to be asked, but crucially always trying to have a potential solution ready for the issues I'd identified. I was so fearful that this could be my only shot at actually making McLaren into a nicer, more successful place to work and so aware of the negative resistance coming from certain quarters who seemed reluctant to change, that I'd decided that preparation was the best tool in my armoury.

And yet, when my 'lucky' break came along a few months

later in that very office, I realised how far short my preparation had fallen.

As time progressed, the improvement programme was going well and most people were positive and grateful for the differences being made. They were beginning to feel they finally had a voice and were being heard, something which had definitely been missing in the past. We were starting to see results in different groups in the factory working more closely together: there was a noticeable air of hope across the 'shop floor'. I was feeling particularly pleased with myself, but also really enjoying the process and learning a lot about team culture and building high-performing teams along the way.

Martin was also very happy. It was him, I think, who'd really convinced Ron to buy into it all, and the small, early successes we were seeing helped legitimise the process. One day, Martin called me up to his office, something that by this stage was beginning to feel almost normal. I went in, he asked me a couple of small-talk-esque questions, then just said, 'We need people like you at McLaren, Marc. If I gave you the choice, where would you like to go in this company?' I was stopped in my tracks.

It was a much bigger question than it seemed. With hindsight I recall he'd been showing more and more appreciation for my efforts, on occasion even suggesting that Ron was hugely grateful too. I should've seen the opportunity coming, but I didn't. Any management team worth its salt should be clambering over themselves to harness the kind of asset I was showing myself to be. And yet for all the preparation I'd done for all the various aspects of the process I'd initiated for the company, I was woefully ill-equipped to respond to this question about what I wanted for myself. I still saw myself as a 'minion', many layers down the pyramid from the COO of the entire McLaren Group, in a place I didn't belong. Imposter syndrome kicked in. I panicked. I 'ummed' and 'argghed'. I giggled in embarrassment. I looked everywhere but at Martin. And then, with my heart pounding and sweat forming on my brow, like a silly schoolboy in trouble with the headmaster, I jokingly said, 'Haha, I really don't know, Martin. I guess I just always thought it'd be cool to have a job here with a laptop!'

I regretted it immediately. I was ashamed of myself. I'm sure I went red. That was my moment, gone. That was my chance to make an elevator pitch, or my opening line on a hopeful first date – it was me missing the last-minute penalty to take my team through to the next round of the cup. I'd fluffed it.

I dread to think what Martin thought. Obviously *I* imagined it was the line that made him rethink his entire opinion of me and realise he'd been duped this whole time. He was of course polite and sent me on my way with a reassuring 'If you do ever think of something, please let me know,' but I was gutted. I could've said I wanted to aim for Chief Mechanic, Team Manager or even higher and I honestly believe Martin would've helped me get there. In truth all possibilities were open and that was my chance to show my ambition. Perhaps an element of imposter syndrome held me back from believing I could aim that high, but the reality is that that too comes largely down to my lack of preparation in that area.

I beat myself up about it for a long time, regretting it for years even, despite moving up in the team naturally to become more senior as years passed by and somewhat ironically being given a company laptop. On that day, opportunity definitely came along, but my preparation just wasn't there to meet it, so there was no 'lucky' moment as a result.

It did of course give me a substantial life lesson. I'd spent considerable time making sure I was prepared for the short-term questions Martin might ask, but was so engrossed in being ready for that, I'd neglected the bigger picture and longer-term time horizon of my own career. Yet, the person I was meeting was exactly the person who could have one of the largest influences upon it.

The irony is, I was working in an industry that puts incredible effort into preparing for the occasions you don't even know exist yet. On a Wednesday or Thursday at every F1 track before a Grand Prix, the drivers, their team of engineers and their race strategist will almost certainly walk the track together to get a close-up look at the features of the circuit around an entire lap. The drivers and engineering groups are looking at kerbs, bumps on the tarmac that might need to be avoided or have the car set up specifically for them. They're getting a feel for overtaking spots, the best places to harvest and deploy electrical energy from the car's hybrid systems. They note any changes from the previous year and examine things like pit entry and exit lines, all in an effort to be best prepared. The strategist is often trying to imagine even the least likely script possible playing out on race day.

They'll be looking at the position of the car recovery gaps in the track barriers, which may be 100 metres apart in some places, and wondering what would happen in a race if a car were to crash or break down at different points around the lap. They might have a chat with volunteer event marshals and ask what it's like to get cars safely off the racetrack if they were to stop there. The marshals might say that if it's wet, for example, it's a nightmare, because the grass next to the track at that point quickly becomes muddy and it's slightly uphill towards the exit, meaning it can take a long time to get a stricken car moving and behind the barriers to safety. Or they might say they have a crane on race day that can literally reach over the barriers and pick the car up within seconds, lifting it away without much disruption.

These are all fanciful plots, as the chances of someone actually stopping in that specific place in the middle of a Grand Prix might be pretty slim, but if it were to happen, the best strategists have already imagined it. They've played out a similar sequence of events in their minds, giving them an idea of the likelihood or otherwise of F1's Race Director throwing in a strategy-altering safety car period in response to the stricken driver and how long the race might then be neutralised for. That of course means a team can factor that risk into its strategy planning and can act accordingly and immediately with their pitstops if the seemingly implausible situation should arise.

MARGINAL GAIN

Even daydreaming about my own future could've helped me in that moment in Martin's office. My advice to anyone, after the disappointment of my own experience, is to do exactly that. No matter what stage of your career or life, imagine yourself bumping into someone who could categorically change it. At some point it will almost certainly happen to you, even if it seems improbable now. You'll be at a party or a work function and be introduced to someone; perhaps someone will find you online, see your work and send a message; a friend from the past could pop up in a new role that opens a door for you and so many other potential scenarios. You could literally end up in a lift with the right person. Try and imagine those scenes in your mind, play them out, envisage the conversations. What would you say? It might seem far-fetched, but I wished I'd done that all those years ago. It's not that events will unfold exactly as you visualised them, but even imagining a vague version of how those moments might become a reality in your world will make you better prepared to meet them than if you'd never even allowed yourself to dream.

The red car theory, or how you can learn to be lucky

This idea of being open to the unexpected and thus ready to grab whatever opportunities it offers leads to another way of looking at the question of whether luck is really beyond our control.

In the field of popular or 'consumer' psychology, there's a concept known as the red car theory.

The phenomenon suggests that if I ask you how many red cars you saw on the way home from work today, the chances are you'd have no idea. But if I suggest to you that I might ask you the same question when you get home tomorrow night, it's much more probable that you'll be seeing red cars everywhere on that journey.

I'm a firm believer that this is exactly how luck works for many of us.

In the red car example, we notice many more red cars on the second day because our eyes and minds are open to seeing them. They were all there the day before too, but simply passed us by as we stared unwittingly into the distance.

The key insight of the red car theory is that if we go through life always open to the possibility of great opportunities coming our way, we're much more likely to see them when they arrive.

If we believe those fantastic things only happen to other, incredibly 'lucky', people, they probably will. It's not that the same chances won't appear before us at some point; it's just that with the very idea of them being closed off in our minds, it's highly likely we won't notice or recognise them.

It's the same reason that if you buy a new pair of Nikes, you suddenly start seeing the same shoes everywhere. The world hasn't gone out and followed your fashion sense; the only thing that's changed is that your brain's now attuned to seeing them as you're focused on them in your own mind. So if we can intentionally create that focus, without necessarily having to actually 'buy the Nikes', the chances of spotting the opportunities in life go up.

One of the challenges to this mindset, as I've already talked about, is the inbuilt 'negativity bias' which our evolutionary history instilled in us for reasons of self-preservation. We're predisposed to expect that bad, rather than good, things will happen to us. For many of us it's easier to assume something won't work out and as a result protect ourselves emotionally and socially from disappointment by pulling out of the race before it's even begun. In doing so, we limit not only the number of potential opportunities that present themselves, but also our ability to respond in a way that can make the most of them.

The 2024 Canadian Grand Prix in Montreal was a spectacular event, with rain and incidents on track all playing their part to ensure the teams and drivers had to be on their toes for the entire race, and it threw up a profound life lesson for me.

My old team, McLaren, after a number of years of struggle and poor results, have made multiple changes to their management personnel and structure and consequently to their team culture, as well as their driver line-up, in a bid to recapture the form of old. In the meantime, firstly Mercedes, then latterly Red Bull, have been through cycles of dominance, winning consistently and breaking records along the way. As a result, McLaren were pushed down the competitive order, at times even slumping right towards the back of the field. Very few people in the current team, until the end of 2024, had won a World Championship and some had never even experienced a race victory. The last F1 title success of any kind before that was our incredible day in Brazil all the way back in 2008.

But the team have found a way back to the top again. They're reaping the rewards of years of hard work and rebuilding and are now regularly taking the fight to the mighty Red Bull. At Canada 2024, as they began to find form again, it was McLaren's Lando Norris who led the Grand Prix, ahead of Red Bull's multiple champion, Max Verstappen, when the safety car was sent out to neutralise the field after another car crashed. Norris was just a few hundred metres from the pit entry road as the safety car was urgently deployed and at first it appeared he'd been very unlucky with its timing. Travelling at over 200mph, he seemed unable to get into the pits at such short notice and make use of the 'cheap' pitstop opportunity that had presented itself now that the field would be circulating under the slower SC conditions. Having missed the pit entry he had to continue for another entire lap frustratingly slowly before eventually making it into the pitlane to get his required fresh tyres from the team. Because Verstappen had been a hundred metres or so behind Norris in the race he had a bit more time to react when the safety car was initially sent out. He could make the required stop for new tyres whilst Lando was forced to crawl around the track one more time. By the time McLaren were eventually able to bring Lando in for his pitstop, that extra slow lap meant he emerged from the pits in second place behind the new race leader and Red Bull's eventual winner.

The immediate post-race media coverage was all about how unlucky McLaren and Lando had been with that unfortunate safety car timing, which looked to have cost him the win. There was huge sympathy from almost all quarters of the sport, yet I'd seen it quite differently.

I looked at the data and video footage and listened back to the team radio calls between the guys on the pitwall and the driver and thought that McLaren did in fact have more than enough time to bring Lando in for his pitstop at the same time as Red Bull brought in Max. It was definitely a tight call and, make no mistake, decisions like this are always harder to make when you're the first one coming through in the lead of the race, but it was a call I was sure could have won them the Grand Prix.

Knowing what I know about how the race strategy systems and software work at the team, I knew that as soon as the Race Director presses the button to deploy the safety car, the team's predictive simulations instantly update with the new preferred plan of action. The team then need to decide very quickly whether they can execute it in the real world. They didn't have long, a few frantic seconds, but crucially there was enough time to make the call before Lando passed the entry to the pitlane. Of course, there's always risk. Would the mechanics be able to have the new tyres ready and out of their heated blankets in time? Could the pitstop crew deliver under huge pressure at such short notice? Was it even the right call to make?

My feeling in the aftermath, and one that was later validated by the team itself with their own analysis, was that, with hindsight, by hesitating too long they effectively made the wrong decision. They weren't quite sure enough to commit in the moment.

So had they been 'lucky' or 'unlucky'?

The truth is you can spin it both ways, but they *did* have the chance to win the race because the SC was deployed immediately after the crash. That's pretty 'lucky'. It gave them the opportunity to take that pitstop whilst the rest of the race was slowed down. Had it been a few seconds later, they'd have already passed the pit entry lane and the 'luck' might've gone to Red Bull to take advantage of. So the opportunity was there, but they didn't take it. Why not?

Although Red Bull had a somewhat easier decision to make in those vital moments, given their position slightly further back on track, my guess is that had the roles been reversed and it was them leading with McLaren in second place when it happened, F1's most recent dominant team might've made a different call.

This is meant in no way to be a criticism of McLaren by the way, just a common observation that I've made across many industries and sports when a company or competitor is learning how to win, either for the first time, or after a long spell away from the top like McLaren were at the time. It's a natural part of the process of switching from being 'unlucky' to 'lucky'.

That moment in Montreal didn't reflect the fact that McLaren aren't competent enough to win, nor that Red Bull are simply a better team. In my mind, it's a reflection of the preparation that both teams have had over recent years and how that preparation met the moment of opportunity on the day.

By preparation in this case I mean the recent history of the two organisations. One's struggled to get out of the midfield for the most part, whilst the other's continually broken long-standing records for the amount of races they've won. One's reaching for the top after a long period of poor results and criticism; the other's been at the top for some time, being held aloft by success and the continual praise of those around them.

The evidence residing in the collective minds of the two teams of people is very different. If, like McLaren at the time, recent history tells you the decisions you've made often haven't worked out for you, you're less likely to make a decision at all, and less likely still to make one that seems like a risk. This would have been just as true for prehistoric man: if history tells you that lions often live in caves, you're less likely to want to go in and explore one, even though it could make the perfect home.

By contrast, Red Bull's recent form tells them that they make good decisions, that they can trust in their own processes and personnel, and so when a split-second opportunity pops up, they're far more likely to be confident enough to take it.

McLaren were learning how to be lucky again after years of feeling pretty unlucky. That they were in a position in the Canadian GP to even be fighting with Verstappen and Red Bull is testament to the fact that they're getting lots of things right again. That in itself feeds into the stack of evidence they're building, and this will help shape moments in future races which I am confident they'll go on to win. What we know now, and they couldn't at the time, was that as the 2024 season went on, McLaren grew stronger and stronger as a team. By the end, they'd overhauled Red Bull Racing and become F1 Constructors' World Champions for the first time in twenty-six years. What incredible 'luck'!

So how can we accelerate the process of building a stack of positive evidence without having to spend years lost in disappointment before finding our way towards success?

McLaren's hesitation in that race, when we really boil it down, almost certainly came down to a lack of confidence. Because they'd rarely been in that situation before, they weren't confident enough to immediately trust their process and make the crucial call. We've all been there. Perhaps early in your career you were presented with a complex challenge and you shied away because you couldn't fall back on the experience of having succeeded in a similar scenario before. Maybe even now, years later, the experiences that have stuck in your mind are predominantly the ones where things failed and it all went wrong.

We have a habit of doing that as humans. When we succeed we celebrate the result and move on; when we fail we come up with all manner of stories and reasons to explain our failure, many of which continue to undermine our self-belief.

This is where the red car theory and its connection to luck comes back in: if we want to be more open-minded to the possibility of good things happening, we need to build self-confidence.

Confidence can come from many places, including practice, like in Gary Player's golf situation, or the support of those around us. When people recognise our achievements, like when an F1 team's awarded trophies and championships, or a business begins to turn a profit or leaps up the rankings, we gain confidence. Those things become evidence telling us that we're good at what we do. On an individual level, it could simply be friends or family appreciating something you've done and telling you so. It could be being promoted at work and so on.

But relying solely on the accolades given to us by others, or what we call external validation, is also something that can be largely out of our control. A back marker F1 team can do a remarkable job in a given set of circumstances and finish a race eleventh, just outside the points. They go home empty-handed and, if that was their sole measure of success, they'd understandably feel pretty low after the event.

If we want to take some control of our destiny and find our own ways of building confidence to help us to become 'luckier', we need to create reward mechanisms based on internal or intrinsic validation rather than relying on the world around us.

Even the biggest and best F1 teams see the benefit of bringing validation 'in-house', as opposed to relying on the traditional rewards system of F1 points, trophies and championships.

F1's very much a data-driven industry, so a team will always look to measure as many metrics as possible to understand and track performance. But whereas in days gone by the only metric that mattered was lap time, today we quantify everything from employee happiness and satisfaction to design and production deliverables, sustainability impacts to fan and media engagement and almost everything in between. Each of those has targets. If they're achieved we celebrate them, loudly, so everyone hears and can appreciate what we've managed to do together as a team. As I said in Chapter 4, celebrating success feels amazing! We let everyone in the organisation know that what they're contributing to is working and we're winning, even if not on the racetrack quite yet. We show everyone internally that we're getting better and better and closing in on the external public success of topping the Formula One time sheets. It builds that evidence stack again and, in all the ways we've already touched on, eventually shapes the decisions being made all the way through the company. That can help lead a team to being a bit 'luckier'.

In our own lives, setting the kind of short-term goals we talked about in Chapter 1 is a great way to aid this. The level you need to start at will very much depend on how you feel right now, but if your confidence is low, if you don't feel very lucky, then perhaps starting really small could help. One of the important effects of this is to gradually, even if only in small ways at first, build your confidence by continually celebrating achievements set and measured by only you. You're not relying on anyone else to recognise that you made your bed, or cleared the email inbox, or whatever the list entailed: it's intrinsically motivated and internally validated.

It may seem like a far cry from making your bed to winning a Grand Prix or making the bold decisions in life that can lead to those unfathomably 'lucky' moments happening to you, but this is where things need to start if you feel close to rock bottom. Whatever your current position, I'd suggest that you should make your goals manageable. Treat it as a tool which evolves as you grow. If you're able, curate the tasks so they become progressively more challenging, so that each 'win' gives you the motivation you need to complete the next one. You'll end the day seeing an array of proud ticks as you write tomorrow's goals. That's a satisfying and affirming feeling (and useful too, if you got some important jobs done). But the true value of these achievements is that behind the scenes, deep in your subconscious, you're building confidence. The messages your brain hears and sees are all about *your* success. If it gets them every day, it'll change the way you think about other aspects of life, without you even realising.

These changes might lead to you making different, braver decisions than you might have made just weeks or months earlier. Suddenly, as the consequences of those decisions play out in your favour, you feel 'luckier'. With small good things happening in your life, you might become more open to the idea of bigger good things happening too; you'll begin to notice opportunities springing up around you. Except, of course, they were always there.

Control amid the chaos

So, let's go back to that question I posed near the beginning of this chapter: 'Is luck really beyond our control?'

There will always be elements of complete chance in our world, things like the weather, or a seed passing through a bird's stomach and being deposited somewhere with the right conditions for it to grow into new life. As humans, we can't realistically attain control over these natural occurrences. But beyond that there's a spectrum of phenomena which happen all around us that we can either exert some influence over or, at the very least, control how we react to them.

Occasionally the line between these is more blurred than you might think. Some might argue that an F1 team shouldn't worry itself about the actions of its competitors in a race, because they can't do anything about them. Often that's true, and the only thing to do is focus on how we respond to whatever moves our opponents make. But there are occasions when our actions do in fact influence what others do.

There've been many Grand Prix where my teammates and I have been called out into the pitlane to get ready for a pitstop, even though the team has absolutely no intention of actually bringing the driver in. We burst out of the garage because we want to persuade our competitors to pit *their* car as it would help our race strategy to have them off the track and out of our way. Drivers move to 'dummy' overtakes to incentivise the car in front of them to move off line and compromise their corner entry in a bid to get past on the way out of the turn. And of course there's the much wider context of how we behave, both good and bad, impacting the way others respond to us. Treat people well and they're much more likely to treat you in a similar way; the opposite of course is true if you don't.

In business we mould our behaviour to convince people to buy products and services, to invest funds or to support us, and it's the same in politics. Even in our own small social circles, both online and at home, our behaviour is often designed to nudge others in certain directions. We want 'Likes' and 'Follows' in the virtual world; we want friends, partners and lovers in the real one. Those behaviours can have an effect on how 'lucky' we are, or at least how 'lucky' we feel we are.

But the one true factor that, with practice, we can exert

total control over is that of our own actions and reactions to the world around us. Try as we might to master it, the world is always going to do things we may not have been expecting. In those moments it's our responses that matter most when it comes to determining an eventual outcome. The mistake is to think of our response as purely a product of *that* moment, that it's simply 'reactive' to the situation in front of us and therefore uncontrollable in advance. If we believe, like I do, that pairing opportunity with preparation is the key to becoming 'luckier', then surely luck really isn't completely beyond our control. It's our ability to pre-empt and practise those reactions, even in the most simple form of daydreaming, that can help dictate how they turn out. At the very least, like the best F1 teams, we must be able to nudge the odds in our favour.

Be lucky.

PITLANE LESSONS

- If you think that lucky moments only happen to other people . . . you'll probably end up proving yourself right.
- Daydream and speculate about the kinds of chance moments that could change your life in the future and play them out ahead of time. If you met a potential investor in an elevator and had thirty seconds to pitch your big idea, what would you say?
- Your behaviours and actions can shape those of the people you meet and it could be those people that open the doors to opportunity for you now or in the future.
- Keep an open mind – luck is all around you. Every day could be your lucky day.

9.

WE'RE ALL LEADERS – WE JUST DON'T KNOW IT YET
How to Be a Twenty-First-Century Leader

I recently sat down with experienced Finnish FI driver Valtteri Bottas, on my *Pitlane Life Lessons* podcast, and asked him about some of the great leaders he's worked under at the different teams he's raced for in Formula One. It made me realise how profoundly the leaderships at FI teams have changed in the years since I first became involved in the sport.

FI's an innovative industry and that's in everything from the tech on the cars to the management structures that run the teams. As a result we tend to be constantly operating at the forefront of the latest concepts with everything, and leadership's no different. But with continuous innovation comes continuous change, so it was fascinating to reflect on how that's impacted team leadership over time.

Frank Williams, the eponymous founder of the famously successful Williams Team, was the man who gave Valtteri his big break and debut drive in the sport. Sadly no longer with us, Frank was respected by pretty much everyone in the game for his passion for racing and fighting spirit, which kept him battling on in FI as a much-loved independent team for decades, up against major automotive OEMs (original equipment manufacturers) and corporate giants. He loved his team and had committed most of his life to helping them become one of the most successful in FI history.

As a result, he led by example, showing the people who worked under him the kind of passion and dedication he expected by living it himself on a daily basis. As Valtteri told me, 'When Frank rolled into the garage in his wheelchair, everyone's back went straight and they tried to be a bit more precise with everything. Everyone was racing for Frank and working for Frank because they felt like he deserved good results.' The respect he commanded from those around him wasn't asked for or ordered down the hierarchical chain; it had developed naturally because of his history and sincere love for the team. He'd earned their respect through his own actions over time. When we see a leader willing to commit everything to the cause, when defeats hurt them deeply, but they get back up and keep fighting because they care, we're much more likely to grow an affinity towards them. We see a window into their character, not just the professional role they play at work, and if we can relate to it – something that's easy to see happening in a team full of fellow racers – we develop respect.

From Williams, Valtteri's career moved on to a new team and a new leader in Mercedes and Toto Wolff. Although Williams had been a dominant force in F1 many years ago, helping to create a success legacy and the respect which that spawns, Mercedes were the current dominant force when Valtteri arrived. Toto was a new type of leader, a modern thinker coming from the dynamic world of entrepreneurship and finance. His leadership style wasn't forged through decades in F1, but through time in other industries, combined with a fresh take when he arrived in the sport.

Valtteri described him as a great 'people person'. He said, 'He's a top, top leader because he's very good at working with different people and getting the best out of them. He's also very good at figuring out if they're actually in the right role or not.'

For me this is modern leadership in a nutshell. Every business is a people business long before it's ever a product business, or a service business, and an F1 team's no different. Toto would be the first to admit he's not a technical expert, he's no engineer, whereas Frank Williams literally used to build his own F1 cars in the garage years ago. Toto's spent his career doing deals and structuring teams to build or grow companies, which means getting to know and understand people. Negotiating any big business deal's almost always as much about how you make the other party in the negotiations feel as it is about the numbers involved. Get them to like you and make them *feel* like they're getting a good deal and you'll likely end up walking away happier. To do that effectively, you need to really try and understand exactly who it is you're dealing with.

Perhaps that's carried over into his F1 team management and leadership. Getting to know your team is one of the most valuable traits you can display as a modern leader. By showing empathy towards his team, but also getting to know them and placing trust in them, Toto's been able to build a group that's thrived in almost every area over many years. When he got to know who he had in his organisation, learning what their strengths, weaknesses and character traits were, he wasn't afraid to offer, or even encourage, those people to find a progressive route through the company that might suit who they were better. Valtteri said to me that sometimes it felt like Toto knew even before an employee did that they might be happier and better suited to a new role. Over time, that has the potential to build a very strong team . . . and so it proved during Mercedes' record-breaking years when they won an unprecedented eight Constructors' titles on the trot.

Bottas's experiences resemble my own.

When I first arrived on the scene, Bernie Ecclestone – the man who over decades had built the sport into a global TV spectacle – was still all-powerful. Bernie was a dictator. He used his power and influence to divide and conquer any potential threats to his reign over the sport and as such created a controlled environment where he was very firmly in charge and everyone else was under no illusion that that was the case.

And then there was the McLaren boss, Ron Dennis, whom I've spoken about at great length already. A man who I had firsthand experience of working under. He was nobody's idea of a 'modern leader'. He was flawed, as we all are, yet brilliant in so many inspirational ways. His leadership style would be considered 'old school' by many today and there were elements of it that left me feeling frustrated, even despondent at times. The communication he had with me and many of my colleagues was almost non-existent for much of my time at the team. Lots of what did filter down to me was often abrupt, unemotional and impersonal and his instructions, no matter how strange they might've seemed to me, came often without explanation. I feel like he believed in building a team of people who could fit into the Ron Dennis way, because he knew that if everyone just did what he expected, it would bring results. And quite frankly, it often did back then. But I'm not sure many of us who worked with him would ever describe him as a 'people person'.

The truth is that there's no absolutely right or wrong way to lead; what's required varies greatly depending on the situation and people involved. The autocratic styles of some of F1's 'old school' have elements that can still be effective today. For example, there's an argument to say that when the proverbial shit hits the fan and the pressure's on, which happens every now and then in all walks of life including F1, a dictatorial leader with an obedient and compliant workforce can make a quick decision without having to consult committees and board members, costing valuable time in certain scenarios.

On the flip side, running a modern business such as an F1 team like that *all* of the time stifles creativity and innovation and breeds a disaffected group of people who have very different expectations today. To some extent, my own experiences at McLaren all those years ago were the beginnings of exactly that, where the team, despite being generally successful on track, were growing more and more disengaged and unfulfilled off it. Winning F1 races on its own wasn't enough any more to keep people happy. We wanted the same thing as Ron, which was to be the best F1 team out there, but as individuals, in my first few years, we were starting to believe we had more to offer than Ron looked like he'd given us credit for.

This desire for greater involvement, to contribute more, was intensified by our sense that the world around us was changing. The internet and social media began to give us more of a window into how others were running their businesses; and more than that, the cultural and technological evolutions all around us were posing questions that the old ways of leading were struggling to answer.

F1 became a globalised sport, which meant that not only did we travel to more and more places and cultures across the planet, but also that the teams were now populated by people and cultures from those places and beyond too. A modern leader has to be able to effectively respect, include, empathise with, and adapt to, all of that. But also to recognise that whatever challenges this presented have been far outmatched by the opportunities the change has created: diversity of cultures leads to diversity of thinking and that can mean spawning the kind of innovative ideas that create new advantages.

Social responsibility and ethics have become increasingly important to businesses and Formula One teams. I could imagine that Bernie Ecclestone might've scoffed at the idea, saying something like 'How much are Social Responsibility and Ethics going to pay for me to consider them?' But the truth is they do pay. As well as the obvious, well-meant reasons the world is taking them seriously today, the result is that consumers, brands, partners, sponsors and fans factor them into their decisions and that affects where they spend their money and what, or who, they get behind. A modern leader needs to consider the impact of business decisions on society and the environment.

All of this social change has been accompanied by the exponential change in technology's evolution, which has also profoundly impacted how an F1 leadership team operates. Whilst the leader of an F1 team isn't required to be familiar with all the tech on their cars, they employ others to do that, they do need to familiarise themselves with the way in which technology development is evolving the workplace. From rapid prototyping, or 3D printing, to advanced simulation, robotics, global connectivity and remote working, the way in which F1 teams operate has changed and with the wave of machine learning, or AI, coming at us faster than we can appreciate, it's going to change beyond belief in the coming years. So a modern leader needs to evolve the way they communicate and be open to new ways of making decisions that rely less on their direct experience and much more on massive amounts of data.

Taken together, these developments mean that today's leaders can't just dictate that their teams give their all and force them to comply. They have to create an environment that both enables them to and means they want to.

This focus on the morale and general well-being of staff isn't just being demanded by an ever-more-needy workforce.

It's driven by an understanding that just as a Formula One car needs to be looked after in order to deliver its peak performance, so human beings need care if they're to perform at their best. Human performance comes from a mixture of things including physicality, experience, skills, knowledge, emotions and psychology. How someone feels in the general sense, as well as specifically about what they're actually doing, plays an enormous role in how they perform.

Formula One operates on its own timescale, at a rapid pace dictated by the intensity of global competition at the highest level. As a result, leaders within the industry are constantly in search of any means possible to eke out another percentage point of performance over rivals at almost any cost. Of course, the natural place to put resources is into the core product, the racing car, but the somewhat obvious realisation over recent decades is that the car never gets designed or manufactured, let alone funded or developed, without the huge team of people behind the scenes. Dedicating substantial resources into managing, leading, looking after and developing them, the company's biggest and most influential asset, is the smartest way to make the car go faster in the end.

That's why, as soon as Liberty Media purchased the Formula One Group at the beginning of 2017 for $4.4b, they put in place a more modern structure. The new owners appreciated that whilst Ecclestone's way of running the company had led it to enormous triumphs during the previous era, times, as well as expectations, had changed. It needed a new, more modern leadership style.

Similar revolutions took place at McLaren. Life is very different now. They understand that, whilst a strong-minded leader like Ron can have a very clear vision, with ideas that can bring about success when executed perfectly by a team of followers, if those people simply *feel* like followers, many of them will experience the things I touched on earlier. Frustration. Despondency. Confusion. In the modern world of elite sport or business particularly, we know that a team collectively feeling these things will never achieve the highest levels as they're only being tasked with carrying out orders for someone else and consequently only utilising part of their capacity for performance that they *could* bring to the operation.

Because, ultimately, high performance in any industry is still powered at some point by human performance. The best leaders today find a way to tap into that as a critical resource. F1 teams have learnt to do that, and so can you.

Familiarity brings success

> You can't lead people if you don't know who they are;
> people won't follow you if they don't know who you are.

The changes McLaren made helped create a team that felt like a team who are all in it together, as opposed to a team simply following a leader and obeying orders, and they saw their fortunes change as a consequence. I don't believe it's any kind of coincidence that almost every single department is now operating at higher levels, producing cars and components of higher quality, more efficiently, and the on-track results reflect that.

There's been a transition, accelerated under new CEO Zak Brown, and recently Team Principal Andrea Stella, following on from the work we started years ago, where *how* people feel is now one of the most important priorities. They conducted regular staff surveys to collect data on previously unmeasured metrics that gave insights into things like happiness and satisfaction and beyond. From that information the executive leadership team could gauge their performance far beyond the traditional measurements of the stopwatch. Over time they gradually improved issues the surveys raised to the point where the team now simply operates an open forum where if anyone is unhappy for any reason they just freely discuss it and address it.

Zak and his team have built an organisation that places emotional intelligence as one of the most important leadership attributes. Emotional intelligence, or EQ as it's often referred to, is a person's ability to recognise, understand and manage their own emotions, but also, and particularly important when it comes to leading teams, the emotions of others too. It's created the kind of environment I described earlier, where people feel heard and valued. They feel important to the team and, as such, feel a sense of loyalty and commitment to the team, which they deliver on by giving more than just the role their job title describes.

The human performance component of the F1 team has expanded and maximised as everyone feels empowered to contribute to, or even make, decisions that affect outcomes. When they win, everyone's played their part; when they lose, collectively they help each other to improve. Each human in the team performs at a higher level because they've been freed up to unleash their full potential, rather than feeling restricted to simply carrying out instructions handed down to them. With each individual performing better, the collective performance of the team rises as a result and the process perpetuates itself. Of course all of this only happens, and is sustained, under the right kind of leadership. In McLaren's case it's taken years to build this kind of culture through the leadership team's consistency in how they've asked their people to grow and shape the new model.

Often when I'm called in to big established corporations the brief is to help them develop a cultural change that looks more like the way a leading F1 team, like McLaren, looks. They want excellent teamwork, they want to minimise ego, establish the highest standards, cultivate innovation and get everyone embracing those changes and pushing towards the same goals. This is often easier said than done. People can be set in their ways, suspicious of change, even if it's supposed to be stuff that will make their lives better. To effect this sort of root-and-branch transformation of their working culture they need a CEO, or leader, willing to embrace the new philosophy, but also someone who is able to carry their employees with them.

A few years ago I was asked to visit the headquarters of a big manufacturing company in the US to help with exactly this kind of situation. Having been the keynote speaker at their annual conference earlier in the year, where I talked in depth about the way F1 and its teams operate at such a consistently high level, the Group CEO got in touch with my office and asked if I'd be interested in working with them over a longer-term relationship. We had a series of meetings to hash out the details and I flew across the Atlantic to begin a six-month initial programme of visits to help them strive for F1-style standards.

I could immediately sense a slight air of arrogance from the CEO, something I'd picked up on previously but instead of it putting me off working with them, I tried to see it as an opportunity for improvement. Our initial conversations highlighted his own belief that he knew exactly what needed to be done, but had struggled to get staff at the company to buy into his ideas for change.

This isn't that unusual. The leader of a traditional big organisation often feels like they need to know everything, or at least be seen to know everything, in order for staff to have confidence in their leadership. It's also one of the first things I try and tackle when the situation arises.

For my initial few visits I didn't sit down with anyone other than the CEO, which frustrated him at first. He didn't believe he was part of the problem. The company was large and successful, so his shareholders and board were very happy with him and he was clearly very happy with himself. But what had become clear was that there was scope to improve further over the medium to long term with some cultural changes that had to start from the very top.

We talked about him at work, as well as him away from work; he often jokingly referred to our sessions as 'therapy', because he didn't understand why we weren't simply looking at the company and what we needed to change to be better. My goal was to understand what kind of person he was, which would determine what kind of leader he could be and for all the bravado and confidence he openly displayed in front of others, over time his personal insecurities began to show.

His need to display such outward self-belief to his staff was, somewhere deep down, the result of a lack of it. He had thousands of people looking to him for strong leadership and, in his mind, that simply meant knowing the answers to everyone's questions and showing ultimate confidence in his decisions. Behind the scenes, he definitely didn't have all the answers and like the rest of us at times doubted himself on a regular basis. Of course that's sometimes a pretty difficult thing for someone in that position to admit and come to terms with, so much so in his case that he almost fired me after a month. Apparently it was only after venting his frustration about me being a complete waste of time and money to his PA after one particular visit that she turned around and nervously told him there might just be some truth in what he'd been told.

He didn't fire me and we ended up working well together for some time. Ultimately, we had to figure out how to get that many people to buy into a change of company culture and, for me, the leadership plays a big role in that. Firstly, the people in the team need to feel some kind of allegiance to the person asking them to make changes. This company had that in some areas, but definitely not in all. Because the profile of the man in charge that everyone saw around the organisation wasn't authentic, as in he was pretending to be the person he thought they needed, rather than just being himself, flaws and all, many people saw through it. If someone suspects disingenuity in one area of someone's character, it casts doubt over all areas of it.

At McLaren, I had total confidence in Ron Dennis because there was never a moment when I didn't believe it was the true, authentic Ron on display in front of us. He 'lived' McLaren through and through and if he ever asked us to go above and beyond, we'd do it for him, knowing he was already doing it himself. That was not where my US-based CEO was at that moment in time, but that was the goal.

I asked how much time he spent 'on the shop floor', meeting with and talking to staff. Not just his senior leadership team, but the people actually making the products or dealing with customers. He eventually admitted: none. It *was* tough to do, this was a big company across more than one site, but I felt it was essential. It allows the boss to get to know their team and, just as key, it allows the team to get to know their boss.

This was something Ron Dennis wasn't so good at, but to some extent perhaps he compensated by communicating through the passion he displayed for everyone to see and by living by the virtues he expected of everyone else. We felt like we knew him.

I didn't need my CEO to personally meet every single person that worked there – it simply wasn't possible in a company that size – but he did need to meet enough, over time, that every single person that worked there began to understand the kind of guy he was. We blocked out two days a month at first in his calendar and I specifically asked him to spend the entire day without any actual agenda, no entourage around him and certainly no marketing team making a media opportunity out of it. His only job was to move around the factory floors chatting to people about anything they chose. I went with him on the first day, just to observe. It was awkward. He didn't feel comfortable doing it, he didn't know what to say, he was very much still giving off his usual, 'in command' aura and, as a result, the people he met felt just as uncomfortable.

At the end of that day we went back up to his office and I asked him how he thought it'd gone. 'Do you know how many important things I didn't do today because I was running around "speed dating" my own employees?' I chuckled.

He *was* speed dating. And just like the mistake so many people make in the romantic dating world, he'd gone in trying to present a version of himself he thought the other person wanted, or needed, to see. I reminded him that following my programme had the potential to add so many benefits to him and his business, including at some point even his all-important bottom-line numbers, and after some muttering under his breath he reluctantly agreed to give it another go.

We went back the next morning. The initial plan had been to go into another department in another facility on the second day, but I asked him to go back to the same team he'd been with on day one and try again. This time I wanted him to forget about the optics and drop his guard. I wanted him to go back and start by openly explaining to the group that when he came down yesterday he'd wanted to get to know them and for them to get to know him. But I asked him to be really honest and admit to them he'd tried too hard to give off a certain image and that image wasn't of the real man. I wanted him to be transparent and open with them. I got him to explain he'd changed plans and come back to the same team because he'd left last time without them seeing the genuine man behind the CEO title. I asked him to be vulnerable and trust that they wouldn't betray that because I knew they'd appreciate it . . . and they did. They needed to know he wasn't giving out orders or instructions; he was effectively being submissive to them and asking for a second chance.

After that initial group explanation of why he'd returned, he gradually relaxed and spent the day talking to complete strangers about how he was trying to get fit, but failing, and how his dog was sick and he'd spent last night crying with his wife about it. As he became more comfortable and saw positive responses, he even shared with one person how he struggled to find the right balance between the pressurised job of running the company and being there enough for his children. He was a different man altogether and because he was willing to open up to these people, they did the same in return. He heard about difficult family situations that made it hard to commit fully to work at times, tales of amazing lifelong bonds created on that very shop floor between workers. He also heard how some felt forgotten by the business as they'd been asking for a production machine to be updated for two years with no response. At lunchtime, instead of rushing back up to his office to eat whilst checking emails, he ate in the canteen with them and learnt and shared lots more. Even I was amazed at the difference.

That evening his demeanour was completely different. He still said to me he couldn't quite figure out how doing this would somehow turn into profit, which was all he thought his shareholders would be interested in, but he did say he'd strangely enjoyed the day.

He continued with his two days a month in different parts of the business and, when my next visit came around, he was enthusiastic about the change. He told me he'd learnt things about areas of the company, and the people within them, that he simply had no idea about before. As a result, he'd been able to help people and teams directly by giving them what he now knew they required to thrive. It was exactly what I knew would happen; I've been through exercises like this many times all over the world. What pleasantly surprised me was just how quickly the team positively responded to the new approach.

I asked him to recognise their achievements publicly, personally giving awards to those who'd stood out for something positive and celebrating them. I asked him to recognise the men and women who worked there in press releases and interviews when he gave them, but to include genuine personal stories that he'd learnt on his travels around the place. I wanted him to start asking for advice and even instruction when needed, instead of just giving it out. They were all things he found hard, but was willing to try.

Our conversations turned to why all this was important.

The mutual appreciation of the personalities in the organisation was crucial on a surface level to make it a comfortable place to have conversations about what they all needed and how best to provide it. It gave workers the confidence to ask questions, knowing the big boss wasn't the terrifying ogre they'd perhaps once thought he was. It gave the CEO an understanding of the human side of his business, appreciating that they had all kinds of strengths, but also weaknesses and lives away from work. With that understanding came empathy. With the empathy came the realisation that everyone needed, but could also offer, different things from and to the business. They could all help each other and collectively they became stronger.

The bigger picture, though, was that as the relationships became more transparent and people got to know each other from the very top to the factory floors, they felt like they were being listened to. Seeing a regular presence from the Chief Exec at ground level told them he cared enough to want to learn more about them. If they had a problem they could share it and believe it would be at least heard. Importantly though, over time, as they began to feel more like part of a team as opposed to simply anonymous worker ID numbers, light years removed from the company's senior representatives, they felt compelled to contribute more.

It broke down the perceived barriers that had previously separated upper management from everyone else and it meant people began putting ideas forward for improvement. Not just ideas that would improve their own working conditions or give them a leg up the corporate ladder, but ideas that would help the 'team' they now felt part of. The business as a whole.

This is the Holy Grail for any business, but what only the best leaders are able to create: a workforce that cares about the business and what they can do to help it succeed. For the CEO or shareholders, the motivation for a company to succeed might be an obvious financial one. The greater the profit, the greater the bonuses or dividends. For most of the staff at the company, though, they normally get paid the same amount each month whether the business is successful or not. So it's easy to see why there might not be much motivation to go above and beyond what's required in your basic job description, yet this team was now doing exactly that.

They did it because they felt like the CEO cared about them and, just like in life, we tend to reflect back the treatment we feel we get.

When we feel valued, we want to show the value we can
add. If we feel like someone has our back, we'll have theirs.
You trust me enough to give me responsibility, I won't want
to let you down.

The reality is it's not rocket science, most of this is basic human behavioural psychology, it's how we tend to operate naturally in social or family circles today. But it's often an alien concept in modern business because we've grown so accustomed to doing things the 'old school' way. Formula One, like many areas, was ahead of that curve. The unprecedented run of form for the Mercedes F1 team under the visionary leadership of Toto Wolff was testament to a team feeling supported and empowered. McLaren are on a similar journey today. They've realised that treating people better, more empathetically, recognising that they are human beings with needs and vulnerabilities, is not just the right thing to do on a personal level – it has huge benefits for every business.

Create leaders, not followers

In my American anecdote above, power was traditionally concentrated squarely in the hands of the CEO. And that was certainly the model in F1 in days gone by. Ron Dennis and other Team Principals like him wouldn't have liked the idea of ceding control to others in the organisation and, in that era, that leadership system did deliver results in many cases.

But today we go to even greater depths to maximise our chances and I've grown to believe that the job of a good leader is to help create more good leaders around them. Although this is often an easier thing to say than it is to do.

The traditional narrative around workplace culture, one that still exists in abundance today, is that you climb the corporate ladder until you get to a position of power and then you get to enjoy the benefits associated with it by sitting back and having other people do the work for you. You spend years climbing the mountain and when you get to the top you get to enjoy the view and look down on those trying to get there too. Of course, there's only enough room at the very top for a chosen lucky few, so why on earth would those at the summit be motivated to reach down and help the climbers for fear they might pull you down from your position to make room for themselves? It comes from a place of fear and insecurity that's created by the company culture itself. If the people around you are *too* good they become a potential threat and who wants that after years of working to secure the good life for yourself?

The alternative approach, the one I subscribe to, is that if you lead an excellent team of people, all performing to extraordinarily high levels, that reflects well on you as a leader. If a leader's able to harness the great attributes of the people they work with and, in doing so, help them to feel great about their contribution, it raises the motivation, the engagement and consequently the standards they're all able to achieve together.

This is the environment created by Toto Wolff at Mercedes; it's very similar at McLaren today under Zak Brown and Andrea Stella and I'm sure at other teams too.

The transition of leadership model at my old team, McLaren, over the last twenty years is nothing short of a success story in itself, bringing modern thinking at the company into the modern world of Formula One and continuously evolving it. Many of the ideas, albeit from a different sector entirely, are encapsulated in one of my favourite books on the subject. *Turn the Ship Around!*, by L. David Marquet, describes how he led a US Navy nuclear submarine in what was, at the time, a truly groundbreaking way. He talks about taking the existing, traditional model of leadership ingrained in the United States military, where leaders gave orders and everyone else often blindly followed them, and turning it on its head.

When he took over command of the USS *Santa Fe* and its poorly performing, low-morale crew, he unknowingly issued an impossible order and yet his sailors tried to follow it anyway. He quickly realised he was leading in a culture of followers and it was significantly responsible for the poor mood in a team that spent months submerged in close confines under the sea in enemy territory.

Captain Marquet's story follows the journey of realisation that what he calls the Leader-Follower model, ingrained in business tradition across the world, could have grave and dangerous consequences in the life-and-death realities of military combat. Such was the level of discipline and obedience that orders were never questioned, even when the leader made a mistake. He talks about how he took the unprecedented decision to move his crew from the traditional Leader-Follower model to an all-new Leader-Leader model.

His idea was to have leaders everywhere, in all positions. He devolved power and responsibility down the chain of command and the effect was transformative. The crew were trained and educated where needed and then empowered to take decisions without needing to go through multiple layers of traditional hierarchy and process. They implemented systems to check with crewmates that mistakes weren't being made and each member of the team was able to make a discernible difference to the way things operated. The results were fascinating.

Over my own years at McLaren I progressed through the ranks of the team into leadership positions myself and I remember feeling an enormous sense of responsibility when it first happened. I'd worked under leaders I'd respected for the way they operated, but also under those I hadn't. As with many things, being shown how not to do something is often more valuable than being shown how to do it. By learning what we don't like it leaves the route forward open to interpretation; it allows for an innovative approach if necessary and gives space to do things your own way, rather than following a prescription.

I'd worked under people who definitely led by ego. Perhaps because of the overall Leader-Follower structure at McLaren at the time, it meant that when some people finally felt like they'd broken out of the lower ranks through a promotion and found themselves with an element of control or power, it went to their head. Ego took over and they simply perpetuated the status quo.

I was determined not to let that happen. I'd started a movement within the company to try and change things because I'd seen how unhappy and unfulfilled many people were, so I knew when my time came to lead my own team, I needed to use the opportunity to put my ideas into place.

I was given the role of Number One Chief Mechanic, leading a team of technicians and mechanics across the garage. There was mixed reaction, as is often the case, because whilst many knew this would be positive, having seen the mission I was currently on with senior management to instigate change for the good of the workforce, others felt like it should've been them that got the promotion. My approach to every challenge in life is always that communication's key to solving problems, so once some time had passed I went head-on to see my detractors one by one.

Of course I understood how some might feel upset, and annoyed even, that they'd missed out on the opportunity themselves, but I wanted to help them understand that I wasn't going to be the same as the egotistical leaders they'd seen come and go for years. I was there to help them and our teammates and my new position gave me an opportunity to accelerate the work I was already doing with Ron Dennis and Martin Whitmarsh. To give them the support they wanted, I needed their help and feedback.

It took more time to convince some than others and I had to prove myself to them by backing up my words with actions in the first few weeks and months. I wanted them to come to the realisation that I was there effectively working for them, as an enabler to help them to better do their own jobs, not what they'd been used to, which would've been the opposite model of them working for me. I knew how good they all were, I'd been amongst them for years, but I also knew their frustrations as I'd shared them for a long time too. So instead of my new position of authority being a ticket to join the privileged ranks of those that went before me, I saw it as a great opportunity to help improve the things I knew were wrong.

My direct reports were given the space to get on with the jobs I knew they were very capable of doing to a high level and I became almost subservient to them, being there as a buffer helping to find solutions to challenges they didn't have time to worry about and protecting them from the bureaucracy that often slowed their progress on what we all agreed really mattered, making the car faster. I wanted them to lead me in the ways I could help them most.

Of course there were many occasions when I had to take control. Formula One's an intense and fast-paced business where the entire existence of team members is highly pressurised. Sometimes that pressure's extreme and we don't have the luxury of time to democratise decision-making, and in those situations we needed a strong leader. Over time I'd built the kind of relationship with my team where they knew that if I was abrupt and to the point, even sometimes raising my voice to make sure I was heard, it was because the moment required it. I was in the position that, on occasion, I just had to dictate what we needed to do right now because that was the fastest, most efficient way. Rarely did anyone get upset by it because for 99 per cent of the time that's not how I operated and they knew that it was what I had to do there and then. I was always open to talking about the decisions I'd made after the situation had subsided if anyone wanted to.

MARGINAL GAIN

Whatever your role as a leader in life or work, try and reframe it as a responsibility to help build and enable other great leaders around you. Share with them what you know, support them; it doesn't devalue your impact on the team but makes the team stronger, and as a leader, that's exactly what you should be aiming for. Too many people judge themselves as leaders through how indispensable they are to their team and, as a result, perpetuate that through gatekeeping. Successful leaders form teams that end up thriving long beyond their direct involvement and that should be seen as the ultimate goal. Your legacy should be defined by the people you help thrive, not their dependence upon you.

Leader-Leader is where McLaren are today and it's something I try and encourage with almost every team I work with. As a parent, I'm trying to implement a similar model with my teenage children. When they were younger, the Leader-Follower model was perhaps the only way to lead them given how little they knew about the world and how few experiences they'd had. But today, they're almost young adults and I've often found myself in the past wondering why the old approach wasn't working in the same way. I was guilty of a similar viewpoint at times to that of my US CEO friend, expecting the children to fall into line with my ideas and just follow orders to get the results I expected, but it didn't work. They began pushing back and feeling disgruntled, even becoming confident enough to challenge my authority on occasion. Of course, I now appreciate that they're evolving themselves, needing different things from me as their dad. More often now they want me to listen, rather than speak. To hear them, rather than instruct them. My role's morphing into the kind of leader that asks questions, rather than gives answers, because they want to learn through having a go themselves. They want to be given more responsibility to make their own decisions and find their own solutions to problems and I need to be OK with that. At times I need to be their leader and help guide them, but on more and more occasions now I'm able to be led by them in a variety of areas. We're transitioning into a Leader-Leader model in the Priestley household.

> The best leaders in Formula One create leaders all around them in their teams by understanding what they need and helping to provide it for them.

We all have a responsibility to take more responsibility

That Leader-Leader structure was incredibly empowering, and helped unlock qualities that many of McLaren's staff didn't know they possessed. That's partly because most people have a fundamental misunderstanding of what leadership is.

For some people it's the thing their boss does at work. It's what a prime minister or a national football team captain does. For some it's the reserve of those in charge, or those responsible for others. Very often it's something done by the people who've been around the longest and worked their way up to 'leader' status. The hierarchical nature of societies we live in and companies we work for means that many people have become conditioned to believe that the leaders are those at the top of the structure and everyone else falls into the category of being led. They think that leadership is something that *other* people do.

I believe in an ideal that's quite different.

All the things I've discussed above have helped me see that leadership qualities, or skills, are prevalent in all of us, just at different levels on an infinite scale. That scale isn't linear across all aspects of our lives either. In some of the roles we play, we might require someone else to take the dominant leadership position, because we lack experience or confidence in that field, for example. In other parts of life, we may have no choice but to step up and lead ourselves, perhaps as a parent, because others are far less equipped than we are. Some people want to lead through ego; others don't due to anxiety. Some want to share what they know; others want to learn what they don't.

The same insight has driven many of the changes to the way that modern F1 teams approach leadership. Today's McLaren no longer has one supreme leader and many followers, but leaders everywhere, in all areas. The environment's changed dramatically and it's had an equally dramatic effect on everyone in it. Responsibility's been disseminated throughout the organisation, giving empowerment to those without the term 'leader' or 'manager' necessarily in their job titles.

If you look at McLaren's 'org structure chart' today, it's much more 'horizontal' or flattened than it is 'vertical' and tall, as in days gone by. It means there's less distance between the 'top' and the 'bottom', making the leadership group appear far less removed than it was. I can imagine it means that anyone wanting to bring an idea or concern to Zak or Andrea would feel far less daunted than I did plucking up the courage to go and see Ron and Martin back in the day. But it also means there're more channels through which leadership qualities emerge.

The beauty of a team is the variance and diversity of characters it's made up of, which in turn demands a profusion of different things from their leaders. That's as it should be. But one thing we all have in common, something that I believe is deep-rooted in the human condition, is a desire to feel an element of control over the direction our lives go in. The more agency we have, the more we feel like leaders in our own working and personal lives, the better we perform.

A leadership model, like the Leader-Leader one at McLaren, at other F1 teams and now emerging in the Priestley household today, gives a sense of agency to those inside it. This cultural shift, in which job titles alone no longer identify leaders in the group, has handed power to those who might once have been expected to quietly follow orders. We all have more responsibility for the shape of our existences than ever before – it's up to us to make the most of it.

PITLANE LESSONS

- F1's biggest teams show there are lots of different ways to be a successful leader.
- You don't need the words 'leader', 'manager' or 'chief' in your job title to be any of those things.

- In an F1 team, sometimes people need to be led and at other times they need to be allowed to lead. A good leader facilitates both.
- The best leaders in Formula One create leaders all around them in their teams by understanding what they need and helping to provide it for them.
- Great leaders build teams that sustain success long after they've moved on, not ones that are entirely dependent on them being there.

10.

YOU CAN DO MORE WITH LESS
How to Make the Most of Limited Resources

Back when I first joined McLaren in the early 2000s, the amounts of money floating around the sport would make your eyes water. Top teams sponsored by cigarette brands were spending over $400 million just to get through a single season of F1 racing. We flew in private planes, stayed in the finest hotels and had some incredible parties. We literally hired out the entirety of London's Royal Albert Hall one year for our team Christmas bash!

If a team like ours had a potential championship at stake and that season's 'war chest' ran low, we'd just go to our tobacco partner and ask for more. If they wanted to be associated with the best team in the world, they'd come up with extra cash for us. At McLaren, whilst we were in a perennial fight for the ultimate status of being World Champions, our German cigarette sponsor, 'West' at the time, was in its own version of the same intense battle each year trying to topple Ferrari's Marlboro from their perch. Having their name on the winning car was a good way to help that cause.

So it's fair to say that back then, more often than not, the biggest teams had more money than they could dream up ways to spend. But here's the thing: having fantasy-like budgets is not always a guarantee of success. You can have all the money in the world, but if you don't spend it wisely you're unlikely to get the right outcomes.

When Toyota, one of the world's biggest conglomerates and car manufacturers, came into Formula One in 2002, they did so with one of the biggest budgets in the sport, more than $440m for the year. They had high hopes of success on track, which in turn they hoped would translate into selling more road cars to the public (as the old adage goes: 'Win on Sunday, sell on Monday'). So throwing astronomical sums at the project was justified as a sound commercial strategy for the wider company.

Unfortunately for them, it didn't quite work out that way. They scored just two points throughout their entire first season and generally struggled in the years that followed. By the time they decided to finally pull the plug and withdraw from F1 seven years later in 2009, they'd spent billions of dollars, yet never won even a single Grand Prix.

At least part of the problem, which wasn't wholly dissimilar to the experience of Ford's well-funded factory attempt to enter F1 through their Jaguar brand in 2000, was that they came into a specialised elite sport believing they could operate their small, dynamic F1 teams like they operated their giant, slow-moving car companies.

Both hugely successful in their own rights in the wider automotive world, they knew how to run massive global corporations and sell vehicles at scale. Their management structures and governance frameworks, which determined how they ended up spending their resources, were quite different to the majority of F1 teams and this hurt them. At the end of 2004, also still without any wins, Ford decided to sell up and leave the sport. The American giant of the global automotive industry sold their struggling team to an innovative energy drinks company . . . Red Bull . . . and as F1 fans will know, the wins eventually came.

Money is important, then; in fact, it's essential, but it has to be used in the right way.

In today's Formula One, the regulations now stipulate a 'budget cap' that's way below that of those hedonistic days of old that I walked into as a young mechanic. The idea is to prevent annual spending from getting out of control and to protect the teams and companies involved from their own competitive obsessions. It's an attempt to make the industry more sustainable and also a way of allowing smaller teams to be able to compete on a more level playing field with their larger, more established competitors. So whereas in days gone by the question was 'How do we make the budget as big as possible?', now teams are asking themselves 'How do we get the most out of the budget we have?'

These changes in F1's financing will almost certainly help secure a better long-term future for the sport. But money's just one of the multiple resources that F1 teams need, firstly to survive, but then of course to generate success by maximising their effectiveness. Everything from the best people to engineering equipment and facilities, strategic and technology partnerships and lots between. It all matters. The same's true for the rest of us. We all have limited quantities of time, money and energy, but the difference between us and an F1 team is that we don't always think about how we can deploy them most efficiently.

In this chapter I'll explore the methodology of how F1 teams deploy their now limited resources to maximise performance and how we can all think about the resources in our own lives in a similar way. At McLaren, or any F1 team, we never wanted to be left with any regrets about the way we used our resources when the chequered flag waved, and I want the same to be true for you at the end of your own race.

Establish your priorities

The modern cost-capped era of Formula One has forced a lot of the big teams to come to terms with the idea of building an existence within the means available. Because they can't spend more than the rules allow them to, they've been pushed to develop new budgeting and efficiency skills as a result.

The teams now take the decisions about where to place resources to achieve the biggest impact very seriously. Like everything else they do, there's science behind each decision. Advanced simulation tools and machine learning systems, or AI, have been in F1 for decades, but today much of the focus is on working out the most efficient use of a team's budget. Running multiple simulations on different ways to commit financial resources to technical developments across a season, for example, can be a quicker way of getting to the right answer than simply trying them all out in the real world.

(Note that efficient isn't always the same as cheap. A team will spend considerable sums on developing these types of programmes, money which might otherwise be spent on the car itself, but the efficiency they *lead* to makes them a must-have, albeit often expensive, tool.)

We may not all have access to these kinds of systems to help us in quite the same way, although advances in the consumer AI tools available are accelerating weekly at Formula One-like pace. But the principle of efficiency is a good general baseline to work from.

For me, being efficient with money, or anything else, brings an enormous sense of satisfaction. If I manage to achieve something without excessive wastage, it makes me feel good, but in turn also frees up more resources to apply to something else, the next-level priority.

The idea of efficient spending means thinking differently about how decisions are made. It means not opening your wallet immediately, but pausing and trying to think in a bigger way about the problem, or problems, you're trying to solve with the money you have. This leads, inevitably, to a consideration of priorities.

Almost everything a Formula One team does is assessed and then executed through a lens of 'performance'. This is their number-one priority. Of course the performance of the car is the obvious assumption to make, but to an F1 team today the word refers to their operations as a whole. Every person, department, piece of technology and the company itself has their performance measured and analysed to see how it fits into the bigger picture.

If they're deciding whether or not to invest in an expensive new piece of manufacturing equipment for the factory, one of the first questions will be 'Is it going to contribute to, or detract from, our performance?'

A state-of-the-art piece of equipment is likely to be 'better' than whatever the factory currently has, so if you're an engineer or designer who'd directly benefit from buying it, then you'll undoubtedly believe it would improve performance. But what if the new machine will take up space currently used by another department? Or perhaps the cost of the new equipment's so great that it can only be afforded by pulling money from another part of the team's budget?

With multiple perspectives at play, the question no longer seems simple. In order to make the right decision, the team has to zoom out and consider the big picture. Years ago, the solution might have involved trying to convince a sponsor to buy the equipment. Now, with every team operating under stringent restraints, and where efficiency's king, they need to think hard about whether the overall impact on performance justifies the expenditure.

The same principles apply whether the team's hiring new personnel, redecorating the company restaurant, making travel arrangements, cleaning the floors, or designing the team's clothing. Do you design a team uniform so it looks great on TV, or is it more important to consider how it feels and functions in the environments in which it needs to be used? If a sponsor's logo doesn't stand out to the hundreds of millions of viewers watching, they're not likely to be happy. That could impact whether they renew contracts or how much value they perceive they're getting and therefore how much they're willing to pay for the exposure. Which in turn would have a direct effect on the ability of a team to perform at the highest level. But the same could be said if the members of that team are all overheating or uncomfortable in the impractical clothing the team provided for the season . . . believe me, I can speak from experience on this one. The team doesn't have unlimited time, money or energy, so it has to measure the trade-offs of every decision against each other as they assess what will offer the greatest benefit to the team's ultimate performance.

Many of our own decisions around deploying resources in our lives can be helped by thinking along similar lines. But whilst F1 teams use 'performance' as the key metric to help them decide what they prioritise most in their businesses, it's possible you might want to focus on something else.

Because what we prioritise in life is rarely a fixed thing. My thinking on this has been greatly impacted by the ideas contained in *Finite and Infinite Games*, by James Carse, which were further developed in an article by Nam Nguyen. (This is something else I learnt from F1: be a magpie. When you're in a race to get the edge over your competition, you need to take inspiration from wherever you can.)

Carse would categorise Formula One as a 'finite game' with fixed rules and players, and an end-point at which we hope to be crowned winners; it is a relatively controlled environment and so in that context it makes sense to prioritise 'performance'. Whereas our own personal goals change on a constant basis. We play in what Carse would call the 'infinite game' of life, where the boundaries aren't fixed in the same way; the moment never comes when we can say we have 'won'. Rather, the aim is generally to stay in the game for as long as possible. And within that larger framework, we of course play myriad other 'games' too, which means it doesn't make sense to prioritise only one thing all the way through. At times it might be your career, or relationships; at others it could be experimentation, fun and beyond.

When tackling a tough decision about how much or where to spend our money, for example, determining the game we're competing in is a good place to start. What do we need to optimise for and therefore what should our priorities be? It could be 'performance', but it could be 'happiness', or 'longevity', or anything else. Are the goals long or short term, or somewhere in between? For some people, spending a few pounds on fast food might optimise for short-term satisfaction, but comes at a cost to medium-term health and fitness. Either might end up being the basis of a correct decision – it just depends on what you prioritise highest at the time. Using the first-principle reasoning techniques we discussed earlier here might be an effective way to come to some conclusions.

Build a flexible strategy

Once we have some sort of order for our priorities, we then need a strategy around which we can execute our actions. Strategy's the way we get from where we are now to where we want to be: it's a plan of actions and behaviours that help us to achieve something. So to figure out a decent strategy, we need to know what we're aiming at.

What you ultimately want is to come up with a plan, or budget, for achieving the things you need, want and would like to accomplish.

So, for instance, when it comes to our finances, there'll be longer-term priorities, like saving up for a house deposit or to buy a car perhaps, that need be balanced with every day and medium-term priorities. Having a strategy allows you to do this.

There are a number of basic ideas for modelling a financial plan. I know many people who work off a 50-20-30 strategy. In that case 50 per cent of their monthly after-tax income is spent on the things they need, like keeping up with the mortgage or rent, buying food and paying bills, etc. Twenty per cent is put into savings for the longer term and the remaining 30 per cent is there to be spent on things they don't necessarily need, but that they want. It's for enjoying life, having fun and doing whatever helps them to feel good on any given month. It can be a pretty good starting point and works well for lots of people, but feel free to adjust the numbers to fit your own situation.

And yet, having created that strategy, you also need to be ready and willing to change it.

One of the things I've learnt through my time in F1 is that flexibility's key in almost every area. Creating a meticulous strategy, then sticking blindly to it, won't win you a Grand

Prix when all of a sudden you get a puncture and have to make an unscheduled pitstop. You need to be adaptable to what's going on around you at the time.

The same applies to F1 budgets. You might start the season with a set portion of the team's annual budget designated for technical upgrades to develop the car as the season goes on. That would typically allow for a number of staged introductions, often designated at key strategic races, of iterative advances in performance parts like aerodynamics. No one can afford to bring major upgrades to every race any more, so it has to be planned out over the season.

Another lump of the budget pot might be set aside for the inevitable crash damage that'll occur over the course of a long, hard-fought championship. (Though this proportion might be increased if you've a young rookie who is likely to crash more, or reduced if you're a front-running team whose drivers are less likely to get caught up in the busy and often messy mid-field pack.)

It's here that luck, or lack of it, can play a big part in what happens next. If after ten races there've been a few occasions when other drivers have crashed into your cars, or your drivers have hit the walls themselves, or parts on the car have failed, causing damage, the repair bills might be way higher than first predicted. With more than half a season left to go, you might need to adapt your financial strategy to cover the extra damage bills coming in. You might have to look at the other 'pots' and rethink your projections. Again, it comes back to priorities. Back at the beginning of the season, there was probably a lot more focus on pushing performance. But now, with your spares stock depleted, the priority might be simply to ensure you have enough parts to go racing. So perhaps some of the money that was originally supposed to cover technical upgrades needs to be reallocated to help cover repairs. The financial split or model now looks quite different.

Of course, if there's been almost no damage in those first ten races, the team might find themselves in the unexpectedly lucky position of being able to send money in the other direction within their budgetary plan and bring more performance upgrades to the track as a result.

In my own life I try to think about things in a similar way. Having a plan helps me to feel a sense of order and control when it comes to money; I ideally never want to feel as if *it's* controlling *me*. But that plan absolutely needs to be flexible. Whatever the changes to my situation, I try to always remember to consider the big-picture view. My short-term goals might therefore take a temporary hit in order to accommodate something that's become more important to me at the time. I recently started a new business with my wife and because it quickly became a top priority in our lives and took some investment, we chose to shelve short-term plans for a long-awaited holiday whilst we got it off the ground. We had to move resources from something that we'd have liked to be able to do, into something we saw as more important in the bigger picture.

Every time I need to make a decision I work out what I need to prioritise. If I focus on getting that right, the decision becomes easier to make. The new priority might be completely different from the one I identified when initially coming up with the budget or plan, but because I've accepted that priorities are fluid things, forever in flux (like race strategies), I can square off the U-turn in my own mind and sleep comfortably at night.

Time is precious, so use it wisely

Money is, of course, just one of the resources we have at our disposal when playing in the 'games' of life, sport, business and beyond. Many of us think of it as, and certainly behave as if it is, our most precious and valuable resource.

But it's not, not by a long shot. The most valuable things in life are generally the scarcest and most limited and money isn't either of those things, even if most of us will have had times when we felt like that was the case. It's not always easy, but it is always possible, for us to make more money.

Instead, the most valuable resources are the ones we can't create more of. Being efficient with them should be amongst our highest priorities.

The most obvious is time. Each day's limited to twenty-four hours, each year to 365 days and each of us has a limited number of both. No matter how we live, or how much money we have to deploy, we can never change that, making it by far the most precious resource we will ever have. None of us can escape the fact we only have a relatively short period of existence here with which to do whatever we want, before we one day disappear forever. The clock is ticking. As such, you'd think we'd all be super careful and meticulous about how we spend our time, but in fact the opposite is often true.

In Bronnie Ware's thought-provoking book *The Top Five Regrets of the Dying*, she talks about how, having spent years supporting and caring for terminally ill patients in the last three to twelve weeks of their lives, she began asking them if they had any regrets. Almost all were somehow related to not making the most of the time they had. Every single one of the male patients the author asked, and many of the women too, regretted spending too much time working and not enough with loved ones, and when I first read this a few years ago it had a sizeable effect on my own mentality. I'm lucky enough to love how I earn a living, I almost always have, but if I'm honest with myself, my near ten years working for an F1 team took up ninety-something per cent of my time during that period, when I had a family at home that deserved more than whatever was left. Today, I still love the various roles I have, running my own businesses and helping other people to run theirs. Presenting TV shows, commentating on, speaking about, or writing books on the subject of F1 brings me so much joy, excitement and fulfilment, but by far my most important role is as a husband and father and it always comes first. It doesn't mean I can't still do the things I love to do, which help pay the bills and give us the freedom to make choices in our lives, but I now weigh up the cost of doing them much more consciously and carefully.

Earning a living almost always comes at some sort of cost to us and often to those around us too. We literally trade our most valuable resource of time for money. The fact that I need to travel for many of my roles inevitably means I'm away from my family and that can be hard. So now, instead of just immediately saying yes, even if I'd really love to take the job on offer, my wife and I try and have an open discussion about whether it's actually worth it to us as a family or not. There're a couple of ways to look at it. Obviously having enough money means you might have more options on how much you need to, or want to, work. But whether or not you have 'enough' money is also often a question you can ponder.

The very idea of whether spending time on something's worth it or not is perhaps the key question to ask, and hopefully answer, when deciding how to 'budget' the precious and limited time we have.

It's not always the easiest one to answer though. In exactly the same way I described an F1 team weighing up the different competing opinions within the organisation of how best to spend their budget, the same challenges apply to our time. Once again it comes down to having a set of clear priorities and optimising in line with them – only with this, the consequences of getting it wrong can be profound.

F1 teams are very good at being efficient with time in the short term. After all, the entire business is literally about trying to save time without compromising quality. We want the fastest lap times, the shortest overall race times and to complete pitstops in under two seconds. We have to be very clear about what we want to achieve and how we're going to do it as quickly as possible. Of course that's because we're optimising for speed in those scenarios. Everything's geared towards our number-one priority.

But not everything in F1 has to operate at 200 miles per hour. A Grand Prix weekend, for example, runs on a very strict timetable that everyone has to adhere to. International broadcasters in almost every territory and country across the world build schedules around it and the teams themselves strategically use the time they have within it to maximise their results.

When I worked for the team, my weekends were run to an almost unbelievable level of efficiency. The days were governed by immovable deadlines, such as getting the cars prepared for scrutineering to ensure they complied with technical rules, conducting our pitstop practices in the pitlane's specific available window of quiet time and of course making sure the cars were ready to roll out of the garage when the sessions started. There is no movement in the race weekend timetable. They won't delay the Grand Prix if you're not ready. But within those deadlines, just like in our own lives, we had total freedom to decide how best to use the available time we had.

If you're already beginning to think like an F1 team you'll

have guessed that we break everything down into its smallest possible parts and see how we can get the best out of each of them. Time's no different. We look at the competing requests for time, then make decisions about where to allocate those precious resources.

For example, there is a two-and-a-half-hour fixed gap between the end of FP3, the third and final practice session on Saturday morning, and qualifying on Saturday afternoon. In theory, there is a huge amount that *could* be done. Even assuming that nothing's gone wrong and the car's in one piece, the mechanics need to go through a whole bunch of time-consuming procedures to ensure it's ready and prepped for Q1. Most of those are safety and legality checks.

But as engineers, we of course want to try and improve the car too. So, after debriefing the driver and looking through data, we decide which, if any, changes we can make to improve the way it performs. (Long before we get into the competitive season we've already practised making all of the possible mechanical changes to the car's set-up and configuration, and would know how long it takes to do each task.)

The tyres we intend to use for qualifying, plus all the spares, need to be put on heat in the electric tyre-warming blankets at the back of the garage hours before they're required on the car to ensure they're up to the very specific temperatures needed. There'll be strategy and engineering meetings that have to happen, engines and gearboxes that need pre-heating, fuel to prepare and deliver into the car, pitstop equipment that needs checking and setting up, media and sponsor commitments and myriad other things too.

Every one of these is super important to someone in the team. How do we decide which of these things we've got time to do?

Each activity has to be graded in terms of importance to the task in hand and then prioritised as such. Time is apportioned based on how mission-critical each task is. Not dissimilar to the way we looked at personal finance earlier, we end up with 'needs', 'wants' and then, if there's time left over, the 'nice-to-haves'. The car simply 'needs' to be ready to roll out of the garage when the pitlane opens for qualifying, or we fail spectacularly and start the race at the back of the grid.

We desperately 'want' to make it as quick as possible to get the best grid slot we can and help our chances on Sunday. It might be 'nice' to be able to get out of the garage early to get to the end of the pitlane first so we can get out on a clear track before it gets busy with traffic. In that basic example the first two scenarios take precedence over the third and therefore the available time is dished out accordingly.

Most of us will face similar dilemmas when it comes to short-term time management, even if we don't think about it in such a structured way. We're all faced with competing demands on our time. A problem that's exacerbated by the fact that the powerful technology in the palm of our hands is literally designed to steal our attention and, therefore, our time away from us. It's also incredibly clever about how it does it without us even realising, tapping into scientifically grounded psychological and emotional cues which prompt us into making automatic decisions. So if technology companies are hijacking our most precious commodity and dramatically affecting how we feel, how do we take that control back?

Here, too, it all comes back to understanding priorities. If we want to maximise our own time, we can do so by deciding first what we want to optimise for, or what we'd like to achieve, and then strategising around it. If we know we're susceptible to distraction, and we all are by the way, and if avoiding that's important to us on a particular day, then we can plan around it. Look at what you absolutely *need* to get done and decide how long you need to dedicate to that – even specify the time slots in your day if that helps to keep things on track. This list will include non-negotiables like eating, sleeping and work, etc. Then look at the things you *want* to achieve, the things you'd be proud of yourself for getting done at the end of the day, and do the same for them. That might be things like going to the gym, calling your parents, tidying the house. Those are your two biggest priority groups and so probably need the most time dedicated to them to be able to do a good job. After that you have whatever time's left to use in whichever way you choose. These are often the spells when most people get lost in distractions because they don't have a clear goal in mind. There's nothing wrong with scrolling social media or getting lost down a YouTube rabbit hole, as long as it isn't distracting you from a higher-ranked priority in your day, but for many of us that's exactly what it does do and that's where lots of regrets emerge from. You might decide to build some 'scrolling' time into your schedule as part of your relaxation and as long as you stick to the period you've allowed for it, it might be valuable, but the apps we open are all there waiting to pounce on the slightest weakness, so being aware of it can really help to avoid succumbing.

MARGINAL GAIN

It might sound extreme, or even a bit prescriptive and corporate, but if you are struggling to avoid distractions in your day and as a result feeling down, techniques for scheduling your time could help. In the same way an F1 team works to detailed timetables as a measure of progress and productivity, we can do the same. Often called time-blocking, splitting your day into hourly or half-hourly chunks can be really useful for some people.

(The people in an F1 team, operating in the way I described earlier, making the very best use of time to achieve their goals over a race weekend, all have phones with them like you and me. The social media firms aren't stealing their time away from them in between practice and qualifying on a Saturday because they have a very clear mission, with high-priority status, that's competing for, and winning, their time. The same probably applies to many situations you find yourself in, where you're engrossed in something important to you in that moment, so there's never even a consideration of looking at your phone or becoming distracted. You might describe yourself as being 'busy', but in truth it's just another thing you've decided is more important to you and therefore worthy of your time.)

There're many variants of this, but the basic premise is that before your day starts you look at the things you need to achieve and prioritise them. Once that's done, you allocate the amount of time, or number of time blocks, on your schedule that you think each one justifies. It's essentially what the Formula One weekend timetable does for the teams. It's also what happens in schools. When we have a formatted day, dedicated to achieving certain things at certain times, we're much more likely to stick to it than if we're just left to our own devices. If you are struggling, my advice would be to turn off all phone notifications and build in a time slot for checking emails, messages and social media if you need to. Make sure you build in breaks too.

Doing this gives some structure and order to your day. I've also often found it can really help with motivation in the same way that physically ticking one job off a list can psychologically help to push you on to do the next one. The great thing is that the very device in our pockets that can so easily distract us from getting things done can also be a useful tool in being more productive with our time. The most popular calendar apps from Google, Apple and others are all designed with time blocking as a very simple-to-use functionality. Give it a try.

Boundaries work – use them

The other benefit of time-blocking is that it prevents what's often called Parkinson's Law from taking effect.

This states that work will always expand to fill the time available for its completion, so if the timeframe's open-ended, the work, or distraction, never stops. I remember a very clear example of it when I was working for the team.

Back in the day, Friday nights at the track were long. We'd had two practice sessions and then the cars needed almost completely stripping down, checking, rebuilding and replenishing with new engines and gearboxes. Then there was a full weight balance and geometric set-up to be done on the suspension, including any changes we wanted to make to improve the car for the next day. After all of that, we had to push the car down to the FIA official weighing scales and flat patch, join what was sometimes a long queue of cars waiting to do the same thing, and check it all again for legality. By the time the covers went onto the cars and we finally left the circuit for the hotel it could easily be 2am, sometimes much later. It wasn't unheard of to not actually make it back to the hotel and work straight through to the following day.

Then in 2010 the sport announced it'd be introducing a paddock 'curfew' to prevent this from happening – it clearly presented safety issues for everyone involved in operating cars that carried a driver at well over 200mph.

The new 'curfew' rules meant that everyone had to be out of the garages and paddock by midnight and weren't allowed back in for at least six hours to ensure they had the chance to get some sleep. We still had the same amount of work to do, nothing changed with the cars or the amount of running they did, and yet somehow every team managed to complete everything they needed to and get out by midnight. Today the time by which teams need to evacuate the paddock is even earlier and yet cars don't grind to a halt or fall apart on track, which was always the original concern against implementing it. F1 teams just work to the time blocks they have available, still to the same exacting standards, but the mindset changes when there's a boundary in place to work up to. They became more efficient in budgeting their time because they had to. I almost guarantee that whilst you might say there's no way you have time to learn a new language or start a fitness regime, I could find fifteen minutes a day just by looking through the screen-time analytics on your phone. The truth is we could probably all find much more than that if we're honest about our priorities. The reason you don't do those things is because they're not important enough to you and not having enough time is an excuse you're making to yourself and others. That might sound harsh, but it's highly likely to be true for many people. If you genuinely made them a priority, time-blocked and added fifteen or thirty minutes to the beginning or end of your working day for learning or fitness, you'd find a way to achieve them because they'd suddenly become important enough and you'd have a boundary to work up to. F1 teams had to become even more efficient with time, and/or prioritise the most important tasks to fill the new time boundaries they faced after the introduction of the curfew rules. You can do the same.

How race strategy can help you plan your life

As we get older, the desire to use our time more efficiently grows more urgent.

When we're young we find it harder to look very far into the future. Middle and old age seem so far away we can't even imagine them, and so we tend to live much more like there's no tomorrow. We're happy to use all our time for something we want now, rather than delay it with a view to revisiting it at a later date. We work crazy hours trying to get rich, then spend it, and we party hard trying to have fun, then feel terrible, all of which may well affect our long-term health, wealth and happiness. I did all of this myself and loved it. I wouldn't change a thing.

> Our twenties are supposed to be fun; they build characters and relationships, they give us incredible experiences we might only be able to have to the same extent when we're in that sprightly, energetic period. I highly recommend going for it!

My only advice here would be the same as a young racing driver gets when heading out for the first Grand Prix of what they hope will be a long career. Enjoy it.

But the moment will always come when we need to put the valuable lessons we've learnt into practice and start thinking about longer-term time management. This is especially true when it comes to two other really valuable resources, energy and health, which often go hand in hand. Energy and health are hugely important to us for making the most of our lives, not least because losing them can literally bring our entire journey and all the time we once had to an abrupt and permanent end. And also because they become apparently ever more valuable as the years roll on.

The first law of thermodynamics states that whilst universal energy can neither be created nor destroyed, it *can* change form or be transferred from one place to another. For us, that's crucial. We may not be able to *create* more energy, but we can harness what's already there in the universe to help us achieve what we want to achieve. Staying fit and healthy, both physically and mentally, eating well, getting enough good-quality sleep and recovery, and any number of other measures that work for us, can all increase our ability to harness energy we can then deploy for personal gain.

For most people, just living a long life isn't enough; we want to be healthy and happy enough to make good use of those extra years. Reaching ninety, but being bedridden for the final decade, doesn't seem like much fun to me.

One way of avoiding this is to try to think about the big picture of your life, or any of the smaller challenges you face along the way, in the context of how an F1 team manages their people, drivers and cars over a gruelling race distance. Emulating an F1 team's race strategy can really help give perspective.

Let's take the idea of a human lifetime as an example. If we imagine the years we might have, let's say eighty for argument's sake, and think of them as laps of our own Grand Prix, we can break it down into phases like we do in F1. The goal might be to get to the end having used up everything we have in the best way possible, achieving all we want to along the way. In F1 we use up fuel, hybrid electrical energy, tyres and the driver's stamina to get maximum performance from our package whilst making sure we don't run out of those things before the race is over. In life we use up our own expendable resources to maximise the journey whilst also trying to make sure we don't use everything up too soon.

So we could never run an F1 race on a Sunday in the way we run a qualifying lap on a Saturday. It's the same car, driver and team, but optimised for something very different. In qualifying the focus is all about ultimate one-lap pace; nothing else matters. We want the fastest lap time possible and we're willing to deplete everything we have to achieve it. Drivers take all of the grip from the tyres over that one important lap; past the finish line they're good for nothing much beyond the Pirelli recycling heap. Energy Stores, or the car's hybrid batteries, are full at the beginning of the lap and completely empty at the end of it, having increased the power unit performance. The drivers take risks because the whole game's just about that ninety seconds or so; so they push with everything they have.

On Sunday, it's a different game altogether. We spend much of the weekend, and especially Saturday night, formulating a series of plans to get from our position on the grid to the chequered flag at the end of the race as quickly as possible. If we approached the race in the way we did qualifying, not only would we likely not make it to the end, but we'd actually compromise our performance. It requires a very different way of driving, with patience and restraint. The drivers all know we rarely win a Grand Prix at the first corner of the first lap, but we can easily lose it then, so they manage risk very differently.

Tyres need to be preserved long enough that we can make our pitstops at the optimum times. The same applies to electrical energy use. We need to spend some time harvesting energy under braking, in the same way your electric or hybrid road car does, even though it's actually slower for lap time, so we can deploy it to either defend or attack later in the race. If we do decide to use a lot of it because we're in a tough fight for position, we might be compromised on the next lap and have to fall back into a slower, energy-harvesting mode for longer. Knowing when to push and when to hold back's an important part of executing a good race and we have to think about driving to manage fuel usage with this mindset too. If we run out of that, it really is game over.

The idea is that it's only when we reach the chequered flag, having completed *every* lap, that the battery and fuel tank are pretty much empty, the tyres we're on have yielded all the life they had and the driver's got not much more than just enough mental and physical energy to climb out of the car and lift a trophy in the air.

I imagine you can see where I'm going with this. Think about your life, or even your business, in the context I've just described. Where in a hypothetical Grand Prix weekend are you?

When I ask big organisations this question, they often reach surprising answers. They might think they're in a tyre- and fuel-saving phase of their 'race', plodding along cautiously to preserve resources, but a bit of honest assessment reveals there's an opportunity to move forward by increasing risk and pushing on whilst competitors are easing off. It works the other way too. If a business is going flat out, giving it everything, it's worth questioning if that's actually the right thing to be doing at that time. Is there a potentially big opportunity on the horizon, like the AI revolution for example, which might be so valuable it's worth backing off a bit and preserving energy and preparing, so you can strike when the time comes?

We can do exactly the same thing in our personal lives. Are we on a qualifying lap, perhaps building a career or business, where all that matters in the short term is going hard to get everything we can out of the time and energy we have and not worrying about what's left over afterwards? Like in F1 qualifying, that might be exactly the correct strategy if that's what's most important to you at the time. Acknowledging this, or even documenting this somewhere like a journal, can help absolve feelings of self-doubt that often creep in.

Asking the same kind of question on a daily basis is also interesting. Which kind of day is today? You could look at each day as if it were a Grand Prix, managing how you spend your time and energy to be able to get to the end having achieved your targets.

It's all about spending what you have in the way that's going to benefit you most in the timeframe you're focusing on. When is the best time to take a pitstop?

As always, there's a balance between formulating plans in advance and responding to events. F1 teams prepare a number of strategies, or plans, for race day, trying to cover as many scenarios as they might expect to happen, but they always remain flexible and adaptable to cope with the unexpected too.

If an F1 driver knows at the start of a race their tyres need to last them twenty laps until their first planned pitstop, they can't go flat out for the whole twenty laps. They need to spend that tyre life wisely, looking after them by driving more cautiously when they're not under threat from a car behind. But if they're forced to use up more of the tyre's performance early on – perhaps by fending off a challenge from another driver – then they need to adjust the way they drive later in the stint to get to the end in good shape. For me, it's a great metaphor for life and the various tools we have to play with.

The importance of budgeting our resources is rarely, if ever, taught in schools, which feels like a missed opportunity – especially at a time when the lessons of having used up our planet's most valuable and irreplaceable assets so profligately are only just being learnt.

But it's useful for us all to understand that budgeting our resources is not about being boring or metronomic, simply spreading them out evenly over the time we have. An F1 driver doesn't settle into the same middle-of-the-road average lap time for every lap of the Grand Prix. Rather, there'll be times in our lives when we absolutely should be going flat out and giving it everything, even though it might be risky, because what we want most at that time requires it. At other times it's OK to want to take it easy, to disconnect from the social and societal pressures and just slow down and recover or prepare to go again when the time's right.

Similarly, learning the way money works in the world and what value it actually has to us is also important. The number on the face of a banknote means very different things to different people and even varies significantly at different times in our lives. Even the relatively affluent teams in F1 have had to re-evaluate what their now limited financial resources mean to them in the context of their overall performance. They've been forced to think more strategically about how they spend what they have, which I believe is a great lesson for us all, no matter how wealthy our bank accounts and assets suggest we are.

So make sure you're clear on the priorities for each stint of your race. Formulate a strategy to get to the end in the best shape possible. Be flexible on that strategy. Take the pitstops you need; avoid the ones you don't. The resources you have are amazing – you're lucky to have them. Budget and deploy them wisely to achieve whatever you want. The laps will tick away quickly, but when you finally get to the chequered flag, whatever regrets you have about the way you ran your race, don't regret the way you spent your time.

PITLANE LESSONS

- Money isn't the key to success or happiness, even in F1; learning how best to deploy what you have is.
- Come up with a plan, or budget, for achieving the things you need, want and would like to accomplish.
- Have you got your resources in the right order of priority?
- Think about spending the precious resources you have like an F1 team thinks about its own resources at different times in a race weekend to maximise performance.
- When the chequered flag's waving, don't regret how you spent your time.

11.

YOU CAN USE STORIES ABOUT YOUR PAST TO HELP SHAPE YOUR FUTURE
How to Harness the Power of Legacy

When I first arrived at McLaren as a young, bright-eyed and starstruck twenty-two-year-old, I of course knew who McLaren were. I was aware of those famous red and white Marlboro cars of the past, but much more front and centre was my recent experience of watching the black, grey and white 'West' liveries of recent years on television. The team had the World Champion's number '1' on the car when I got there, with Mika Häkkinen having won the drivers' title for the previous two years and, alongside Ferrari, McLaren were one of the two most prominent forces in the sport's history. But I was young and history, in F1 or otherwise, wasn't a major topic of interest for me. I loved the modern cars, the technology, the drivers of today and the storylines playing out now. I knew the names of most of the sport's greats of years gone by, but certainly didn't really know much else.

My early years at the team didn't really change my perception of any of that. We were so busy, engrossed in the day-to-day, travelling and fighting for more World Championship success: it was all-consuming. I'd joined a technology company that was all about innovation, progression and science. The past was gone; this was all about the future. We worked in an industrial estate in Woking in the UK, nothing that impressive from the outside, but super clean, smart and modern once you walked through the dark glass front doors. The team had been there for years and when I turned up for the very first time for my initial job interview, I was blown away at just how cool and futuristic it was.

As I slotted into my new dream-come-true role as a Number Two Test Team Mechanic and got to know more and more people, I found a fascinating mix of characters at the company. I discovered a group of older guys at the team, spread out across a number of different factory-based roles, who'd been there for many years, decades even, some of them. They'd been track-side in the days of Ayrton Senna and Alain Prost and stayed in the company ever since. The younger majority referred to them as the 'dinosaurs', or 'heritage department' and although some had gained respect after years of service, it felt like they were often jokingly denigrated for being old and slow in amongst the new dynamic, bright, young workforce. Of course it was all part of the 'banter' amongst the lads, but it felt harsh at times.

The factory itself was astonishingly well equipped compared to anything I'd ever seen before coming up through the junior categories of racing, but there was definitely a feeling that we were running out of space as the team continually grew. McLaren had already swallowed up most of the industrial estate on which we were based over the years, as well as keeping hold of the previous factory building down the road to use as an extra storage facility.

A couple of years into my tenure, Ron Dennis made the bodacious announcement that he intended for us to move to a new purpose-designed and -built facility in serene countryside surroundings a few miles up the road. Just a couple of years later we moved into the facility that became known as the McLaren Technology Centre, or MTC. It was breathtaking. It still is today, more than twenty years later. It looked like a spaceship from a movie. Futuristic, science-fiction-like, innovative, beautiful.

The new building was the very essence of modernity, from the way the integrated lake was used as a clever and energy-efficient cooling system for the state-of-the-art wind tunnel, to the next-generation equipment and facilities packed inside its artistically sculpted form. But it was also McLaren's first-ever permanent, self-designed and -built home. It brought the Formula One team, with all of its departments and people, along with McLaren's blossoming automotive supercar business and their other subsidiary companies, together under one solar-powered roof for the first time. That new-found sense of connection gave us all a much bigger appreciation of who we were.

On one hand we could see the scale of McLaren's operations and that certainly took me by surprise. I'd been so seduced by the glamour and excitement of being on the race team that for a long time I'd thought that the world began and ended with us. It was sometimes easy to slip into the delusion that it was us and us only that won races. But it was now abundantly clear that those victories were won through the efforts of everyone in that building and that, of course, it had always been that way.

With the appreciation of just how many people were involved, and how big an operation McLaren really was, came an acknowledgement of where all this had come from. When Bruce McLaren Motor Racing Ltd was founded back in 1963, I later discovered, it was from a small dirt-floored shed. I've heard it described as the motor racing equivalent of the biblical stable. From those incredibly humble and basic beginnings came this behemoth of the future in which we all now resided, MTC. That story alone was remarkable, and yet many people, including me, didn't know much about it. Perhaps that's why one of the first things Ron did was to use some of our new space to display a line-up of cars from the team's history. On the new MTC Boulevard in front of the enormous glass wall looking out onto the lake and manicured grounds we had the first racing car that Bruce McLaren ever built with his father at thirteen years of age. It was a small, red, unassuming 1929 Austin 7 Ulster, which today looks like a toy car in comparison with what we're all familiar with. A little plaque next to it explained what it was, but also its importance in our history as the first time Bruce McLaren had that little spark of a love of engineering combined with competition. But I gave it little more than a fleeting glance on my way somewhere in an undoubted hurry, probably chuckling to myself at its simplicity in such high-tech surroundings.

As the collection grew over the next few weeks after moving into MTC, the tiny car became dwarfed in scale by the huge sports cars of McLaren's early days, including the M1A, the first to be designed and developed by McLaren back in the early sixties. Again, they really didn't grab my interest, partly because I didn't have spare time to go and look at them, but partly because they were just so old and I was so young. The line-up expanded to include some of the much more recognisable icons of F1 history, with Ayrton Senna's famous cars alongside those of other World Champions, up to our most recent hero at the time, Mika Häkkinen. This became more interesting to me as at least I knew what I was looking at from a technical point of view, even if it was still outdated tech that I was now actively involved in superseding. It was a lovely display and nice to look at. It brought some life to an otherwise quite sterile and colourless environment and I'm sure, for the many guests that were constantly shown around, it was a real treat to see up close. But for me they were still just museum pieces, and I've never been a huge fan of museums.

What I didn't appreciate then, but do now, is that a legacy like McLaren's has a power that doesn't just reside in the past: it can play a dynamic role in the present and future. Legacy's something that connects us all across time. It gives us a deep need for, and reliance upon, those who've come before us and an important responsibility to those who come after. You can think about that in the personal context of your own family, a business like McLaren and sport like Formula One, or at scale on a humanitarian level. It has the same importance for those it affects. I'm going to use powerful examples from my time in the sport to try and explain how legacy can be an effective tool for improvement and that, rather than actually being morbidly emotive, it's really all about life and living.

How I came to understand that, and how you apply those same principles to your own life, is the story of this chapter.

How to stand out from the crowd

A problem that many of the organisations I work with today experience is encouraging the workforce to give the 'extra' effort and commitment the company needs to harness when chasing excellence. There are lots of high-performing businesses out there and the truth is that, with some guidance and good leadership, that's not really too difficult to achieve. But when I get called in to work with executive teams, it's often because just being high-performing isn't enough for them. They want to be more than that. They want to out-perform everyone else in their sector. To do that is much harder in some industries than others and Formula One, where everyone's constantly operating at an elite level, is a perfect example of how to achieve it.

To attain true excellence that stands out in a crowd of slick operators requires something extraordinary, something most companies can only dream of having. One of the key elements for me is a team of people who aren't just motivated by personal gain or achievement. It's easy to say, but much trickier to manifest into existence as the reality, for most working people, is that they do it for the money they receive at the end of the week or month. It's perfectly reasonable: we give up our own valuable time to do work that someone else either can't or doesn't want to do, generally to further someone else's goals or ambitions and on someone else's terms . . . all in exchange for being paid an amount of money we can use to firstly survive, then hopefully help service our own goals and ambitions in the future. In that very common basic scenario, there's not normally much incentive or value for us to start *really* caring deeply about that work so much that we're willing to go above and beyond what's required in order to help our boss achieve their dreams and make them more money. Typically the amount we get paid isn't based on how much we care about what we do.

This was a problem we were trying to solve at McLaren too. We already had an excellent team of people, many of whom already did care about what we were doing. The recruitment process had always tried to bring in people like me, 'racers', passionate about, and driven by, winning. I desperately wanted to win a World Championship in Formula One: it was a dream for me, just as it was for any driver on their own journey through the sport, so although being well paid was great and bonuses for success really did help, I had something else pulling me towards the same goals that McLaren had always had too. The challenge in that regard was that every other team in the pitlane had similar people motivated by similarly competitive passions as well. That wouldn't be enough to create something world-beating on its own.

When we looked at this at our team, it became clear that not *everyone* in the organisation felt the same way about the racing part of what we did. In hindsight that was quite understandable. My Race Team colleagues and I left the UK factory every other week to fly around the planet to incredible destinations and compete in one of the world's biggest and most spectacular sporting events. We were the headline acts, creating the stories the world talked about in pubs and offices in the weeks that followed. We lived it and competed in it whilst hundreds of millions of people watched on and at the end of the weekend we either celebrated or commiserated as a group. We felt it. Back at MTC hundreds of people weren't even watching the race. They'd done their jobs, clocked out at 5pm on Friday and gone home to spend the weekend, and the money they'd been paid, with their families. Also perfectly reasonable.

So to maximise the human performance of every individual in the company, which is what we believed we had to do to differentiate ourselves from the high-level competition, we needed to find a way of motivating every single person in the MTC building to really care about the outcomes we created. We needed winning a race or a championship to be the dream that more people were chasing, not just a nice bonus on the side.

We thought about doing that with money. We reviewed the bonus schemes and made increases across the board, particularly for factory-based staff as they'd never been as well rewarded for good results as the travelling race team. But we knew that wasn't enough. Any well-funded F1 team could offer more money to their staff to attempt to create greater motivation.

There's a lot of research on what really motivates people in their jobs and there're many complex elements to it. As a team we read lots of it and were pleasantly surprised about how much we were already trying to implement. I recently read a paper published in the *International Journal of Innovative Research and Development*, entitled 'Maximising Productivity Through Employee Motivation', which compared many of the theories on the subject. It concluded there's a combination of extrinsic motivations, like money, status and rewards, but also some really important intrinsic motivations, with finding 'meaning', 'purpose' and a sense of agency in what they do, right at the top of the list.

We tried our best to develop the organisation along many of those lines and I've described some of the areas I personally got involved with in my dealings with Ron Dennis and Martin Whitmarsh. I know much of it helped, but it only gave us advantages because other teams hadn't yet caught on to this modern thinking around leadership and human psychology. One day they would.

But at some point during the conversations we realised the significance of something we already had in our 'locker' that no other F1 team had, or could ever have, but that we weren't really exploiting to our advantage. Our own story. McLaren's legacy.

> Our special new home and the appreciation of its interconnection with our past gave us some fresh ideas on strengths we might leverage in our eternal pursuit of advantage.

James Kerr's brilliant 2013 book, *Legacy*, explores the inspirational story of the New Zealand Rugby Team, the All Blacks. He spent an extended and privileged period of time deep inside the All Blacks' culture, and one of the biggest lessons to emerge was how they used the immense power of the legacy of those who'd preceded them to motivate the current team. There was total respect for the formidable black jersey they pulled on for each game, but most importantly for what that jersey represented. The heroes and ancestors who'd gone before were all connected through that uniform and paved the way for the squad of the present day. They were all part of, and proud to be, one of the most successful sporting teams in the world. The All Blacks.

The current players are simply custodians of that shirt for a fleeting moment in time and their purpose is to ensure that when they pass it on to the next generation, they leave it in a better place than when they found it. Apart from that just being great advice for life, it's also, now I think back, a philosophy we tried to work out a way of instilling inside the team at McLaren.

In some of my in-depth conversations with Martin Whitmarsh, I talked about how I personally hadn't felt any meaningful connection to McLaren's impressive history. I had to own up to perhaps looking down on the cars' inferior technology and even, if I was really honest, some of the people involved in creating it. It was a sad admission to make, but not one, I felt, that would've been uncommon had we candidly canvassed much of the current workforce. There was a growing feeling we were missing an opportunity.

It's obviously hard to make a cultural change like that in a team of over a thousand well-established people. You can't just order them to go away and appreciate the past and to come back with a respect that translates into a group of people suddenly willing to 'die for the badge'. That kind of thing can't happen overnight. The story needs to be told, but it needs to be told in a way that the team of today can relate to. That they can understand the significance of, and that they somehow need to feel part of. It needs to inspire.

At McLaren we had the advantage of our back story being pretty well documented. We all knew the names and were even familiar with some of the accomplishments. Modern-day fans still raved about some of those that'd worn the McLaren 'jersey' before we did; we just needed to paint a picture of what all of that meant for us in today's world. The goal was for the people on the 'shop floor' of our impressive facility to feel part of something much bigger than themselves and even than the impressive grand surroundings in which they worked. We needed to create a meaningful and powerful connection between the McLaren of twenty or thirty years ago and 'our' McLaren of the day.

There were meetings and discussions at senior management level about how to achieve it, but the truth is, back then, we never really came up with a clear strategy on how to make it work in the most effective way. We increased the presence of the 'Heritage Fleet' of cars, both on static display at the factory, but also using running cars at events like Goodwood, where many of the original team members, mechanics and engineers who'd worked on Senna's cars, for example, took the iconic machines and brought them back to life. We were all invited to be there and watch. Even when we just got one out and fired up the bone-shakingly loud engines at MTC, we encouraged crowds to gather round and appreciate them. But that was more or less it. I always found myself a bit frustrated that we hadn't gone further, even just from a personally selfish point of view. I wanted to know if I could feel different about what I did today, if I could feel more connected to what our team had done years ago.

Perhaps because I was a little more involved in the process

and had taken a personal interest, I did begin to feel different. I took it upon myself to learn as much as I could and I made a point of asking questions of the older guys in the team. I listened to their stories with genuine fascination and awe. But although I became much more aware, I'm not sure I could honestly say I felt moved enough or inspired enough to instinctively change my behaviours at any sort of scale. That connection wasn't there. I was too caught up in the relentlessness of the right now.

That was until Ron Dennis stepped in with a few powerful words – I'm not even sure he meant to have this effect – during a period of adversity for our 'Class of 2007'.

I've written about the fallout of the 2007 'Spygate' controversy in some depth in my previous book; I've spoken about it on my own podcast and on other people's; I've said many times before that I think it's movie-worthy as a story. But what I've referenced far less are those few words uttered by Ron on a late night inside a Spa-Francorchamps pitlane garage in Belgium on the weekend we'd discovered our fate in the courts and been thrown out of a Constructors' World Championship that we were very much on course to win. As well as focusing on the importance of team spirit in all the ways I talked about in Chapter 5, he gave us an important and moving history lesson.

He said to us that McLaren were a team who'd often courted the wrath of viciously bitter rivals and their fans, the press, and even, as he claimed was the case here, the rule-makers of this sport. We'd always posed a threat to those hoping to have it all their own way. He said that in all the years he'd been fighting on behalf of this team as its leader, no matter what attempt had been made to stop us, he'd never seen anyone who was wearing our famous McLaren logo on their shirt give up. He listed names like Senna, Prost and Hunt, who all faced moments when it felt like the world was trying to stop them winning and yet it only made them fight harder. He talked about the personal struggles he'd had of tragically losing great members of this team along the way and how it only spurred him on with a sense of responsibility, as he couldn't ever bring himself to not give it everything he had on their behalf. He said we were, right there in that moment, just as McLaren had always been on many great and seminal moments in history, fighters. If the world was going to turn against us, which is how he saw it in 2007, then we would do what the greats of this team had done before us, enabling us all to be there in the first place . . . and fight back. He was visibly shaking, as passion oozed from him, forcefully dictating the words coming from his mouth, and for someone so typically controlled and measured, it was incredibly powerful.

I honestly felt chills. I was heartbroken at the outcome of the court hearing, which found us collectively guilty of 'cheating', even more so at the punishment we'd been given. But somehow Ron turned that devastating moment into something that I've no doubt contributed to us coming back and winning the world title the very next season.

It was a short, rousing address, but undeniably authentic and genuine. It wasn't scripted, but driven by Ron's raw love for McLaren. As he spoke, he positioned every single one of us in that Belgian garage right in the heart of the same legendary, half-century-long story as the heroes that graced the record books of our sport. That was the moment when I suddenly felt differently about what we did.

It wasn't that from that day forth I became a new man or anything; I'm sure most people wouldn't have even noticed a difference in me. But deep down, at some subconscious level, I felt a real connection to the legacy of McLaren's past and it meant I had a new-found appreciation of where I fitted into it. I was no different, and certainly not superior, to the people who'd been in my position all those years ago fighting the same fight. The fact that so many of them had won their battles was an enormous part of the reason we stood where we stood, as one of the greatest teams in Formula One. Had Ron, or any of them, given up when times get tough, this team may not even exist, let alone be still fighting at the front.

So how can this help you?

> When you identify, and then tell, inspiring stories of the past, it can be a powerful motivator when you need to ignite a spark in someone, or a team of people, to achieve something.

Find your own legacy story

I work on this with lots of teams that have long histories, which much of the time we're able to unpick future-shifting moments from. But in even the smallest startups, and even in our own families, I believe there's almost always a legacy story to be told that can inspire the behaviours and actions of today, allowing that legacy to continue and grow.

The skill, and that's what it is from a leadership point of view, again meaning it can be practised and developed, is telling the right story, to the right people, in the right way, at the right time.

My McLaren example's a perfect case in point.

- Ron giving the same speech at a different point, even in that same season, would've likely not had the same effect as it did that particular weekend. It linked in perfectly to the raw emotions of the moment and gave a group of people, feeling like an injustice had been done, an 'enemy' upon which to focus.

- It may not have had the same impact with a different group in the team. We were on the ground, in the battlefield, with our rivals / enemies all around us. We were the first responders when it came to fighting back.
- I'm sure had I not seen the passion, grit and determination in Ron's face as he spoke, with my own eyes, I may not have succumbed to its power in the same way. I saw the genuine emotion triggered in him and 100 per cent believed it, so it triggered it in me too.

That's not to say that a speech like this can't be scripted or prepared in advance and still have a seismic affect. Think of some of Churchill's greatest addresses to his people. It's about understanding who you want to hear your message, why you want to say it and what you'd like it to achieve. You might want to inspire a young member of the family to show a bit more gratitude for what they have and appreciate how lucky they are by telling the tale of how a grandparent they love went through unimaginable hardship, or fought in a war, or perhaps built a company against the odds that you all now reap the rewards of. Some kids respond to shocking, or respect-inducing, family history stories, others to the awe-inspiring journeys of a famous footballer, pop star or entrepreneur they look up to. Utilising legacy as a means of improving performance is really about piecing together, and then living, the right story. I've worked with small founder teams in their first two years of business and discovered moments in the struggles to get things going, or even in the multiple business failures that went before it, that now serve as anchor points in their history to keep them fighting onwards. As the teams grow, the stories of what it's taken so far to get there are told to new members and the legacy evolves as part of the culture.

The power of legacy can be immense. The All Blacks, McLaren, Steve Jobs' path to the Apple we know today, amongst millions of others, are all massive stories in shaping how people feel to be part of them. A recent survey of the literature on this subject in the journal *New Ideas in Psychology* has shown that, although some of its deeper psychological impacts remain understudied, they are clearly present and highly influential.

As I experienced first-hand, it can instil a sense of pride and honour, an important interconnection backwards through time along the same path. To feel like you belong to the same story as the greats of your company's or industry's history can morph mindsets, which can have an incredible impact on human performance.

But there's another really important part of what tapping into a relevant legacy does. It's why I said at the beginning of this chapter that instead of the word 'legacy' conjuring up images of death and the end of our lives, for me it evokes a notion of life and maximising how we live it today.

Leaving the jersey in a better place than you found it

It's also why I said that legacy can tie us inextricably to those who've gone before us, but that it also creates in us a responsibility to those who'll follow. The powerfully told legacy of the All Blacks of the past almost entirely shapes the way the team behaves today because of their passionate desire to leave the special black jersey in a better place for the All Blacks of future generations. We can use this tool in a similar way in our homes and teams if we generate that same sense of responsibility. I wish as a human race we'd found a way to think collectively in a similar way; imagine the possibilities!

The McLaren of today in some respects tries to respectfully model that All Blacks philosophy; in fact I know that James Kerr's *Legacy* has been passed around most of the current management team as a guiding set of principles.

MTC, as well as McLaren's trackside facilities, is now adorned with imagery and milestones from the team's history. The first thing anyone sees as they walk into the pitlane garage at a racetrack is the list of honours on the wall. McLaren are currently the second most successful team in FI history, with only Ferrari having won more titles over the years. That long list of names and achievements is proudly there for all to see. The use of historic cars is even more prominent at the factory and the display tells the inspiring story of the journey we're all part of. I use the words 'we're all part of' deliberately there. I left McLaren officially in 2009, but I'll always feel part of the team and enormously proud of that. To see our legacy story being told every time I visit the team at a Grand Prix is powerful.

It's working. I see an enriched passion and pride in the team and there's a feeling that, whilst of course everyone wants to experience the personal success that comes with winning titles, they also want to be part of the history book that'll be written. They want to be the latest winning chapter of the McLaren story. They want to leave the 'papaya' McLaren shirt in a better place than when they found it and nothing makes me happier than to see this playing out as I watch on. 'My' McLaren laid the foundations for the current team, just as the brilliant people that worked alongside the likes of Senna, Prost, Hunt and others laid the groundwork for us. That's how a great legacy works.

MARGINAL GAIN

We can use legacy in similar ways in our own lives. There might be an obvious story to tell around a family struggle from previous generations, like a great-grandparent fighting for freedom in a world war, or escaping persecution, for example. Not unlike Ron's McLaren story, that can be used to inspire and generate a feeling of responsibility within the family because of the way a story's told about their forefathers. The respect needs to be genuinely modelled by parents so children see it, not just get told to do it themselves. Parents set the team culture in their families, like a CEO does for their company

In modelling the right behaviours and showing respect for what's gone before, parents are also building the legacy of the future and this can be an equally inspiring tool for younger generations. Our children are growing up in a world where personal brand is real, powerful and important to them and yet that same personal brand can either form a legacy of its own or build on an existing one. Having the conversation now about what our children's children and grandchildren will think about the legacy we're all building can be equally inspiring to some. An interesting way to do this on a practical level is to review, or debrief, the entire family's social media posts at the end of a week. Ask the question: does the digital trail we're leaving behind align and add to the legacy we're aspiring to build?

So, if you want to tap into this wonderful phenomenon, why not consider the following:

- Look backwards in your timeline. Dig deep; often the best stories are ones that no one's either found yet or told. Find the big moments of great success or monumental failure, of adversity and courage. Pivotal moments, or moments that could be turned into pivotal junctures on the journey when recounted in a new context.
- Decide what's most likely to resonate with the person or people you need to impact.
- Build an inspiring story around the moments you identified; don't lie, but highlight or even embellish the elements you need to – that's what great storytelling is. Relate the story to your audience. You don't want them to feel like it's just a history lesson; you need them to feel like they're a part of that same story so they feel a responsibility to carry it forward.
- Then deliver it at the right time with vulnerability and passion. Let your audience know you also feel the same connection and that it moves you too. Share that responsibility to carry the baton on with them.
- If you want fight and determination from your team, demonstrate it yourself.

It's important to know that whoever's hearing this simply won't believe your words if they're not backed up with authentically aligned behaviours. No one wants to be preached to with a set of ideologies that you're not willing to live with yourself, so don't even think about delivering the message if you don't actually believe it. It won't land. But if you can inspire a child, a team or a workforce to want to fight or strive for the greater good of the family, the club or the business, you're well on the way to creating a high-performance team with a significant advantage over most others.

PITLANE LESSONS

- Think about your legacy, not as relating to your death, but about your life and living it the right way today.
- What are the legacies you're a part of creating today and what do you want them to look like?
- Identify people or moments in the historic story of your family or company that enabled you to be here today and build that story to inspire the current generation. Imagine future generations telling your story and be proud to write it.
- Use legacy as an effective and powerful tool to connect those who came before to the people of today and then to the generations that follow.
- Always leave the 'jersey' in a better place than when you were handed it.

Conclusion

At the end of the day, Formula One teams, international rugby squads, workers at the world's most valuable companies, or the communities and families we live in are simply a collection of people trying to work together to achieve things. To me it makes perfect sense, then, that each one can offer value to, and learn from, the others. So whilst this book is pitched at helping you to think more like an elite F1 team might think about the challenges you face in life, it's also very clear from my experience that F1 teams can learn from people outside the industry. Although arrogance up and down the pitlane probably prevented that happening in the past, I hope the story I tell in this book tells you that it's changed. Now, even in the highly technical world of Formula One, where the machinery's so critical to our outcomes on track, it's understood that the human performance of over a thousand people underpins it all.

Something similar is true of life more generally. If you employ the techniques and examples I discuss in this book, you can not only help yourself to perform better in every aspect of your own existence, but in turn you could end up using them to make a difference in the worlds you live and work in. Maybe you'll end up having an impact on the F1 pitlane. I hope so.

I end every episode of the *Pitlane Life Lessons* podcast with the following line, so it feels like a fitting way to end here too . . . It's a mantra I try my best to live my own life by . . .

DO THE RIGHT THINGS . . . DO THE THINGS RIGHT.

Thanks for reading.

Acknowledgements

Thank you to McLaren Racing and the Formula One community for changing my life for ever. For similar reasons, thank you especially to the incredible and unique Dr Aki Hintsa – you are much missed.

Thanks to Jake Humphrey for his support and wonderful foreword. To Will Buxton and Annastiina Hintsa for their support and kind early words. To Josh Ireland, Fiona Brown, Joe Pickering, Mairéad Zielinski, Ellie Auton, Amelia Tolley and everyone at Penguin Random House for their help and patience in turning my dream of this book into a reality.

Enormous thanks of course to everyone who's taken the time to read this, listened to or watched my podcast or TV shows, or sent me messages on social media. I appreciate you all – it means so much.

Finally, to my family, without whose love and support – and despite my constant travel and dishwasher re-loading – none of this would've been possible. I love you all more than any words can express.